BOOK TWO
Modules 4, 5, 6
Vocabulary, Fluency, and Comprehension

LETRS

Language Essentials for Teachers of Reading and Spelling

Louisa Moats, Ed.D.

Presenter's Edition

07 06 05 04   6 5 4 3

Proofread by Susan Defosset
Cover design and text layout by Sue Campbell
Slide design by Christine Kosmicki
Production assistance by Sherri Rowe and Kim Harris

ISBN 1-57035-995-4

Printed in the United States of America

Published and Distributed by

SOPRIS
WEST
EDUCATIONAL SERVICES

4093 Specialty Place • Longmont, CO 80504 • (303) 651-2829
www.sopriswest.com

191PRESENT2/5-03/BAN/1M

Acknowledgments

These LETRS modules have been developed with the help of many people. During the production of these first modules, we have treasured the experience, knowledge, and editorial contributions of Bruce Rosow, Kevin Feldman, Susan Lowell, Carol Tolman, Patricia Mathes, Marianne Steverson, Lynn Kuhn, Jan Hasbrouck, Deb Glaser, Marcia Davidson, Anne Cunningham, Susan Hall, Susan Smartt, and Nancy Eberhardt. We also thank those professionals from all over the country who attended the pilot institutes and who shared their ideas so that we could produce a better and more useful tool for professional development.

Many professionals in reading and language education have journeyed with me through this content or have requested materials that would help teachers reach *all* children in their classrooms. You are too many to name, but our shared learning experiences are, in one way or another, reflected in these modules. I hope you see yourselves on every page.

I am grateful for the daily support and energy of the Sopris West office staff, editors, and designers including Keri Stafford, Sue Campbell, Sandra Knauke, Christine Kosmicki, Kim Harris, and Sherri Rowe.

Stu Horsfall, Steve Mitchell, and Steve Kukic are the vision, guidance, and energy behind this enterprise. I am so fortunate to be working with all of you.

—LCM

Contents

Introducing LETRS: Language Essentials for Teachers of Reading and Spelling

Our national goal of "every child a reader" requires teachers with expertise in reading instruction. The research-based, comprehensive instructional programs called for by Congress are necessary tools to reach the goal, but are not sufficient without continuous, long-term, professional development for teachers. Teaching reading is a complex discipline that requires in-depth learning beyond the use of a program manual.

To reach *all* learners, teachers must understand how students learn to read and write, the reasons why some children fail to learn, and the instructional strategies best supported by research. Teachers need an understanding of the language structures they are teaching. The American Federation of Teachers' *Teaching Reading Is Rocket Science* and the Learning First Alliance's *Every Child Reading: A Professional Development Guide* endorse these core understandings. LETRS modules are designed to teach teachers the content outlined in such consensus documents on reading instruction. These modules use professional development methods successful with diverse groups of teachers: regular classroom and special education, novice and expert, rural and urban.

The three stand-alone modules in each of the four LETRS books teach teachers the meaning of scientific findings about learning to read and reading instruction. The modules address each component of reading instruction—phoneme awareness; phonics, decoding, spelling, and word study; oral language development; vocabulary; reading fluency; comprehension; and writing—and the foundational concepts that link these components. The characteristics and the needs of second language learners (ELL), dialect speakers, and students with other learning differences are addressed throughout the modules. Instruction in assessment and evaluation of student performance will be embedded in the topical modules. An independent module on the DIBELS assessment (Dynamic Indicators of Basic Early Literacy Skills) will also be offered. The format of instruction in LETRS institutes allows for deep learning and reflection beyond the brief "once over" treatment the topics are typically given.

Modules provide material for each teacher-participant and are ideally delivered by professional developers at the state, district, and building level. They are also suitable for university courses that lead to teacher licensing. Each module can be taught to experienced staff developers in one day. Teachers in the field may need extended time to learn and apply the knowledge and skills, depending on their background and experience.[1] Each module is written so that teacher participants will engage in questions, problems, and tasks that lead to understanding. Teachers of all grades and all subjects learn best if they explore new concepts, information, and skills and then apply the new learning as they solve instructional problems encountered every day. This is never

---

[1] Future optional technology supports (online and CD-based instruction) can be used to decrease the necessary class time.

so true as it is in the teaching of reading. A number of commercially available reading curricula provide appropriate classroom content for the teaching of structured language. The LETRS program is not intended to replace these comprehensive reading programs, but to make their implementation more effective, and to help teachers overcome any gaps in their instructional materials.

The LETRS Modules

- ◆ Book One, Modules 1–3: *Foundations for Reading Instruction* (For All Grades)
  1. The Challenge of Learning to Read
  2. The Speech Sounds of English: Phonetics, Phonology, and Phoneme Awareness
  3. Spellography: A Road Map to English Orthography

- ◆ Book Two, Modules 4–6: *Vocabulary, Fluency, and Comprehension* (For All Grades)
  4. The Mighty Word: Teaching Vocabulary and Oral Language
  5. Getting Up to Speed: Developing Fluency
  6. Digging for Meaning: Teaching Text Comprehension

- ◆ Book Three, Modules 7–9: *Teaching and Assessing Beginning Reading and Spelling* (For Kindergarten, First Grade, Second Grade, and Remedial Instruction)
  7. Teaching Phonics, Word Study, and the Alphabetic Principle
  8. Assessment for Prevention and Early Intervention (K–3)
  9. Teaching Beginning Spelling and Writing

- ◆ Book Four, Modules 10–12: *Teaching Reading and Writing* (Third Grade and Up)
  10. Reading Big Words: Syllabication and Advanced Decoding
  11. Writing: A Road to Reading Comprehension
  12. Using Assessment to Guide Instruction (3–adult)

- ◆ Supplementary Modules:
  - A Paraprofessional's Guide to Effective Tutoring
  - Teaching Adults to Read
  - Preschool Preparation for Reading
  - Classroom Management and Organization
  - Using the DIBELS Assessment
  - Developing Classroom Coaches

Module 4

The Mighty Word: Building Vocabulary and Oral Language

Contents for Module 4

Objectives for Module 4

◆ Understand the many facets of word meaning

◆ Appreciate the role of vocabulary knowledge in reading comprehension

◆ Identify the ways in which word meanings are learned, in oral and written language

◆ Experiment with the role of context in word learning

◆ Develop a rationale for choosing specific words for direct instruction

◆ Generate multiple meanings for words and understand why instruction of multiple meanings and multiple uses is important

◆ Practice semantic feature analysis to appreciate how words are related in meaning

◆ Practice categorizing and understand its importance

◆ Sketch a lesson plan for teaching vocabulary in or related to a specific text

Key Ideas, Module 4

- Word meanings are multi-faceted
- Vocabulary knowledge is essential for reading comprehension
- Word meanings are learned from direct definition and exposure to contextual use
- Specific words should be selected for direct teaching
- Teach word meanings in relation to one another and the contexts in which they are used

Slide 3

Review these "big ideas" briefly, as a preview; note that we are going to develop a rationale for moving beyond the traditional practice of simply matching a new word to a definition or telling children to go look a word up in the dictionary.

Content of LETRS: The Language-Literacy Connection

Components of Comprehensive Reading Instruction	Organization of Language						
	Phonology	Morphology	Orthography	Semantics	Syntax	Discourse and Pragmatics	Etymology
Phonological Awareness	2	2					
Phonics, Spelling, and Word Study	3, 7	3, 7, 10	3, 7, 10				3, 10
Fluency	5		5	5	5		
Vocabulary	4	4	4	4	4		4
Text Comprehension		6		6	6	6, 11	
Written Expression			9, 11	9, 11	9, 11	9, 11	
Assessment	8, 12	8, 12	8, 12	8, 12	8, 12	8, 12	

What does it mean to know a word? Module 4 begins an inquiry into this question. We consider that words are known in relation to one another, that word knowledge has many facets, and that vocabulary growth can be indirectly and directly influenced. Other modules have addressed the organization of language at the levels of sounds, symbols, meaningful word parts (morphemes), sentences, and discourse, but this one is all about words.

Word meanings are multi-faceted. That means that when we talk about "knowing a word", if we know it well, we know many things about it. If we know it partially or in a limited way, we are probably missing knowledge of one or more of these dimensions of the word:
- *Phonology—if you don't recognize the sound difference between "anecdote" and "antidote," you may not know the meaning difference*
- *Morphology—if you know "persuade," you might then infer the meaning of "dissuade"*
- *Spelling gives away the difference between "passed" and "past"*
- *In a meaning network about golf, the words "green" and "putt" and "stroke" have special meaning*
- *Words that end in "al" are adjectives—special, imperial, feral*
- *"Metamorphoses" is from Greek and is a plural form*

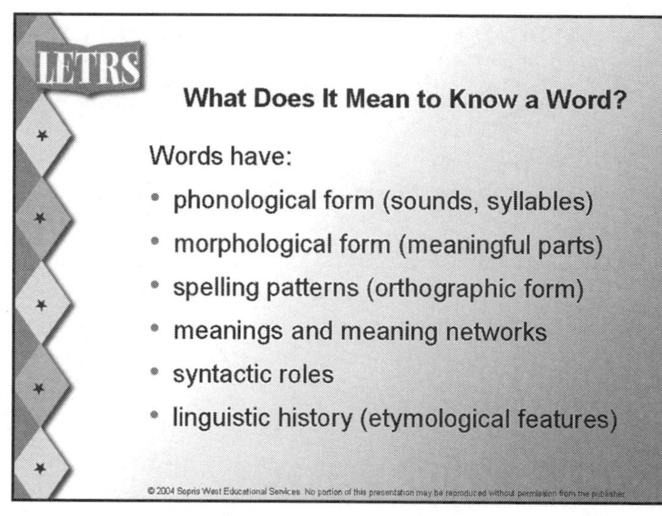

Vocabulary and Learning to Read

Slide 5

Knowledge of individual word meanings is essential for comprehension. Since the research of John Carroll, Jean Chall, and others in the 1970's, we have known that word knowledge accounts for about 50% of the variance in reading comprehension.

Knowledge of word meanings is a major contributor to text comprehension. The National Reading Panel (2000) confirmed that the depth and breadth of a learner's vocabulary contributes substantially to proficient reading. Consequently, explicit and implicit exploration of word meanings should occur often during reading instruction.

Slide 6

The ads that claim you will increase your IQ by studying vocabulary are, in one sense, true: the ability to define words completely, out of context, and to use them appropriately in context constitutes the most representative measure of verbal intelligence on traditional IQ tests (Wechsler and Stanford-Binet). If researchers want a "proxy" for Verbal IQ, they give a vocabulary test, because other measures of verbal ability usually correlate very highly with vocabulary, and vocabulary correlates highly with overall intelligence.

Getting at the meaning of a written passage requires knowledge of the individual words in the passages. Vocabulary tests predict and are highly correlated with general reading comprehension tests. Vocabulary also correlates very highly with the overall verbal reasoning quotients of IQ or cognitive ability tests. If psychologists need to estimate the verbal abilities of a student, using one quick measure, they often use a vocabulary test. Vocabulary is said to be a proxy or stand-in for verbal reasoning ability.

It is also true that children with better vocabularies tend to do better on measures of phonological skill and to learn to read more easily than those with low vocabularies. In addition to the phonological abilities and decoding skills necessary for early reading success, the size and depth of a child's vocabulary helps to predict reading outcomes on high stakes tests at 4th grade and beyond.

Slide 7

If children do not know the meanings of words they are decoding, they may pronounce them but not understand the gist of the passage or how phrases go together. Recognition of a new word in print is easier and faster if the word already has an identity (a pronunciation and meaning) in the mind of the reader. The child who is a good decoder nevertheless must identify the meaning and use of a word in a specific context in order to comprehend.

Children who are learning English (ELL) or who have limited language development will require intensive, deliberate instruction in word meanings in addition to phonics and word recognition. Children learning English may be more adept at decoding than they are at interpreting what they read. The size of the child's vocabulary in his or her first language will affect how readily he or she learns the vocabulary of a second language. Word learning in the first language and overall language proficiency in ELL children is related to the ease with which they learn English.

Defining "Vocabulary"

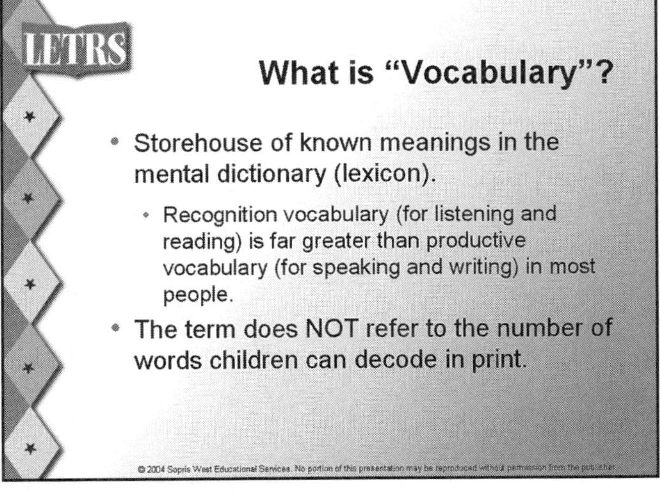

Slide 8

The lexicon is the memory system that stores word meanings. It is located in the left cerebral hemisphere—the language hemisphere for most people.

Receptive or recognition vocabulary is much larger than expressive vocabulary—the words we use for speaking or writing.

The term **vocabulary** refers to the storehouse of word meanings that we draw on to comprehend what is said to us, express our thoughts, or interpret what we read. The **lexicon** is the mental dictionary, the storage file of the **meaning processor** that Module 1 explored. The meaning processor makes sense of word parts, phrases, sentences, illustrations, and punctuation marks. Meaning also resides in the context surrounding specific words; otherwise, we would not be able to pronounce and interpret word forms such as *object* (n.) and *object* (v.). In other sources, the word "vocabulary" is sometimes used to refer to the words that students can pronounce or recognize in print. That is a misuse of the term, as students may pronounce words they see in print without knowing their meanings.

Size of Young Readers' Listening and Reading Vocabularies

Although unusual content words are only 5% of running text, they carry most of the unique meaning in a passage; they must be decoded accurately and interpreted for comprehension to occur. The most common 5,000 words constitute a minimum, essential vocabulary for young learners.

Slide 9

Somewhere between third and sixth grade is a "cross-over" between size of listening vocabulary and size of reading vocabulary. At this point, instead of knowing most of the meanings of the words they can read, children expand their vocabulary from reading itself (to learn from context, exposure, and teaching).

Slide 10

When children begin formal reading instruction at the end of kindergarten or beginning of first grade, their listening vocabulary is far greater than their reading vocabulary. By third or fourth grade, normally progressing children begin to encounter more words in print than they already know for listening and speaking. At that point, growth in vocabulary depends more and more on reading itself and the ability to derive meanings of new words as they are encountered in context. Let's consider why that is the case.

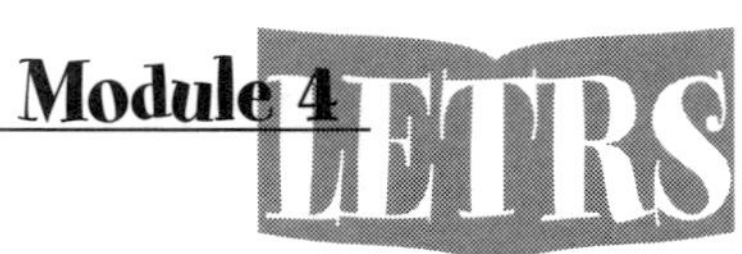

How Do Children Learn the Words They Know?

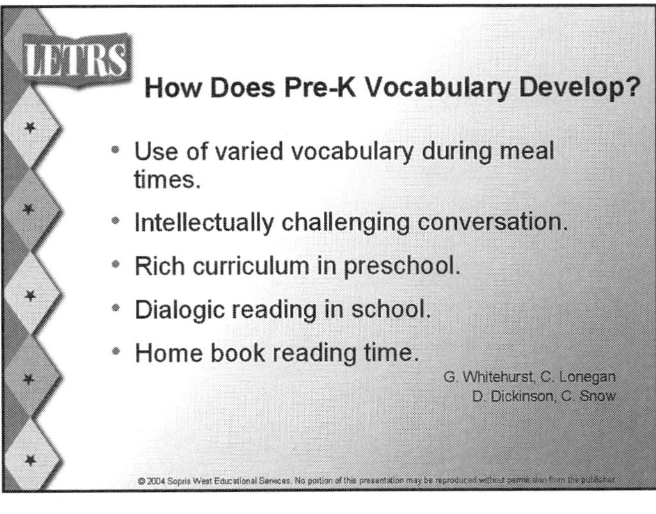

Slide 11

Act out and talk about the verbal styles of different kinds of households; refer to the Hart and Risley study "Meaningful Differences" (Brookes Publishing, 1995) in which extensive transcriptions were made of families at different socioeconomic levels, and low SES families were found to use many fewer words and use them for control purposes rather than conversation.

Children in the preschool years learn language rapidly— several new words per day—if they are exposed to it and engaged in meaningful conversation around a shared experience.

Emphasize that language learning is socially driven; more than "exposure," language interaction is the vehicle for word learning.

Learning of word meanings occurs rapidly from birth through adolescence within communicative relationships. Everyday experiences with friends, care-givers, and community members shape speech habits and knowledge of language. The human mind latches onto new words as it hears them because the words are the tools of communication. Humans have an intrinsic need to understand what is said to them and to share experience through language, and the brain is biologically adapted to support language acquisition. Before school and before learning to read, children learn most of the words they know through daily oral language with adults. Adults facilitate that process when they introduce new words in a shared experience, elaborate what a child has said, confirm and clarify the child's attempts to use new words, deliberately repeat new words in conversation, or read aloud.

Great differences exist, however, in the exposure to language of children with highly verbal or nonverbal parents. Imagine the verbal styles of three mothers taking their children to the grocery store.[1]

---

[1] The author is indebted to Phyllis Hunter, reading consultant from Texas, for her dramatization of these styles at a Reading First meeting.

Mother #1 (low verbal). [Child in the grocery cart.] Sit still. [Child reaching toward the avocado]. Keep your hands to yourself.

Mother #2 (average). [Child in grocery cart.] What should we have for dinner? See anything good, honey? We haven't had carrots for a while. [Child reaching toward the avocado.] Put that back, now.

Mother #3 (high verbal). [Child in grocery cart.] Oh, what do we see here? Organic avocado? Do you know what "organic" means, sweetie? It's when the farmer says she doesn't put any pesticides on the plants. What's a pesticide? It's something that kills pests. Pests are insects that eat up the green leaves on the top of the plant. The plant needs the green leaves for all that green chlorophyll that goes into that yummy green mushy stuff we make guacamole with. Guacamole? That's a Spanish word!" [Child says, "Mommy, you talk too much!"]

Exercise #1: How We Learn Words

Think of a word you have learned recently. What was the context for that learning? What motivated you to learn and remember that word?

In the discussion, these points should arise: word learning occurs for a variety of reasons, including curiosity alone, the need to comprehend a passage, or the need to communicate with someone around a shared experience. Most people have to hear or read a word several times before they try to incorporate it into their own speaking vocabulary.

Even when we are 70, we are still learning a few new words each year! Vocabulary tends to "hold" with aging, or even improve with age. Ask the participants to talk about any recent vocabulary learning experiences. Reflections that usually emerge from the discussion include:

• Motivation to learn the meaning of a new word resides in curiosity, competitiveness, and/or the need to know what other people in the language community know and use

• To belong in the language community, one wants to know the meanings of any new words so that communication is possible

• Contextual use and the dictionary are both important sources of meaning

• Several exposures usually occur before a word is learned

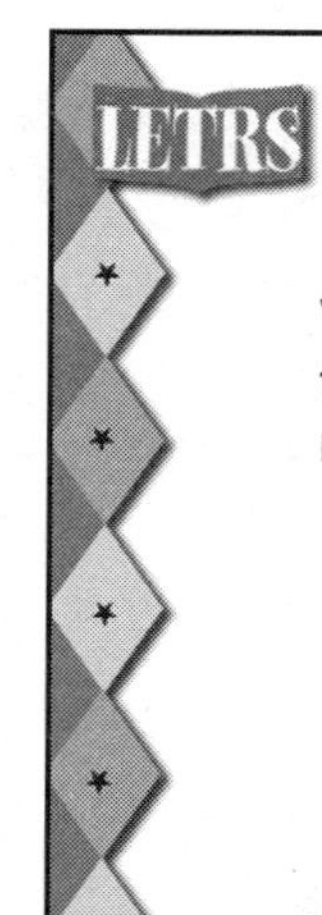

Slide 12

How Many Words Do Children Know on School Entry?

Highly verbal adults may enrich their children's vocabularies continually. But children whose chief exposure is to nonverbal adults or adults who do not engage them in reading or conversation have many fewer opportunities to learn new words. Hart and Risley's (1995) study of verbal-linguistic adult behavior in households with high socioeconomic (SES) and low SES parents documented that low SES children are exposed to one-third of the verbiage that children from high SES, highly verbal families are exposed to. By the time they enter school, low SES children may know one-half or fewer of the word meanings known by typical middle class children, and far fewer than more privileged children. Once that gap is established, it is very difficult to make up. Normally progressing children who already have an advantage in word knowledge are continuing to learn words at a faster rate than less verbal children. This widening gap is what Stanovich referred to as the "Matthew Effect," whereby the verbally rich get richer and verbally poor get poorer.

Slide 13

The rate at which children have to learn new words is truly astonishing. The important point here is that the "gap" between high verbal and low verbal children will tend to widen, not decrease, if natural influences prevail.

Estimates of how many words children know at certain ages vary quite widely, but Andrew Biemiller has supported his with meticulous research. Biemiller has assembled a list of the basic words children need to understand and use to be successful with grade level work in kindergarten through third grade (in his book, Language and Reading Success).

Slide 14

Andrew Biemiller, who has studied the number of words children typically know by each age and grade level, estimates that by third grade, advanced children's word knowledge is equivalent to that of average children in fourth grade (Biemiller, 1999, p. 1). Slower children, at about the 25th percentile in third grade, are similar to average second graders. Less verbal children begin school knowing perhaps 1,000 root words and 2,000 meanings for those words, but an average child knows roughly 2,000 words and 4,000 meanings for those root words in first grade.[2] To make up this "language gap," as it is called by Hirsch (2001), the less verbal child would have to learn vocabulary at a considerably faster rate than his average classmates. The average child increases his or her knowledge of root words to about 8,000 by sixth grade, but verbally limited children may have learned about 4,000 in the same time span.

Point: The vocabulary we want children to learn (as educators) is a literate vocabulary, not a conversational vocabulary. It is in well-written children's literature, and children's informational text. Select and read a passage from a classic children's story, such as Peter Pan *or* Black Beauty, *in the original version, and note the use of vocabulary that children were expected to know before the age of television …*

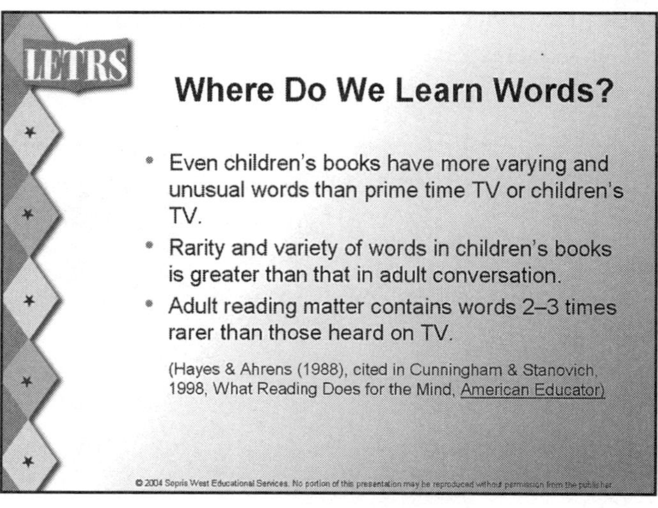

Slide 15

What role do books play in preschool word learning? The Hayes and Ahrens study from 1989, reported again in Cunningham and Stanovich's (1998) essay, "What Reading Does for the Mind," documents that well-written children's books are richer in unusual vocabulary than typical adult conversation, peer conversation, or typical television programs. Books embody more uncommon and content-rich words than any other verbal medium, right from the beginning. Thus, word learning requires exposure to the language of books. Furthermore, the language of books is most attainable when adults pause while reading and engage children in conversations about new words and concepts and relate those concepts to their own experience. As children learn to read themselves, reading begets verbal growth; new words can be deciphered more easily from context as vocabulary and verbal fluency increase, and more new words are encountered when text exposure is high.

[2] Biemiller's vocabulary list of root words known by most children by grade 4 is listed in the appendix of *Language and Reading Success* (1999).

What Does "Knowing a Word" Mean?

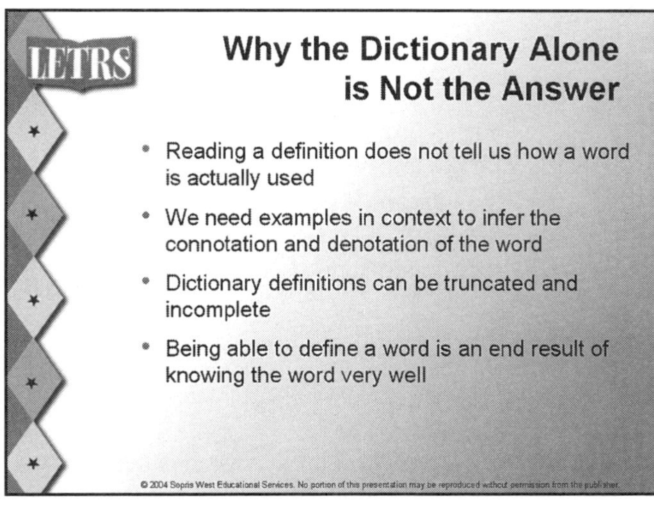

Slide 16

The dictionary is a resource—a repository of "word fossils" that always has to be updated to accommodate constantly changing patterns of word meaning and word use.

The dictionary typically does not give enough contextual examples of a word's use for us to know how to use the word.

The dictionary is great for checking meanings derived from exposure or context, for finding synonyms, or learning the history and structure of the word.

Words are learned through both indirect and direct processes. The mind indirectly constructs the meaning of words that are encountered in various contexts. Beck et al. (2002) have estimated that children typically need 10 to 12 exposures to words used in multiple contexts in order to learn their meanings indirectly. During that process of acquiring and consolidating a word's meaning, children are unsure and groping for evidence to confirm their idea of the word. Partial knowledge of a word is a sample of an incomplete and unelaborated entry into the mental dictionary. Students also learn a smaller number of words from direct teaching or from being given a definition from someone else. Direct teaching of vocabulary succeeds when it deepens and enriches knowledge of word meanings and when it emphasizes the relationships among words and concepts. Good instruction often does not begin with a definition; rather, the ability to give a definition is often the result of knowing what the word means.

The dictionary has been described as a repository for aging words, a historical record of words' origins and evolutions. We cannot learn to speak from memorizing the dictionary. Definitions do not tell us how a word is used. "Precious" is defined as "having great value" and being "costly" in Webster's New World dictionary. A child learning "precious" from a definition is likely to misuse the word ("His leather jacket was precious") unless its use and connotation are demonstrated.

Shallow and Deep Word Knowledge

So, we learn the words we know from reading text that is not too hard—and not too easy.

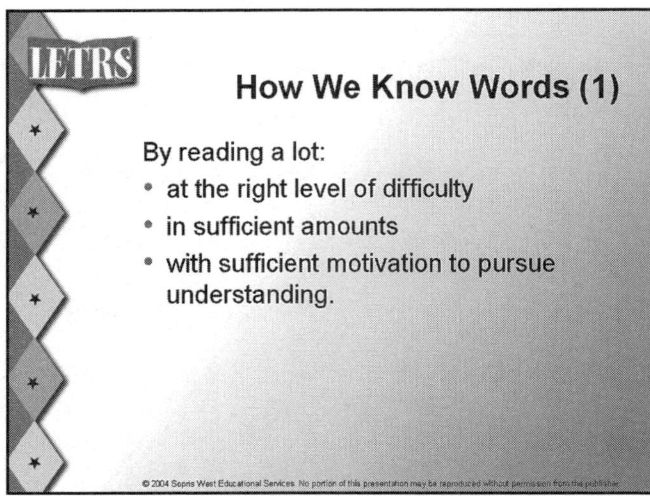

Slide 17

We learn a word from many exposures (10-12) to the word's use in context; then we tend to try to use it ourselves.

Also, we learn from someone telling us what a word means and giving us examples with an explanation.

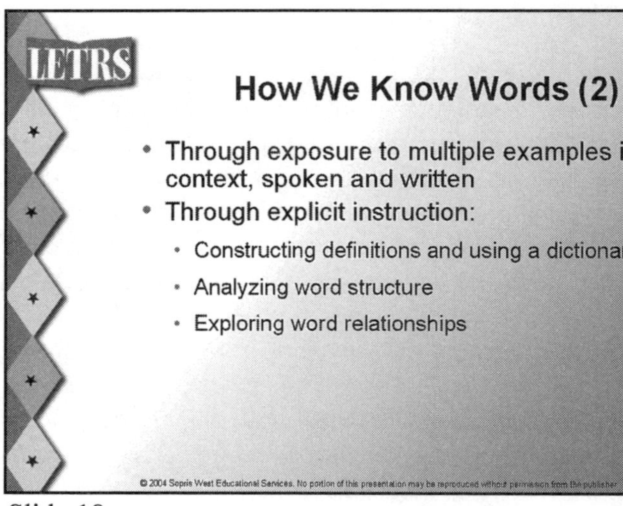

Slide 18

"Word consciousness" refers to linguistic sensitivity—awareness of a word's features, curiosity about them, a need to know where words came from—and this is cultivated in an environment in which adults communicate interest in words.

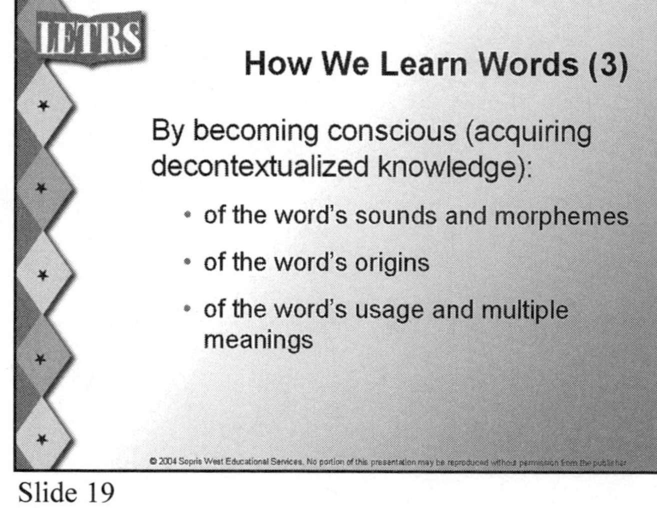

Slide 19

Learning what a word means necessitates multiple experiences with the various uses and meanings of the word. Children (and adults) commonly have partial or shallow knowledge of a word, sometimes because the word has only been encountered in a limited context. For example, from watching an older sibling come home with a friend's belonging, children might think that the word "borrowed" means "given" without an understanding that something borrowed must be returned. The word "designated" might mean "sober" to a child who has only heard the phrase, "designated driver." The word "job" might mean only what the child's parent does, not the whole category of various jobs. A grasp of deep meaning is signified when multiple meanings and uses are understood, when the word can be used with precision in writing or speech, and when a definition can be generated. The ability to define a word is a *result* of word knowledge.

Exercise #2: Exploring the Use of Words in Context

Work with a partner. Choose an important word that is specific to a hobby or area of special knowledge that you have—a "jargon" word that a layperson would not know. Make up several sentences that use the word. Can your partner figure out what the word means? Could he or she define the word on the basis of the contextual uses you gave? How close was the meaning your partner came up with? What are the advantages and limitations of context use in word definition?

Context can help to a greater or lesser extent depending on the amount of redundant information that the surrounding text gives about the word. Context can be misleading. Exposure to a single contextual use of a word may not be enough to get the meaning; several exposures are often more helpful for narrowing down the word's meanings.

The points that usually emerge in discussion after this exercise are:
• *Context must be forthcoming and informative to truly give away a meaning*
• *It's possible to be "in the ballpark" with a contextual derivation of meaning and not be right on target*
• *Unless the context is rich, it's possible to be way off base in the derivation of a word's meaning (e.g., the child who thought that "designated" meant "sober")*

Slide 20

Locate the Kipling example in the story; take 1 or 2 minutes to let people surmise what "nubbly" means. Look at the second contextual use toward the end of the story and see if that helps narrow the definition. The context is not quite forthcoming enough to be certain of the meaning in this case. Thus, more examples would be needed to form a clear enough idea of "nubbly" to be able to use it.

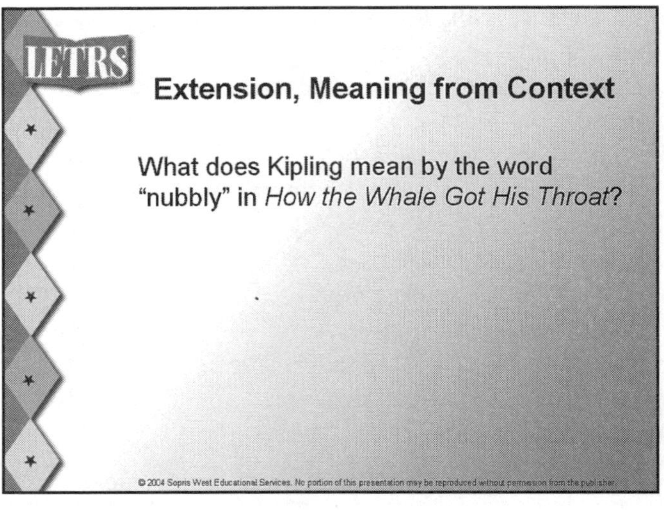

Slide 21

Point: the oldest words have the most meanings—they've been evolving the longest. Newer words such as "residence" have fewer. Check out Appendix A. Listings are based on the Oxford English Dictionary— *the most complete history of the words of our language—which had over 60 listings for "house."*

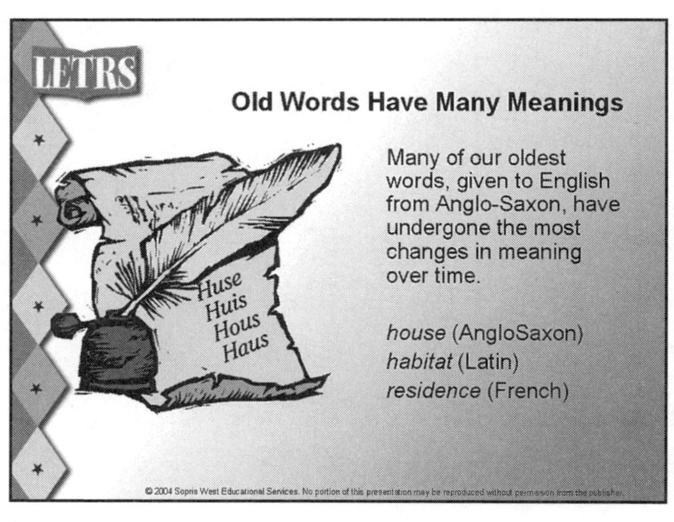

Slide 22

Words have connotations and denotations that determine how they may be used in specific contexts, and many have more than one meaning. Our oldest, most common words seem to have developed the most varied meanings over time (see Appendix A). Looking at the Oxford English Dictionary, for example, one can see that the word "house" has dozens of definitions and that it entered our lexicon from Anglo-Saxon. Its first uses were noted in Beowulf in the 800's A.D. The word "residence," however, entered our language from Norman French about 500 years later, was used by Chaucer in the 1300's, and has only a few meanings.

Exercise #3: Multiple Meanings

How many meanings and uses can you think of for the following common words: frame, check, pitch. Take one word and list all the meanings you know without using a dictionary. Then, check the dictionary for others you may have missed.

Frame: frame a picture; build the skeleton of a house; frame an innocent person accused of a crime; a sheltered box for growing plants from seeds

Check: bill at a restaurant; winning move in chess; body blow in ice hockey; check mark on paper; explore or look into (check up on…)

Pitch: throw a baseball to the batter; the angle of incline; black tar; try to sell an object or idea

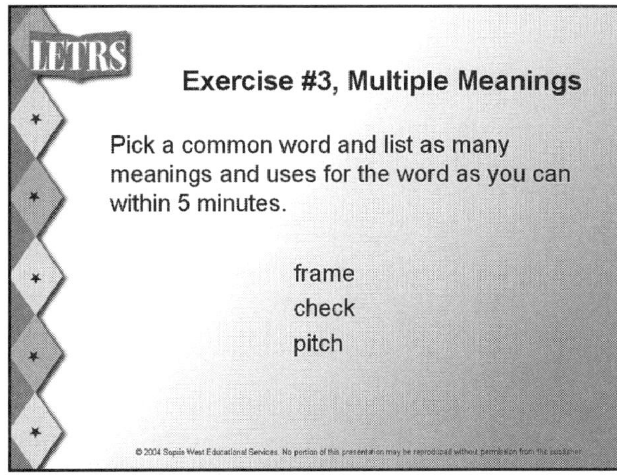

Slide 23

Let individuals or small groups work for no more than five minutes. Debrief quickly by having people call out meanings for each word.

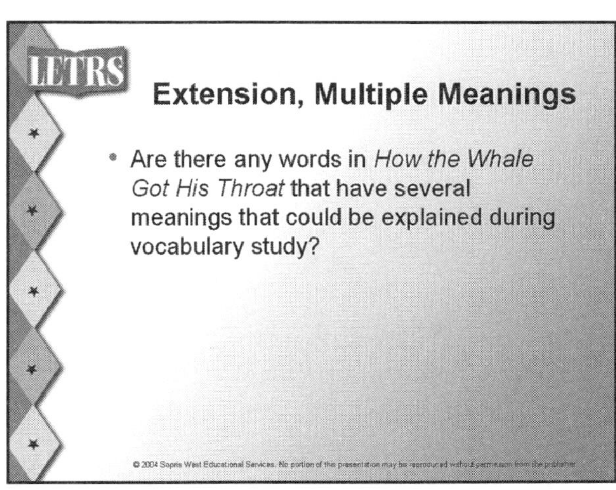

Slide 24

This is optional—take only a few minutes to identify one or two good candidates.

The construction of meaning around a word is also individual and personal. Two of us might interpret the word "republican" very differently depending on our prior experience, beliefs, and acculturation. The sense we have of our own understanding or misunderstanding is **metacognition**. Comprehension depends upon knowing when and what we have not comprehended, for example recognizing when our understanding of a word may diverge considerably from understandings shared by others. If we are adaptive and willing to search for more information, we can readily adjust our internal definition of a word.

Our knowledge of words, or lexical knowledge, is organized in networks of meaning. Thus, we are able to remember and recall words that are associated with the same topic more quickly than we can recall words that have no meaningful connection. Those meanings are often organized in hierarchical networks; that is, we spontaneously categorize or group ideas together and recognize categories that have intrinsic similarities. In turn, the reality of meaning networks and categories can be exploited in purposeful teaching. Words and concepts should be learned in relation to one another and in relation to a topic of interest, not as isolated units. New words are remembered and retrieved more easily if they are filed in a meaning network whose structure is familiar. Effective teaching will:

- elaborate various connections among better known and less-well known words,

- deepen and enrich existing knowledge, and

- build a network of ideas around key concepts that are well elaborated.

If each person has a word on a card, then ask the group to arrange themselves by categories. Tell them there will be several levels on which they can arrange themselves—high or overriding (superordinate), to major categories, to subcategories. This exercise may take a few minutes as people move about. You may need to prompt the person who has "dogs" to stand up higher than everyone else.

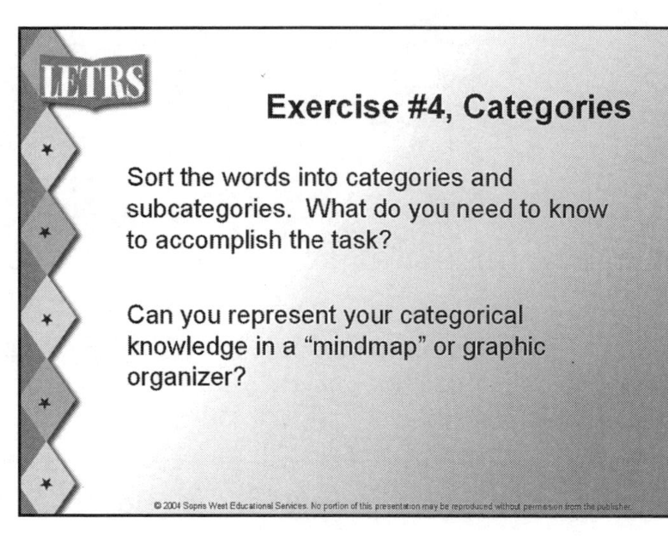

Slide 25

Exercise #4: Categories

Put the following words on cards and then sort them into categories and subcategories. What do you need to know to accomplish this task?

mushing	Bruno	bones	fur/hair
jobs	Lassie	sniffing	retriever
kibbles	greyhound	famous dogs	legs
dogs	Rin-Tin-Tin	leading	spaniel
milkbone	tail	food	Fido
searching	terrier	breeds	body parts

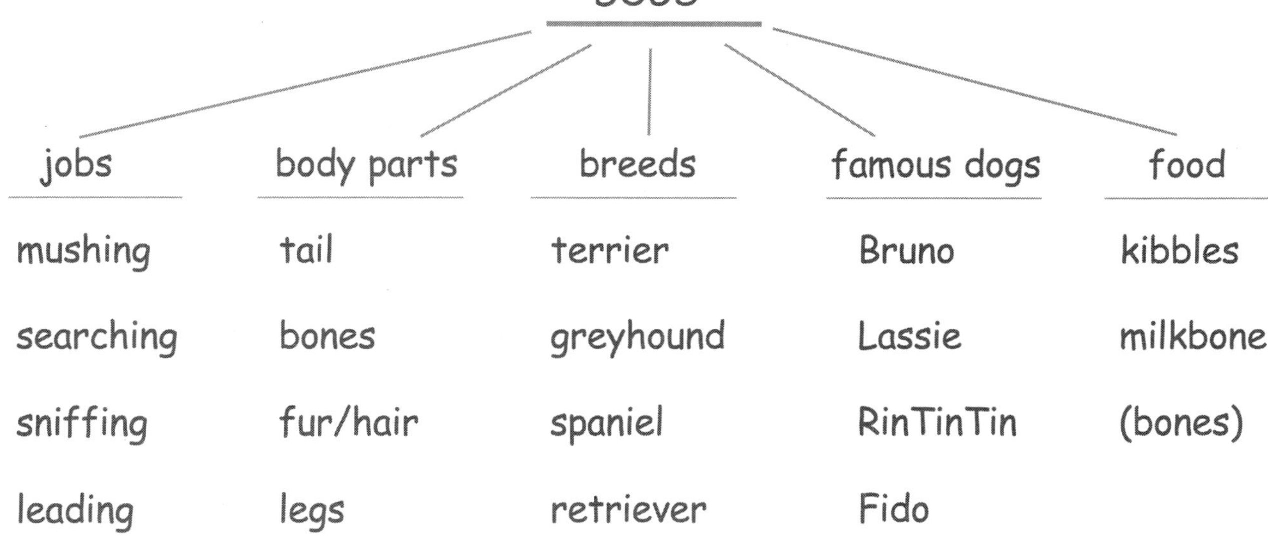

Which graphic organizer in Appendix B would be most suitable for showing these word relationships?

When children are first learning a word, they typically define that word in terms of a few meaning features without giving a category or synonym. As they learn a word better, they can give a complete definition. This "classic" or "formal" definitional pattern can be a helpful framework for instructing children in how to define a word.

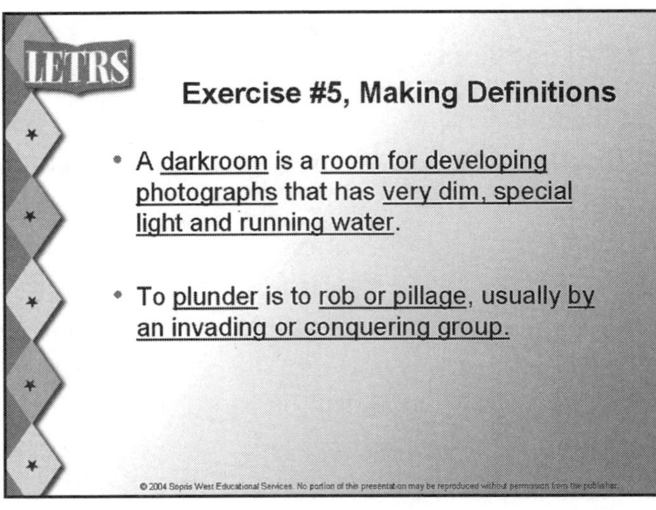

Slide 26

More on definitions. Dictionary definitions often follow a formal structure. They denote the category to which something belongs, provide a synonym, and then elaborate the concept's distinguishing features or properties. For example, *granola* is a *breakfast cereal* of *rolled oats*, *wheat germ*, and *other grains*, that is considered a *healthy* "*whole food*."

As children learn vocabulary, their incomplete knowledge of a word may be reflected in their ability to give only part of a definition. For example, if asked to define "lake," they may say "it has lots of water." A goal of instruction is to give them a complete and elaborated definition.

© The New Yorker Collection 1998 by Tom Cheney. Reprinted with permission.

"It all depends on how you define 'chop.'"

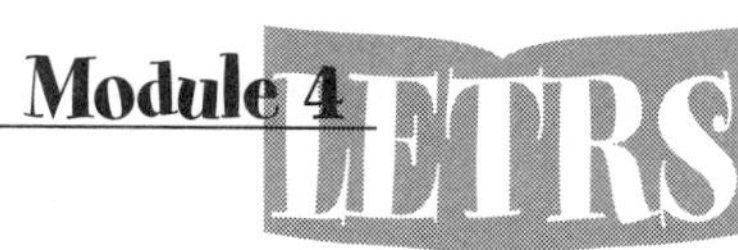

Exercise #5: Structure of Definitions

Use the following format to make a definition for each word below.

A _________________ is (a) _________________ that (is, does) _________________.

(critical features)

Words to define:

River: A river is a long, flowing body of water that goes downhill and that gets its water from many tributaries in a watershed.

Phoneme: A phoneme is a single speech sound that combines with others to make words. Every language has its own inventory of phonemes. Phonemes may be consonants or vowels.

Bison: A bison is a buffalo, a large brown animal with woolly fur that lives on the grassy plains of the Western United States and that once ran wild in very large herds before the west was settled.

Semantic feature analysis. The critical or defining features of words are sometimes formally presented or analyzed in charts that show the contrast between two similar or overlapping concepts. Content words (nouns, verbs, adverbs, adjectives) have many attributes known as **semantic properties**. The better a word is known, the more of its properties or features are known. Words that overlap extensively in meaning qualify as **synonyms**. Words that overlap very little and have opposite connotations qualify as **antonyms**. Many words have semantic overlap but are not synonyms for one another.

Be sure to do this exercise. If possible, bring a variety of drinking vessels to class and ask the class what they would be called. The points to elicit from the activity of checking the features of cup, glass, and mug are:

• Not everyone agrees on every feature, but there is general consensus on how these names are applied to various objects.

• Many words share "semantic overlap"—they have meaning features in common, but they differ on several others.

• Words with semantic overlap are not synonyms, but they are related enough to be in the same category or to have associated uses.

Slide 27

Exercise #6: Semantic Feature Analysis

If the object at the top of a column has the feature designated on the left, mark a (+).
If the object does not have the feature, mark a (–). How extensively do these meanings
overlap? Are the words synonyms or not?

	OBJECTS		
FEATURES	**cup**	**glass**	**mug**
Have a handle	+/–	–	+
Made from clay			+
Made from glass		+/–	
Round shape	+	+	+
Taller than round		+	
For hot liquid	+/–	+	
For cold liquid	+/–	+	
Made from paper	+/–	–	–
Used for wine	+/–	+	–

Exercise #7: How Groups of Words Are Alike

In what way are the following groups of nouns the same and a little different?
In what ways do their semantic features overlap?

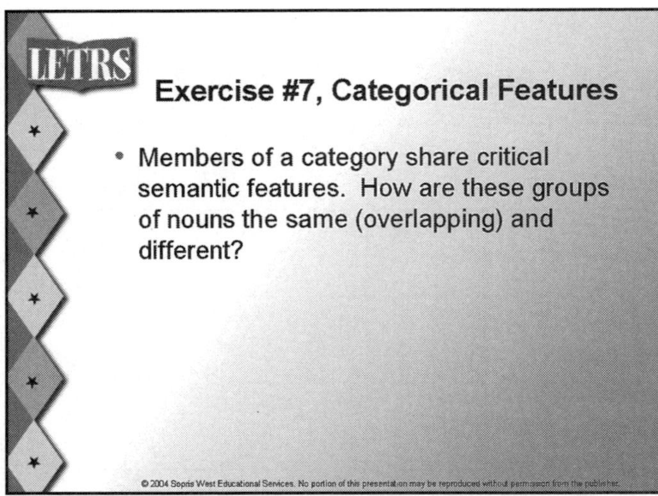

Tell the participants that this exercise is for them—it is more difficult than an exercise that would typically be used with elementary students. It is to stretch their minds a bit. The exercise reveals some other properties of nouns, such as animate and inanimate, concrete and abstract, countable and non-countable.

Slide 28

1. daughter, sister, niece   vs.   nun, waitress, actress
    <u>Both groups are female; the first group are relatives.</u>

2. rooster, bull, ram   vs.   hen, ewe, cow
    <u>Both groups are farm animals; the first are male.</u>

3. table, chair, pencil   vs.   water, cream, sand
    <u>Both groups of objects are inanimate; the first group are solid and can be counted; the second are fluid and cannot be counted.</u>

4. table, chair, pencil   vs.   faith, hope, charity
    <u>Both groups are nouns; the first are concrete, the second abstract.</u>

5. husband, brother, son   vs.   clerk, preacher, judge
    <u>Both groups are people; the first are relatives, the second are professionals.</u>

6. grandfather, mother, nephew   vs   brother, sister, cousin
    <u>Both groups are relatives; the first are multiple generations, the second are the same generation.</u>

The Mighty Word: Building Vocabulary and Oral Language

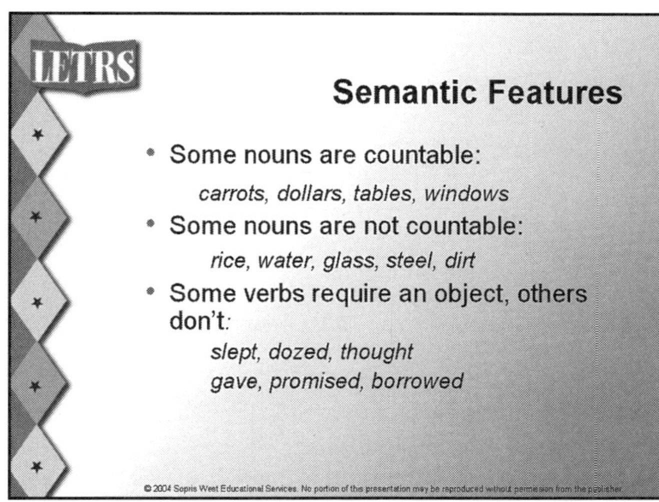

Slide 29

Countable nouns take the adjectives "few" and "fewer," while non-countable nouns take the adjective "less."

Countable nouns take "many," while non-countable nouns take "much."

Other kinds of semantic features. Words also have other properties or features that determine how they can be used in sentences and what words we combine with them or substitute for them. For example, nouns may be subdivided into those that are **countable** and those that are not. Countable nouns take the quantifier adjectives *many* and *few*; non-countable or mass nouns take the adjectives *much* and *less*. You can eat *too many carrots* but not *too much carrots*, or *too much rice* but not *too many rices*. You can have *too few dollars* or *less money* than you'd like. The word *more* can modify either type of noun.

Verbs may be subdivided into those that must take a direct object and those that can stand alone without an object. Verbs are "marked" as needing other words to go with them. The **transitive property** of a verb means it requires an object. For example, I can *subject* someone to something but I can't *subject* (with no object). I can *reject* someone for something but I can't just *reject*. On the other hand, I can *procrastinate* all by myself, without doing anything to anyone but me. Other intransitive verbs are *sleep*, *think*, and *hesitate*. *Sleep* and *think* can be followed by prepositional phrases (*I will sleep* until *9:30. I thought* about *what you said...*) But the word *hesitate* must be followed by an infinitive (*I hesitated* to call *you...*). Content words, including nouns and verbs, contain grammatical properties that most speakers of the language know just by hearing the words spoken often in context.

Tip for Teaching

Teaching a word's meaning may necessitate explaining its part of speech and showing how it must be used in a sentence.

Scaling of nouns, verbs, and adjectives is helpful to children who are looking for the best word to express their meaning or trying to understand what a word conveys. A property of antonyms that invites scaling of words is that some are gradable—they are points on a continuum, not absolute either/or qualities.

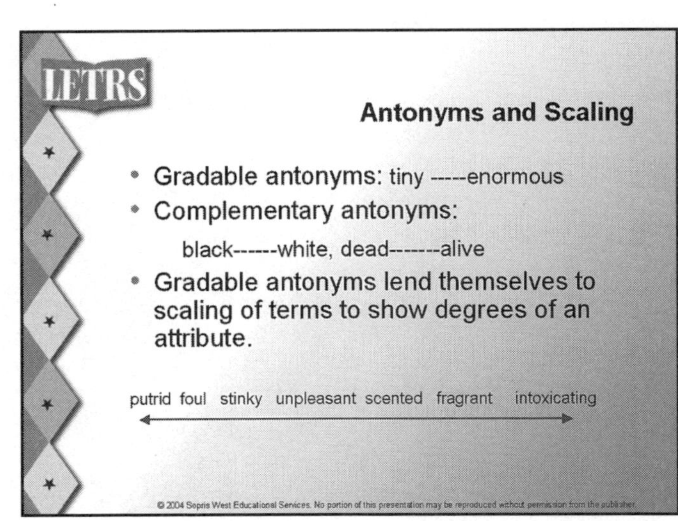

Slide 30

Types of opposites. Antonyms are words of opposite meaning, but there are two important subtypes to consider: **gradable** or **complementary** antonyms. **Gradable antonyms** take meaning from the context in which they are used. Their meaning is relative and expresses the degree to which an attribute characterizes a person or object. For example to say that one house is "enormous" and the other is "tiny" does not convey any fixed amount of space occupied by either house. The words refer to points on a continuum that vary according to one's perspective on houses. Gradable antonyms lend themselves to the activity of **scaling** or putting words on a continuum to express degrees of meaning. *Enormous, huge, large, average, small, tiny,* and *miniscule* convey a scale of size. Scaling is a verbal exercise that can help a writer be more precise in word choice and help young readers refine their knowledge of word meanings.

Complementary pairs of opposites are dichotomous and do not represent points on a scale. The qualities exist in a complementary relationship; if one condition exists, the other cannot, and vice versa. There are no gradations between the opposite conditions. One can be married or single; dead or alive; male or female. The expression, *he sees things in black and white* means, he thinks that if something is one thing it cannot be the other. This type of person thinks of opposites as complementary when in fact they are gradable; there is a continuum of qualities between the points on a continuum that we refer to as the "gray."

A common way of forming antonyms in the language is to add prefixes including *un, in, non, mis,* or *dis* to words as permitted: *happy/unhappy; hospitable/inhospitable; conformist/nonconformist; identify/misidentify; allow/disallow.*

Exercise #8: Antonym Pairs and Scaling

Check the antonym pairs as complementary (either/or) or gradable (opposite ends of a continuous scale).

	Complementary	Gradable
dead – alive	✔	
hot – cold		✔
above – below	✔	
fat – skinny		✔
married – single	✔	
fragrant – putrid		✔
angry – delighted		✔
hideous – gorgeous		✔
straight – bent	✔	
honest – devious		✔
winner – loser	✔	

Now take one of the *gradable* antonym pairs and fill out the scale from one extreme to the other with words that show degrees of meaning.

honest   straight   fair   dishonest   devious

⟵————————————————————⟶

Figure 4.1: Dimensions of Word Knowledge

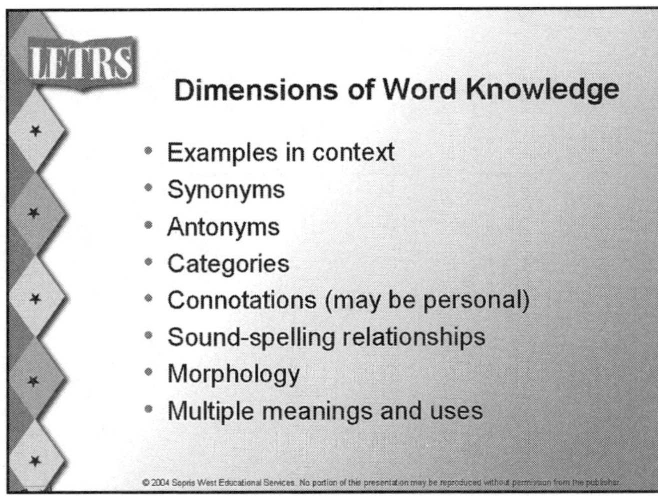

The diagram or conceptual map of facets of meaning can be helpful in considering how to teach vocabulary. First, multiple examples in context are necessary. Then, all other properties represent aspects of meaning that are possible to discuss and explore to deepen word knowledge.

Slide 31

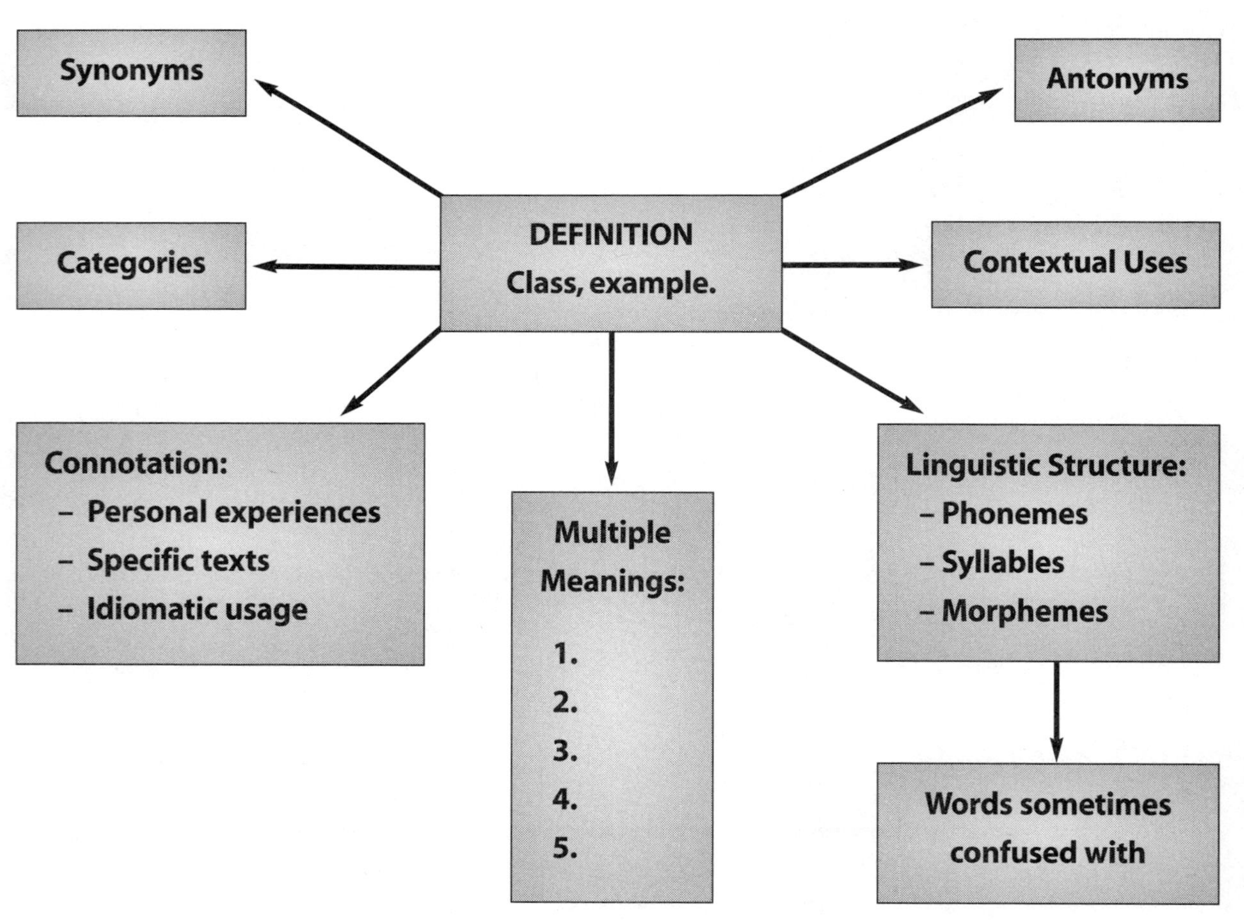

Teaching Vocabulary

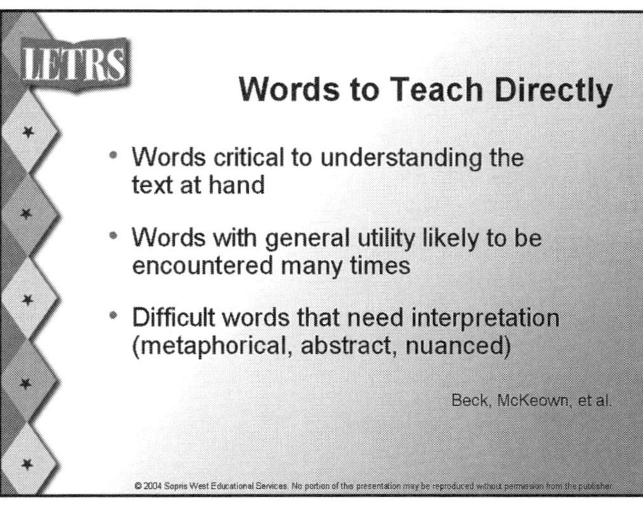

Slide 32

Beck et al. emphasize that words for instruction must be selected judiciously because we have time to teach only some of the words children should know. Topic-specific or rare words should be explained briefly and directly, then instruction should move on. Words with general utility deserve the most instructional focus. Figurative language often needs explanation.

Which Words Should Be Directly Taught?

a. *Words important to the theme of a passage read* and discussed in the classroom should be chosen and emphasized first. Those words may or may not be in the written text that the children are reading. For example, in Chapter 9 of *Stuart Little*, Stuart the mouse finds himself in a dumpster covered with wet, smelly garbage. The scene invites a discussion of words for smells, even a scaling of words from *putrid* to *fragrant*, even though they are not used in the text.

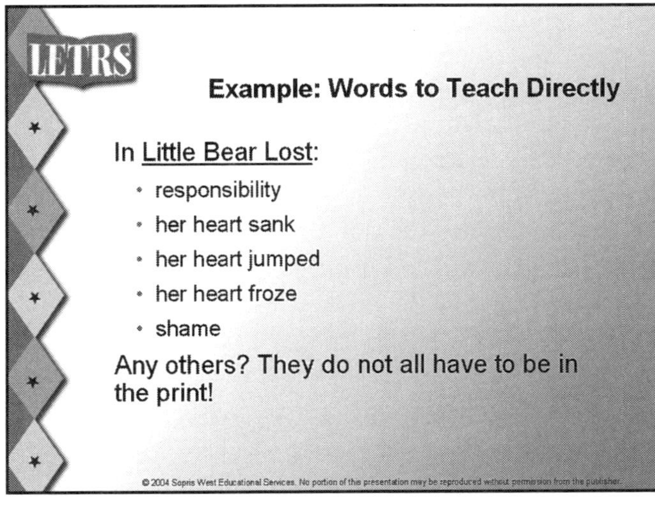

Slide 33

In Little Bear Lost *(see text at end of book), the word "responsibility" is only used once, but it is the central theme of the story and the word most important to explore in multiple dimensions. Are there any others that are not in the print that might be discussed? (forgiveness, regret, immaturity are possibilities)*

b. *Words that are useful and likely to be encountered again* soon can be revisited in other contexts. For example, words for human emotions and relationships will be useful whenever characters in narratives are discussed. *Guilt, gratitude, indebtedness, greed,* and *wisdom* are useful words.

c. *Difficult words that need interpretation,* such as figures of speech, idioms, or words that refer to background information that is central to understanding the text must be tackled directly. More time should be spent elaborating their meanings. For example, if a passage is about animal habitats, the concept of habitat and words describing habitats should be directly presented.

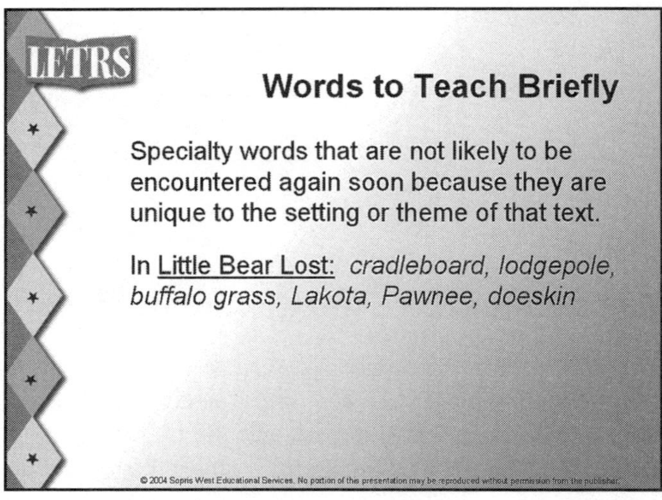

Slide 34

Which Words Can Be Explained Briefly?

Children's texts often include specialty words needed to understand the topic at hand that will not be encountered again soon. Those words can be sorted out and explained briefly before reading and during reading itself. Elaborate exercises or memorization are not worthwhile for words with a limited range of use. For example, if the story is about a weaver, terms such as *shuttle* or *spindle* might be used but they do not require instructional focus.

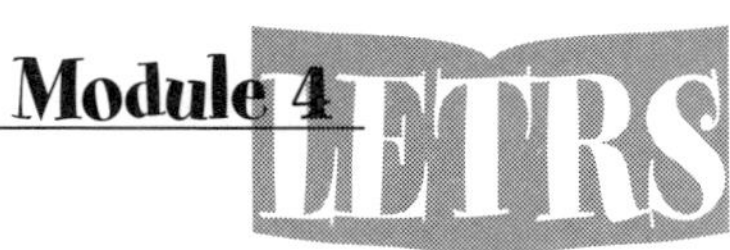

Provide Multiple Examples of Word Use in Varied Contexts

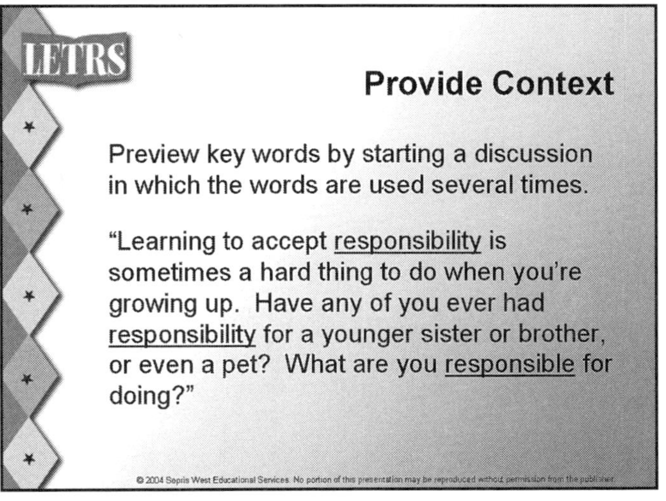

Slide 35

Encourage teachers to use key words in a preview conversation with students, before they list them on the board. Teachers need to realize that their own verbal behavior can be a key facilitator of vocabulary development.

Especially before reading a new selection, preview the most important vocabulary by using the words in spoken sentences and seeing if the students can begin to form an idea of their meaning. Hearing the words spoken and used is essential; if students do not hear them used in their classroom, they may never be exposed. Many published reading programs begin lessons with a list of new words with which a written definition is to be matched. That exercise may be more worthwhile after the children have heard the teacher use the words several times.

Teach the Relationship Between Word Structure and Word Meaning

Teachers should encourage choral responses from the class and the use of words in complete sentences.

Look for opportunities to parse a word into morphemes and link a word to others in its morphological family.

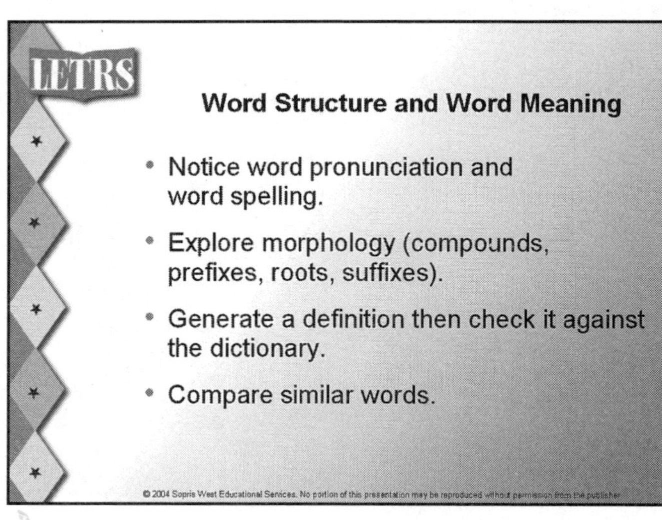

Slide 36

Meaningful parts of words—compounds, inflectional endings, prefixes, suffixes, roots and base words—connect words with other known words. Recognition of meaningful parts can help students figure out meanings of new words encountered in context, and can help them organize their mental dictionary for easy access to words in memory. For example, a second or third grader will benefit from knowing that *misery* and *miserable* are related and to think about why the word *miser* shares meaning with *misery*.

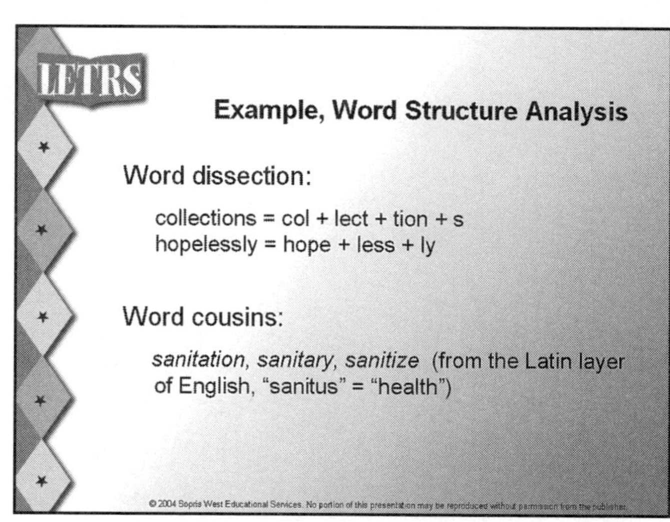

Slide 37

A third grader can learn that the words *bisect*, *dissect*, *intersect*, *insect*, and *section* share a root (meaning to *cut*). They can be asked what each of these words has to do with the idea of cutting or segmentation. They could be asked to speculate on the meaning of "sector" or "trisection."

Be Sure the Students Can Pronounce the Word

Students confuse similar sounding words such as *pacific* and *specific*, *then* and *than*, *shocked* and *shot*, *bisect* and *bicept*. Without an accurate and complete phonological representation of a word (how it is pronounced, with all sounds enunciated) students will have trouble sorting out the meaning. Check pronunciation; always have students pronounce new words accurately.

LETRS

Multiple Meanings and Uses

Stuart Little….
- squash
- duck
- grounds

© 2004 Sopris West Educational Services. No portion of this presentation may be reproduced without permission from the publisher.

Slide 38

In Chapter 9 in Stuart Little, these words are used in ways that students may not know. "Squash" as a vegetable; "duck" as an action; and "grounds" to mean the residuals of coffee-making. Again, the teacher may need to anticipate the possibility that students know only one meaning of several.

Teach Multiple Meanings and Uses

Even the words first encountered in decodable text often have multiple meanings. Students who learn new uses and meanings for known words develop more flexibility and curiosity about words, or greater word consciousness. For example, if the students read "jam," they should be able to think of both a traffic jam and the jam spread on toast. They are also likely to expect other words they know to have new meanings.

Teach Idioms, Metaphors, and Colloquial Uses of Language

Students who are learning English as a second language, who are concrete or literal in their interpretation of language, or who have not been exposed to wide ranging uses of words and phrases, may be stymied by the metaphoric nature of verbal expression. "She's gone to the dogs." "He ran out of luck." "Let's kill some time before the game." "She's taken nothing from nobody."

© The New Yorker Collection 2001 Gahan Wilson. Reprinted with permission.

Use Graphic Organizers to Show How Words Are Related

Especially after reading a passage, word webs and graphic organizers that depict categories and comparisons are very helpful for defining and deepening word knowledge. Word webs and graphic organizers from the *LANGUAGE!* curriculum (Sopris West) provide good examples of the formats that can be devised and are included in Appendix B.

Emphasize again that the process of learning words should embrace a variety of activities that require a student to expand, rearrange, compare, analyze, or write words, and that encourage students to use the words themselves in both speaking and writing.

Word Wizard is a game devised by Beck et al. that rewards students for noticing the use of a learned word outside the classroom and bringing in examples of its use.

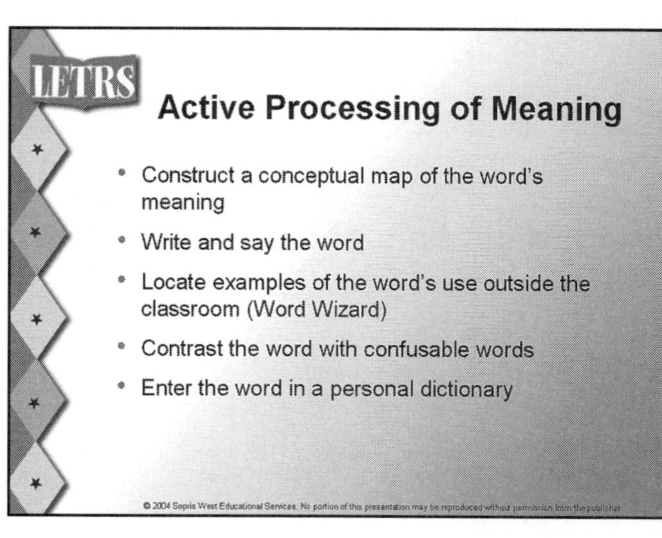

Slide 39

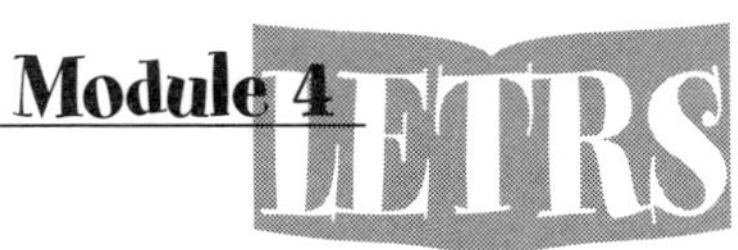

Exercise #9, Plan Instruction

Select one or more of the narrative or expository texts provided at the end of the module.

With a small group, decide on the words that are most important to teach directly and thoroughly (5–10). List words that might be taught more briefly as well.

Outline a few activities that would be useful for building vocabulary before, during, or after reading the selection.

© 2004 Sopris West Educational Services. No portion of this presentation may be reproduced without permission from the publisher.

Slide 40

This is the most important activity of the day. About 1.5 hours is typically needed for the class to break into groups of 3-5 people, read a text, decide on a plan for teaching the vocabulary in the text, and then share with the class in a debriefing session.

Encourage groups to choose either an expository or a narrative text, so that in the sharing time, one of each is covered. It is a good practice to have several groups generate a plan for the same text, so that ideas can be compared and groups can teach one another.

Suggestion: Give each group an overhead transparency to outline their presentation to the rest of the class.

Usually the collective ideas of the group include many good (and different) insights and innovations. There is no "best" plan, so each group will have something of value to offer the others.

Appendix C includes one example of how the assignment can be done.

____

____

____

Exercise #9: Apply Strategies to Teaching Text

Focusing on one or more texts at the end of this module, work with a small group to a) select the words that you would teach directly and b) devise strategies for teaching those words. Indicate whether you are likely to use the strategies before reading, during reading, or after reading.

This exercise can take an hour or more. Select a text that is appropriate for the group. The text on Animal Homes or the narrative, Little Bear Lost are excellent selections for this exercise. Give the groups 20 to 30 minutes to sketch out their instructional strategies for just the vocabulary part of the lesson. Use groups of 4 to 6 people. Give each group an overhead transparency or chart paper to support a brief presentation by the group. There are no "right" answers. Each group's approach will vary and the sharing will enrich everyone's knowledge of potentially productive approaches.

Summary

Point out that those students who don't read need to hear the words in text read to them—thus, taped books and vocabulary instruction are extremely important for the verbal development of students with reading difficulties.

Guided oral reading or small oral reading groups during school time are valuable. Sustained silent reading only "works" if students are able to choose an appropriate book and read to themselves with comprehension. Many cannot use the time well if left on their own.

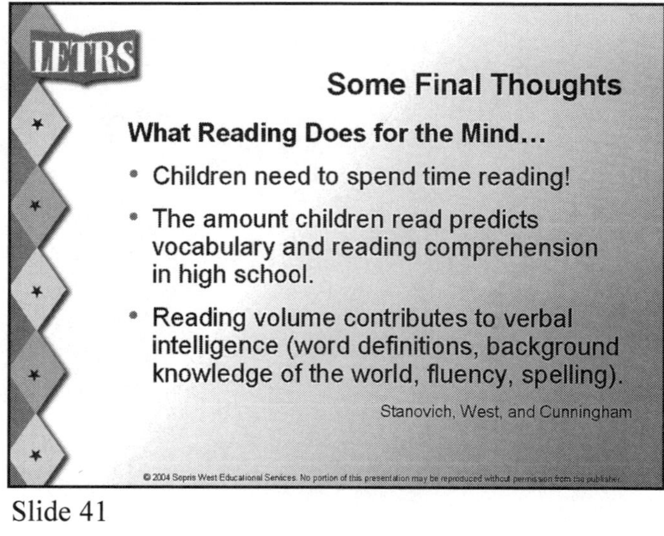

Slide 41

Understanding what we read depends not only on the ability to decode the words in print but also to know their meanings. Comprehension is highly dependent on knowledge of word meanings. Knowledge of a word is learned gradually after multiple exposures to words in speech and print. Students can be encouraged to learn new words by piecing together meanings from context, word parts (morphemes), and dictionary definitions. Many word meanings are learned indirectly from exposure. Thus, there is no better way to build vocabulary than through reading itself.

Incentives for reading outside the school, using the library, and involving parents in home reading are all extremely important to any reading instruction program.

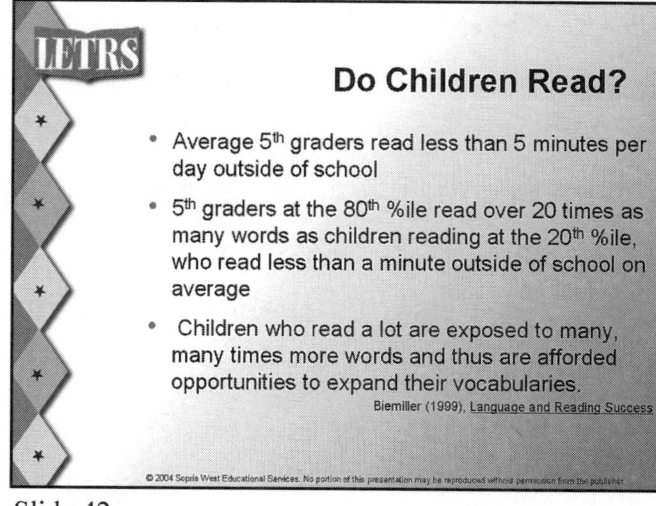

Slide 42

Direct vocabulary instruction targets specific vocabulary that is a) very useful, b) central to the meaning of that passage, or c) difficult to figure out independently. Between 10 and 15 new words a week are usually targeted for direct teaching. Relationships among words should be emphasized. Synonyms, categories, antonyms, overlapping meanings, thematic associations, analogies, class—example relationships, and figures of speech all can be employed in the discussion of word meanings and their associations.

Slide 43

Let's teach reading well from the time students enter school so that problems are caught early and children get on the right track toward reading success. It makes a difference for a lifetime.

The dictionary is an indispensable reference, but dictionary definitions are often incomplete, misleading, or useless for knowing how to use a word. We don't "own" new words until we have been exposed to them, investigated them, and used them appropriately ourselves. Knowledge of word meanings is necessary for proficient reading and writing, and, paradoxically, those meanings will be learned most readily from reading itself and from a stimulating linguistic environment. Teachers' verbal behavior in the classroom is pivotal in providing students the exposure, the models, and the incentives they need to pursue word learning.

Finally, remember these principles:

◆ Motivate students to read or listen to challenging text.

◆ Prioritize critical high utility vocabulary for direct teaching.

◆ Actively engage students in "deep processing"—integrating and applying new words across contexts.

◆ Don't waste time memorizing definitions or telling children to use words in sentences if they do not yet understand them.

Bibliography on Vocabulary

Beck, I.L., McKeown, M.G., & Kucan, L. (2002). *Bringing words to life: Robust vocabulary instruction.* New York: Guilford Press.

Biemiller, A. (1999). *Language and reading success.* In J. Chall (Ed.), *From reading research to practice, A series for teachers.* Cambridge, MA: Brookline Books.

Carlisle, J. & Rice, M.S. (2003). *Reading comprehension: Research-based principles and practices.* Baltimore: York Press.

Chall, J.S., Jacobs, V.A., & Baldwin, L.E. (1990). *The reading crisis: Why poor children fall behind.* Cambridge, MA: Harvard University Press.

Dickinson, D.K. & Smith, M.W. (1994). Long-term effects of preschool teachers' book readings on low-income children's vocabulary and story comprehension. *Reading Research Quarterly, 29*, 104-123.

Flavell, R. & Flavell, L. (1995). *Dictionary of word origins.* London: Kyle Cathie Limited.

Hart, B. & Risley, T. R. (1995). *Meaningful differences in the everyday experience of young American children.* Baltimore: Paul Brookes.

Hirsch, E.D. (2001). Overcoming the language gap. *American Educator, 25* (2), 4, 6-7.

Irvin, J.L. (1997). *Reading for the middle school student* (2nd Ed.). Boston: Allyn and Bacon.

Kacirk, J. (2000). *The word museum: The most remarkable English words ever forgotten.* New York: Touchstone.

RAND Reading Study Group (2002). *Reading for understanding: Toward an R & D program in reading comprehension.* Washington, DC: Office of Education Research and Improvement.

Sable, P. (2001). Vocabulary: Teaching words and their meanings. In S. Brody (Ed.), *Teaching reading: Language, letters, and thought.* (pp. 254-275). Milford, NH: LARC Publishing.

Stahl, S. A. (1999). *Vocabulary development.* In J. Chall (Ed.), *From reading research to practice*, A series for teachers. Cambridge, MA: Brookline Books.

Sternberg, R.J. (1987). Most vocabulary is learned from context. In M.G. McKeown & M.E. Curtis (Eds.), *The nature of vocabulary acquisition* (pp. 89-106). Hillsdale, NJ: Erlbaum.

Instructional Resources

Dictionaries

- Longman Dictionary of American English

- The Basic Newbury House Dictionary of American English

- Longman Basic Dictionary of American English

- http://www.m-w.com/

Software

- www.inspiration.com

- http://npip.com/CBSS/index.html

- Masterminds@graphicorganizers.com

- Power Vocabulary: www.lexile.com

Appendix A for Module 4: Multiple Meanings

"House"[3]

Spellings: hus, hows, hous, huus, houus, huse, huis

Origin: Old Teutonic (huso)

Relatives: German - haus, Swiss - hus, Dutch - huis

Meanings:

a) a building for human habitation (c. 1000, Beowulf)

b) the portion of a building occupied by one tenant or family (c. 1020)

c) a building for human occupation, for some purpose other than that of an ordinary dwelling, usually with a prefix: workhouse, poorhouse, brewhouse (c. 1552)

d) a place of worship (c. 1000)

e) a building for entertainment of travelers, an inn (c. 1550), "on the house" (c. 1889, Kansas City, MO)

f) a building for the keeping of cattle, birds, plants (1503)

g) a place of abode of a religious fraternity, a convent (c. 1375)

h) a college in a university (1536)

i) a boarding-house attached to and forming a portion of a public school (c. 1855)

j) the building in which a legislative or deliberative assembly meets, or the assembly itself (1545)

k) a place of business, as in clearing-house, counting-house (1582), house of ill-fame (1810)

l) a theatre or playhouse

m) attribution of a permanent or resident band or jazz group (1934)

n) the persons living in one household (c. 950)

o) a family including ancestors and descendants (c.1000)

p) astrology—a twelfth part of the heavens as divided by great circles through the north and south points of the horizon (c. 1391, Chaucer)

q) phrases: house of ill repute, house of call, house and home, house-to-house, bring down the house, keep house, set up house, like a house on fire

[3] Listings based on entries for the word in J.A. Simpson (Ed.) (1989). *The Oxford English Dictionary*, 2nd Edition, Volume VII. Oxford: Oxford University Press.

    r)   special combinations: house boy, house arrest, house-bound, house call, house manager, house officer, house physician

    s)   compounds: housekeeper, householder, housebreaking

"Habitat"

Origin: Latin, habitat, habitare

Spelling: no change

Meaning:

    a)   the locality in which a plant or animal naturally grows and lives (c. 1762)

    b)   dwelling-place (c. 1854)

Combinations: habitat form, habitat group, Habitat for Humanity

Relatives: inhabit, cohabit

"Habitation"

Origin: Latin to French to English, abitacioun (habitation, c. 1374, Chaucer)

Meanings:

    a)   the action of dwelling in, occupy by inhabitants

    b)   a place of abode or residence, dwelling-place (1382)

    c)   a settlement

Relatives: cohabitation

"Residence"

Origin: Old French, Latin (residere) (1386, Chaucer)

Meanings:

    a)   having one's usual abode at a certain place

    b)   where a couple settles after marriage

    c)   living regularly at some place for the discharge of special duties

    d)   continuance in some course or action

    e)   the place where one resides

    f)   a dwelling, abode, or house

    g)   the seat of power

    h)   the time during which one resides at a place

    i)   the settling of sediment in liquids

Relatives: preside, president, presidential

Appendix B for Module 4: Graphic Organizers

On the following pages are examples of graphic organizers that can be used before and after reading.

Graphic organizers used by permission from J. Greene, N. Eberhardt, A. Whitney, and L. Moats (2000). *LANGUAGE ! Curriculum, Instructional Resource Guide for Teachers*. Longmont, Colorado: Sopris West.

~~~~ Multiple Meaning Map ~~~~

Unit: _______   Student: _______________________________   Date: _____________

Directions: Use discussion with classmates, a thesaurus, or a dictionary to find multiple meanings for the word that is provided. Write a word or phrase to describe the word's meaning, or draw a picture to represent the meaning. Write a sentence using the word with each of the meanings.

~~~ Map It: Classification Paragraph ~~~

Unit: _______   Student: _________________________________   Date: ____________

Category

Subgroup

Subgroup

Subgroup

(Examples)

(Examples)

(Examples)

~~~~ **Relate It: Word Wheel** ~~~~

Unit: _______   Student: _________________________________   Date: ____________

Synonyms

Antonyms

___________ is to ___________

as ___________ is to ___________

Analogies

Write a sentence to show one of these relationships to the target word:

____

____

____

∼∼∼ Define It (Sheet A) ∼∼∼

Unit: _______   Student: _____________________________   Date: _____________

Directions: Use this graphic organizer to build definitions for words in this unit.

Word		Category		Attribute

1. [Word] = [Category] + [Attribute]

Definition: ____

____

____

2. [Word] = [Category] + [Attribute]

Definition: ____

____

____

3. [Word] = [Category] + [Attribute]

Definition: ____

____

____

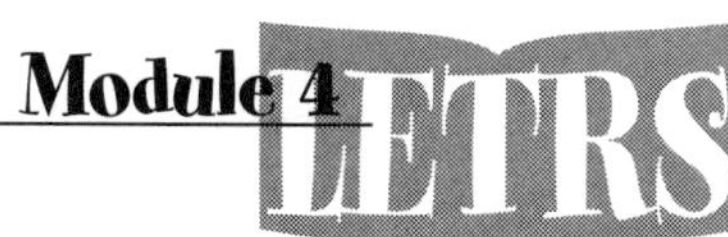

~~~ Define It (Sheet B) ~~~

Unit: _______   Student: _________________________________   Date: ____________

Directions: Use this graphic organizer to build an understanding of this word.

Category

What is it?

Properties/Attributes

What is it like?

What are some examples?

Illustrations/Examples

Appendix C for Module 4: Model Lessons

Little Bear Lost
Vocabulary Instruction

Pre-selected Vocabulary for Direct Instruction

Content-Specific	Key Words For In-Depth Teaching
cradleboard	responsibility
buffalo	silence
Lakota	enemy
Pawnee, Crow	pestered
lodge	terror, terrified
village	sob, sobbing
prairie	search
prairie grass	
doeskin	

Similes

. . . as warm and brown as the leaves that fell when frost lay on the grass

. . . as hot as the lodge fire in winter

. . . strong enough to shake the whole earth like thunder and with hoofs as wide as a cradleboard

Metaphors

. . . Blue Cloud felt her heart sink.

. . . her heart jumped

. . . that made her heart freeze in fear

. . . to find a whole sea of huge, hairy beasts running

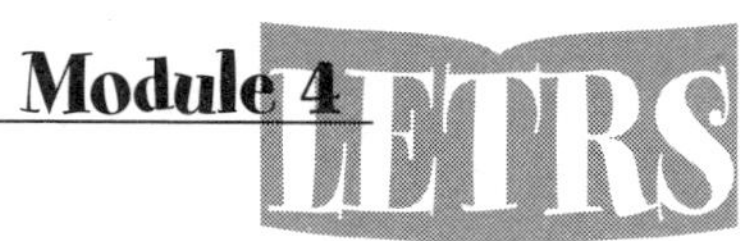

I. Introductory Activities Before Reading

Look at pictures that help depict content-specific vocabulary and introduce it first to paint the setting and context for the story. Discuss Lakota life in the days when Lakota Sioux lived on the prairie, relied on buffalo for food, clothing, and shelter, and traveled continually in pursuit of the hunt. Ask why babies would be put on a cradleboard and why it would be dangerous if they cried. Ask who the enemies of the Lakota might have been; have the students heard of other tribes by the name of Pawnee and Crow.

Elaborate the use and meaning of *responsibility*. Say that this is a story about how a young girl handles a responsibility that was a little too much for her. Use the word "responsibility" many times in introductory conversation with students about their responsibilities. Give an example from your own life about responsibility that may not be easy for you carry out, or about a challenging responsibility you were given as a child. Ask other children to contribute experiences of their own. Use related terms *responsible*, *responsibility*, *irresponsible*.

Ask if students have heard of *pestered*. Give a clue that it has to do with being a *pest*, or bugging someone else until you get what you want.

Explain what *sob* means—to cry uncontrollably because you are very upset about something.

II. During Reading

In addition to other comprehension questions (see Module 6), ask students to paraphrase or interpret the metaphors and similes as they are read aloud. Alternatively, as students read a paragraph with a metaphor, ask students to find the phrases that tell how frightened Blue Cloud is [her heart sank . . . ; her heart froze . . .].

III. After Reading, Vocabulary Consolidation Activities

a) Put words for *crying* on cards and ask students to arrange them according to degree of upset they convey:

> whimper, whine, shed a tear, cry, bawl, sob

b) Create new similes:

as hot as ______________________

as frightened as ______________________

as clever as ______________________

c) Answer each question "yes" or "no" and then explain "why":

Did Blue Cloud forget to be responsible?

Was Blue Cloud's mother responsible?

Were Blue Cloud's friends responsible when they wanted to continue racing horses?

Would it be good if the baby sobbed when Blue Cloud searched for it?

Did Blue Cloud's mother pester her to take the cradleboard?

d) Match the word to another that means almost the same thing:

pester	baby-carrier
enemy	someone who wants to hurt you
cradleboard	search
look all over for	bug someone over and over

e) Create new sentences that use two or three vocabulary words together.

f) Ask students to paraphrase [restate in their own words] sentences and paragraphs in which figurative language is used.

g) Write a personal narrative about taking responsibility—successfully or unsuccessfully.

Mansion for a Mollusk
Vocabulary Instruction Activities

Pre-selected Vocabulary for Thorough Instruction
- mansion
- mollusk
- protect, protection, protected
- prevent
- secrete, secreting, secreted
- sturdy
- mantle
- moist
- flesh

I. Vocabulary Activities Before Reading

a) Introduce title and focus on *mansion* and *mollusk*

b) Discuss different kinds of human homes and functions, listing words such as castle, trophy home, bungalow, cabin

c) Tell what a mollusk is—a soft, squishy animal that can live on land or sea—and ask students what they might know about mollusks (if anything!).

d) Say that mollusks—and all animals—need *protection*. Site examples of the kinds of protection that our houses give us—protection from extremes of temperature, sun, bad weather, predators. What do they use for *protection* when they are out in a storm?

e) Pronounce and write down other key words coming up: prevent, secrete, sturdy, mantle, moist, flesh.

II. Vocabulary Activities During Reading

a) Follow along and underline new words as they are read.

b) Or, put a post-it note where there is a new word they want to know more about. Can go back later and write definition on the post-it, then enter the word on a new words list.

c) Confirm a new meaning with the whole class as a word is read in context and discussed.

III. **Vocabulary Activities After Reading**

a) Rewrite phrases with the new words learned, or complete sentences with the new words. [protect, prevent, secrete, mantle, flesh]

1. The pads on a dog's foot ____________ it from the rough ground and ____________ it from getting sore.

2. The inside of the nose ____________ fluid to keep it moist.

3. An outside cover over the skin is called a ____________.

4. People, animals, and all warm-blooded things have ____________ on their bones.

b) Have students combine two or more words into one sentence that shows the meaning of each. Have them work in partners so that everyone participates and may be called on to share.

> A mollusk seeks *shelter* to *protect* it from enemies.
> *Fleshy* slugs stay under rocks to keep *moist*.

c) Complete the semantic feature analysis chart:

	Soft	Fleshy	On land	In sea	Shell	No shell	Fixed to one place	Can move fast	Slow moving
whelk									
abalone									
squid									
octopus									
Pearl oyster									
conch									
mussel									
snail									
slug									

d)   Sort into categories all the mollusks named in the article:

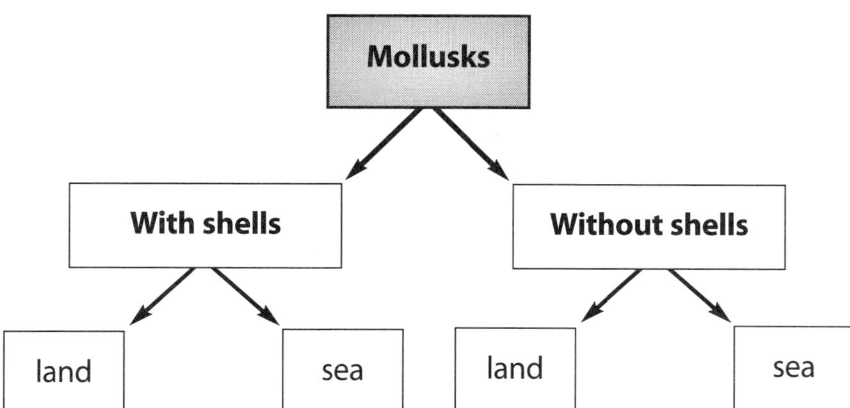

Module 5

Getting Up To Speed: Developing Fluency

Contents for Module 5

Content of LETRS: The Language-Literacy Connection

Components of Comprehensive Reading Instruction	Organization of Language						
	Phonology	Morphology	Orthography	Semantics	Syntax	Discourse and Pragmatics	Etymology
Phonological Awareness	2	2					
Phonics, Spelling, and Word Study	3, 7	3, 7, 10	3, 7, 10				3, 10
Fluency	5		5	5	5		
Vocabulary	4	4	4	4	4		4
Text Comprehension		6		6	6	6, 11	
Written Expression			9, 11	9, 11	9, 11	9, 11	
Assessment	8, 12	8, 12	8, 12	8, 12	8, 12	8, 12	

Objectives for Module 5

- Understand the concepts of automaticity and reading fluency
- Define reading fluency
- Explain why fluency is necessary for comprehension
- Identify several common causes for dysfluency
- Explain the consequences for dysfluency
- Understand poor reader subtypes: single and double deficits
- Explain why fluency-based measurement is important
- Identify who might benefit from fluency-building instruction
- Learn how to calculate, record, and chart fluency results
- Practice several strategies for fluency-building
- Consider some less effective strategies to minimize or avoid

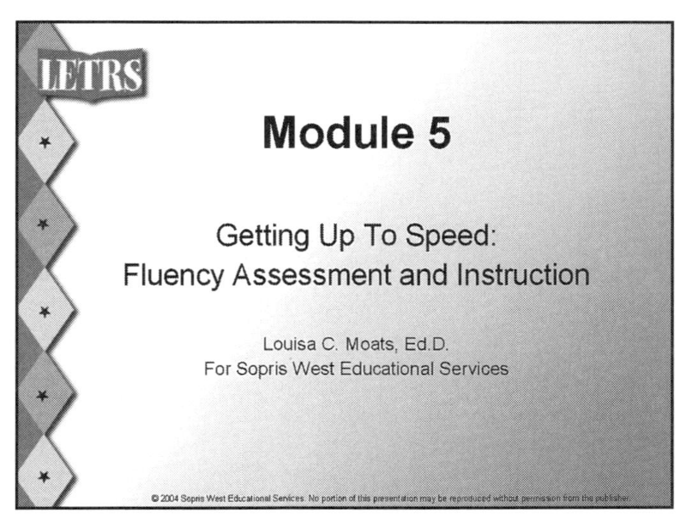

Slide 5

Give examples of how you or others in the group learned component skills of a complex behavior to the point of automaticity.

Reflections may include stories of doing things automatically—when they should have been consciously mediated! Such as taking the turn-off toward work on a Saturday morning when you intended to go somewhere else.

Introduction to Reading Fluency

In addition to the five components of reading in Put Reading First, *a comprehensive language arts curriculum addresses writing, spelling, verbal comprehension, and critical reasoning, and background children need to comprehend.*

Fluency has been a neglected topic until recently, when researchers discovered students could be accurate in decoding, after good instruction, but still could be lacking in sufficient reading fluency to comprehend. To develop into good readers they had to read with fluency and automaticity.

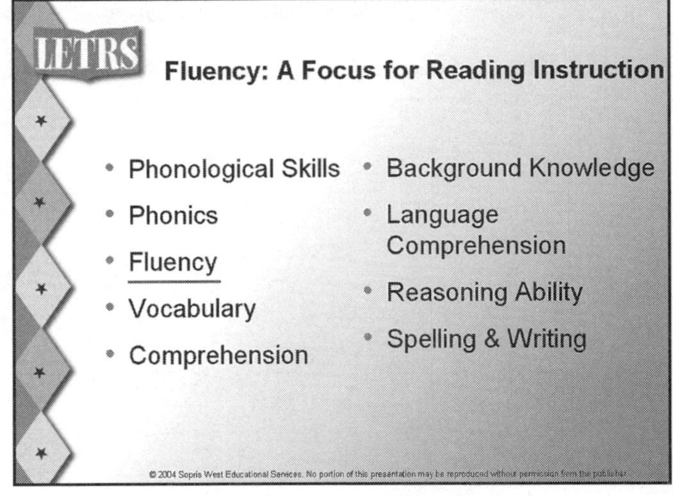

Slide 3

Effective reading instruction enables students to read with comfort, concentration, and comprehension. A productive, satisfying reading experience, in turn, is associated with reading fluency. If students are taught the component skills of reading, including phonics, phonological processing, vocabulary meanings, and comprehension strategies, they will be successful readers only when their text reading is proficient enough to support comprehension. Reading fluency depends on the development of many underlying processes that must be so well learned that they can be carried out effortlessly while the mind devotes itself to making meaning.

Automaticity is a word that describes a characteristic of cognitive processing; fluent performance depends on automaticity.

"Automatic pilot" means the plane is flying itself with no conscious effort from the pilot— it's functioning by bypassing conscious manipulation.

Automaticity refers to the allocation of attentional resources in consciousness.

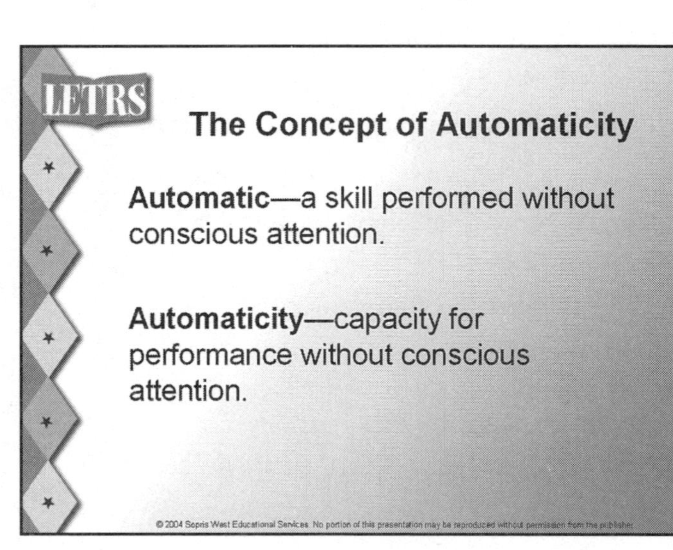

Slide 4

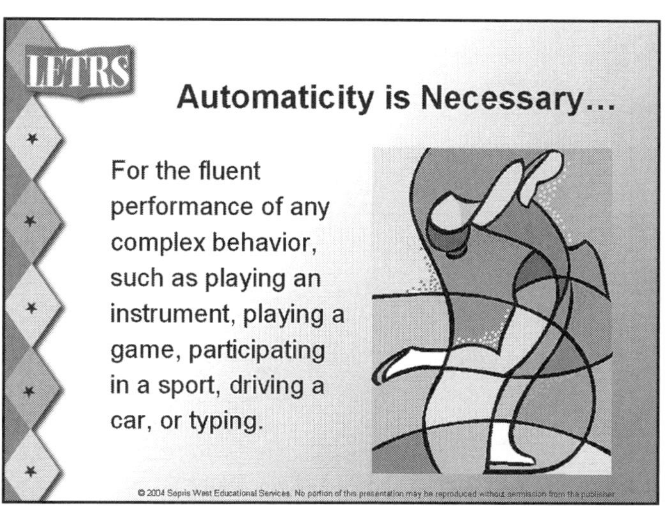

Slide 5

Automaticity refers to the learned capacity to use a skill on demand without having to think it through or use up valuable attentional resources. The brain has only a limited amount of "desk space" or attentional capacity at any one time. Almost all complex behaviors that humans master include a set of underlying subskills that have been learned to an automatic level so that attention is devoted to higher goals. Great basketball coaches ask their players to practice and master ball handling, footwork, court coverage, and other skills until they can use them instantly in the service of complex plays. Pianists learn finger positions, keys, scales, chords and other aspects of musicianship before and during their mastery of challenging compositions. Readers must learn to recognize words accurately and quickly, so that attention can be allocated to comprehension and strategic reading for varied purposes.

Give examples of how you or others in the group learned component skills of a complex behavior to the point of automaticity.

Reflections may include stories of doing things automatically—when they should have been consciously mediated! Such as taking the turn-off toward work on a Saturday morning when you intended to go somewhere else.

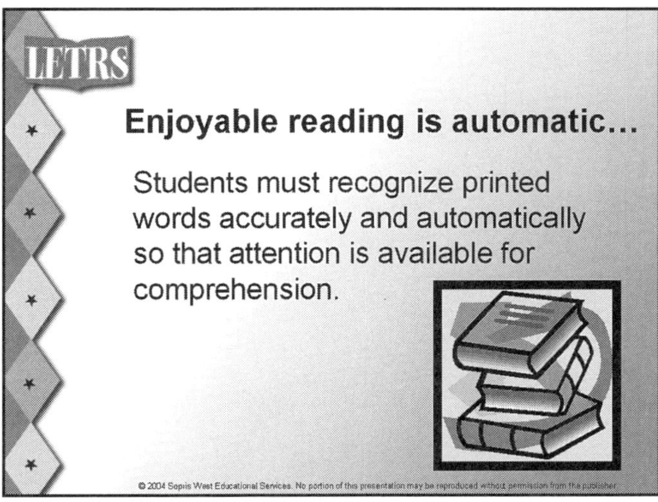

Slide 6

People who are good readers are more likely to enjoy reading, and people who are poor readers are more likely to find reading taxing and aversive.

Poor readers read with too much effort for reading to be relaxing or fun.

In the Connecticut Longitudinal Study, one subject who was a poor reader declared he would rather clean toilets than read!

How Do Children Become Fluent Readers?

These are all terms that reading psychologists use for the idea of exposure to text or number of words read. One of the fundamental principles of learning is that practice is important—that is also very true of reading.

However, practice has to be "perfect practice" to be worthwhile—that is, the students have to know how to read the words accurately before benefits can be accrued from practice.

Exercise #1: Listen to a dysfluent child read on an audio or videotape.

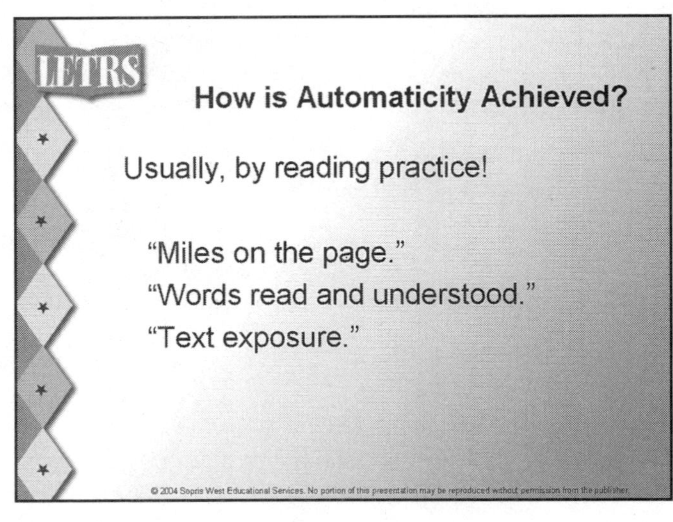

Slide 7

Reading fluency is both a cause and a result of one's reading experience and reading habits. Research indicates that good readers, who recognize words instantly and use phonic decoding skills easily and accurately, read much more than poor readers do right from the beginning of their school career. They practice reading early and often and thus are exposed to printed words far more than children who read very little. Good readers who begin with an aptitude for and/or knowledge of sounds, letters, and words get significantly more print exposure from the first part of first grade.

In contrast, poor readers, who struggle with word identification and decoding, do not like to read because it is effortful and tend to avoid reading. Consequently, they are exposed to far fewer words, get less practice, and remain uncomfortable with a task that is often frustrating and unrewarding. These readers almost always fail to develop the automaticity necessary for reading to become enjoyable and so they practice far less than they should. This cycle must be broken if poor readers are to become proficient readers.

Exercise #1: A Dysfluent Reader

Watch a videotape or listen to an audiotape of a child whose reading is dysfluent.

What is that child's affect?

Does the child seem to understand what is read even though the reading is slow?

Neurological Underpinnings

The brain's cognitive "desk space" has a limited amount of processing capacity (attentional resources) at any one time.

© 2004 Sopris West Educational Services. No portion of this presentation may be reproduced without permission from the publisher.

Slide 8

"Overload" is when more attention is demanded than is available.

If a lot of attention is needed for one task (word recognition), then less attention will be available for others (critical reasoning).

The way to get less attention expended on decoding is to teach decoding accuracy and fluency—NOT to avoid it or try to redirect the child toward comprehension (context) before the child has become proficient in word recognition. Bypass strategies don't work!

Advances in neuroscience, especially neuroimaging techniques, allow researchers to document differences between good readers and poor readers. Magnetic resonance imaging and other techniques illustrate quite concretely that poor readers are struggling with the basics: sounding out and recognizing words bit by bit. Good readers, however, have developed word identification habits that are subsumed by the posterior or back areas of the brain.[1] The "poor reader" patterns change when remediation is successful.

---

[1] Eden & Moats, 2002

All of these parts of the brain are critical to fluent reading, but patterns of activation change as reading develops. As phonological awareness is developed, then sound-symbol connections can be learned. As sound-symbol or phoneme-grapheme connections become accurate and fluent, recognition of whole words is enabled. Then, more frontal lobe capacity is available for reasoning during reading.

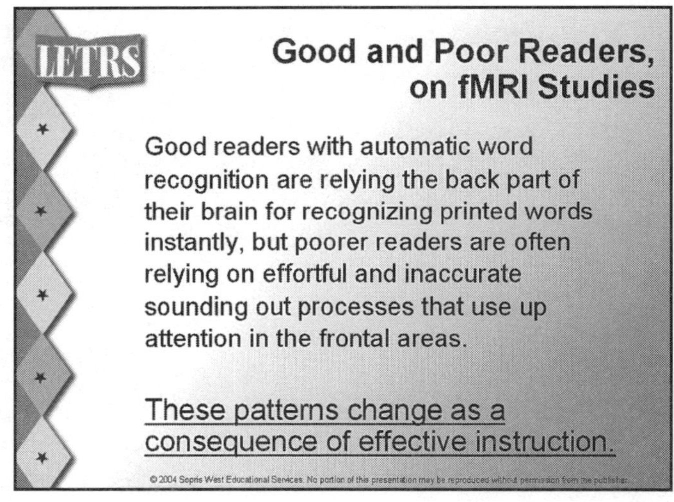

Slide 9

Fluent readers who are automatic at word recognition activate the posterior (back) part of the brain for word reading, and have more attentional resources available in the front part of the brain for higher level verbal reasoning. Beginners or poor readers who are learning to decode allocate more attention to phonological processing and sound-symbol association because these processes are not yet automatic. Again the path to automatic word recognition is through building phonological awareness, accurate sound-symbol association and sound blending, accurate recognition of words by sight, and speed in these sub-processes.

Exercise #2: Have participants time themselves as they read aloud for one minute in each of the two texts. Usually the average oral reading rate for "Alice" that the group reports is about 200 w.p.m., and the average oral reading rate for the reading science article is somewhat slower. Encourage a brief discussion about why most of us are less fluent with the reading science article. Ask participants if they can tell if a person comprehends just by listening to them read.

Slide 10

No one disagrees that the goal of proficient reading is comprehension of text. Thus, as we explore the relationship between reading fluency and reading comprehension, and discuss ways to improve fluency in those children who are too slow, reading speed must always be considered in relation to all other components of and purposes for reading. The following figure depicts the relationship between the skills that go into word recognition and the accomplishment of fluent text reading:

Figure 5.1: The Path to Fluency

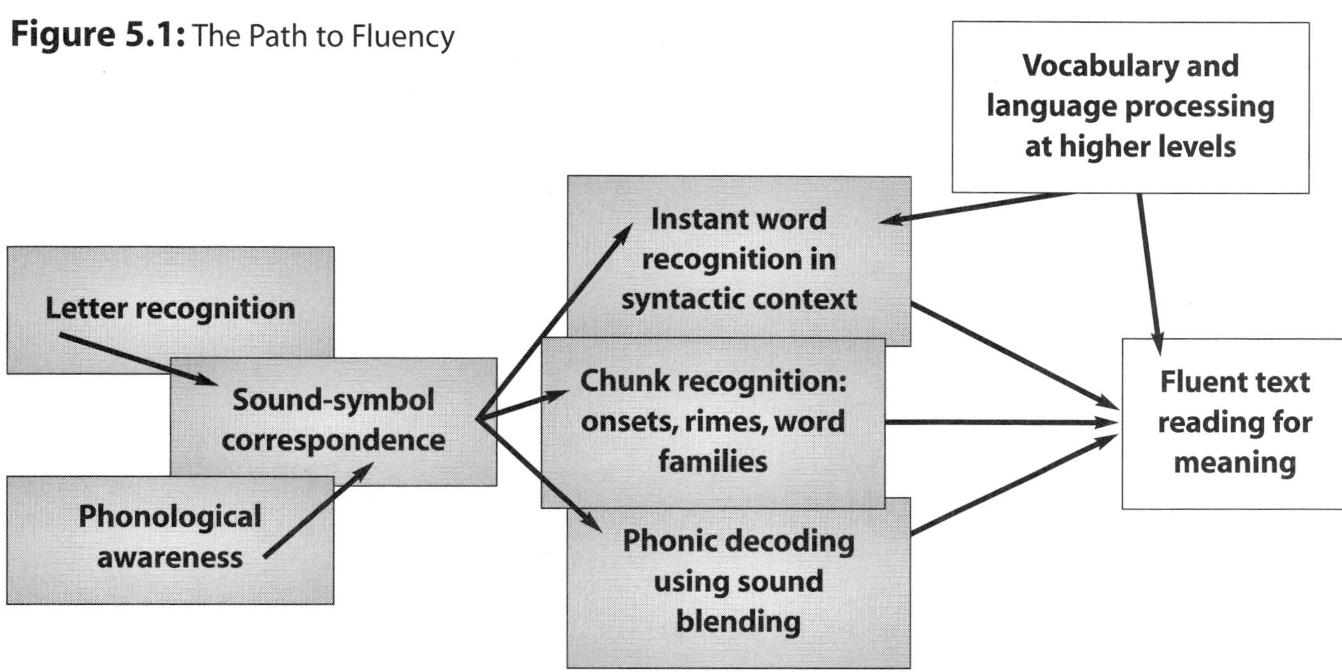

Exercise #2: An Experiment in Fluency

Ask a partner to time you as you read each of the following passages for one minute. Then retell what you read. Was there a difference in your speed or your comprehension? In your enjoyment? What is the relationship between your reading fluency, the type of text you are reading, and your ability to get meaning from the text?

Passage #1: Alice in Wonderland

Passage #2: Excerpt from *Scientific Studies of Reading*

Alice's Adventures in Wonderland
by Lewis Carroll
Chapter 1, Down the Rabbit Hole

Alice was beginning to get very tired of sitting by her sister on the bank, and of having nothing to do: once or twice she had peeped into the book her sister was reading, but it had no pictures or conversations in it, "and what is the use of a book," thought Alice, "without pictures or conversations?"

So she was considering in her own mind, (as well as she could, for the hot day made her feel very sleepy and stupid), whether the pleasure of making a daisy-chain would be worth the trouble of getting up and picking the daisies, when suddenly a white rabbit with pink eyes ran close by her.

There was nothing so *very* remarkable in that; nor did Alice think it so very much out of the way to hear the Rabbit say to itself, "Oh dear! Oh dear! I shall be too late!" (when she thought it over afterwards, it occurred to her that she ought to have wondered at this, but at the time it all seemed quite natural); but when the Rabbit actually *took a watch out of its waistcoat-pocket*, and looked at it, and then hurried on, Alice started to her feet, for it flashed across her mind that she had never before seen a rabbit with either a waistcoat-pocket or a watch to take out of it, and, burning with curiosity, she ran across the field after it, and was just in time to see it pop down a large rabbit-hole under the hedge.

In another moment down went Alice after it, never once considering how in the world she was to get out again.

The rabbit-hole went straight on like a tunnel for some way, and then dipped suddenly down, so suddenly that Alice had not a moment to think about stopping herself before she found herself falling down what seemed to be a very deep well.

Either the well was very deep, or she fell very slowly, for she had plenty of time as she went down to look about her, and to wonder what was going to happen next. First, she tried to look down and make out what she was coming to, but it was too dark to see anything: then she looked at the sides of the well, and noticed that they were filled with cupboards and bookshelves: here and there she saw maps and pictures hung upon pegs. She took down a jar from one of the shelves she passed; it was labeled "ORANGE MARMALADE" but to her great disappointment it was empty: she did not like to drop the jar for fear of killing somebody underneath, so managed to put it into one of the cupboards as she fell past it.

(continued) ...*Alice's Adventures in Wonderland*

"Well!" thought Alice to herself, "after such a fall as this, I shall think nothing of tumbling down stairs! How brave they'll all think me at home! Why, I wouldn't say anything about it, even if I fell off the top of the house! (Which was very likely true.)

Down, down, down. Would the fall never come to an end? "I wonder how many miles I've fallen by this time?" she said aloud. "I must be getting somewhere near the center of the earth. Let me see: that would be four thousand miles down, I think" (for, you see, Alice had learnt several things of this sort in her lessons in the school-room, and though this was not a *very* good opportunity for showing off her knowledge, as there was no one to listen to her, still it was good practice to say it over) "yes—that's about the right distance—but then I wonder what Latitude or Longitude I've got to?" (Alice had not the slightest idea what Latitude was, or Longitude either, but she thought they were nice grand words to say.)

Presently she began again. "I wonder if I shall fall right through the earth! How funny it'll seem to come out among the people that walk with their heads down-wards! The Antipathies, I think—" (she was rather glad there was no one listening this time, as it didn't sound at all the right word) "but I shall have to ask them what the name of the country is, you know. Please, Ma'am, is this New Zealand or Australia?" (and she tried to curtsy as she spoke—ancy curtsying as you're falling through the air! Do you think you could manage it?) "And what an ignorant little girl she'll think me for asking! No, it'll never do to ask: perhaps I shall see it written up somewhere."

Down, down, down. There was nothing else to do, so Alice soon began talking again. "Dinah'll miss me very much tonight, I should think!" (Dinah was the cat.) "I hope they'll remember her saucer of milk at tea-time. Dinah, my dear! I wish you were down here with me! There are no mice in the air, I'm afraid, but you might catch a bat, and that's very much like a mouse, you know. But do cats eat bats, I wonder?" And here Alice began to get very sleepy, and went on saying to herself, in a dreamy sort of way, "Do cats eat bats? Do cats eat bats?" and sometimes, "Do bats eat cats?" for, you see, as she couldn't answer either question, it didn't much matter which way she put it. She felt that she was dozing off, and had just begun to dream that she was walking hand in hand with Dinah, and was saying to her very earnestly, "Now, Dinah, tell me the truth: did you ever eat a bat?" when suddenly, thump! Thump! Down she came upon a heap of sticks and dry leaves, and the fall was over.

Alice was not a bit hurt, and she jumped up on to her feet in a moment: she looked up, but it was all dark overhead; before her was another long passage, and the White Rabbit was still in (continued) ... ***Alice's Adventures in Wonderland***

sight, hurrying down it. There was not a moment to be lost: away went Alice like the wind, and was just in time to hear it say, as it turned a corner, "Oh my ears and whiskers, how late it's getting!" She was close behind it when she turned the corner, but the rabbit was no longer to be seen. She found herself in a long, low hall, which was lit up by a row of lamps hanging from the roof.

There were doors all around the hall, but they were all locked, and when Alice had been all the way down one side and up the other, trying every door, she walked sadly down the middle, wondering how she was ever to get out again.

Suddenly she came upon a little three-legged table, all made of solid glass; there was nothing on it but a tiny golden key, and Alice's first idea was that this might belong to one of the doors of the hall; but alas! Either the locks were too large or the key was too small, but at any rate it would not open any of them. However, on the second time around, she came upon a low curtain she had not noticed before, and behind it was a little door about fifteen inches high; she tried the little golden key in the lock, and to her great delight, it fitted!

Alice opened the door and found that it led into a small passage, not much larger than a rat-hole: she knelt down and looked along the passage into the loveliest garden you ever saw. How she longed to get out of that dark hall, and wander among those beds of bright flowers and those cool fountains, but she could not even get her head through the door-way; "and even if my head would go through," thought poor Alice, "it would be of very little use without my shoulders. Oh, how I wish I could shut up like a telescope! I think I could, if I only knew how to begin." For, you see, so many out-of-the-way things had happened lately that Alice had begun to think that very few things indeed were really impossible.

Excerpt From
Scientific Studies of Reading

To analyze the underlying factor structure of the 16-item Teacher Efficacy Scale for Writing, the responses of the participating primary grade teachers were analyzed through exploratory factor analysis. Initially, an unconstrained principal factor analysis was used to generate the factor matrix with squared multiple correlations as initial communality estimates. Items that exhibited factor structure loadings of .40 or greater were used to define a factor.

Prior to rotation, the unconstrained principal factor analysis produced four factors with eigenvalues greater than 1.0. The four factors accounted for 60% of the total test variance. Their respective eigenvalues were 4.7, 2.57, 1.31, and 1.09. Based on a scree plot of the eigenvalues and theoretical concurrence with models of teacher efficacy, a two-factor solution was rotated by using the varimax solution.

Results for the forced two-factor solution revealed that the varimax rotation accounted for 38% of the total test score variance. As can be seen in Table 2, 10 of the 16 rotated items loaded at .40 or greater on the first factor. This factor appeared to reflect teachers' beliefs about their ability to teach writing and affect change in their students. Consistent with prior research, we labeled this factor personal teaching efficacy. The other six rotated items loaded at .40 or greater on the second factor.

Graham, S., Harris, K.R., Fink, B., & MacArthur, C.A. (2001). Teacher efficacy in writing: A contract validation with primary grade teachers. *Scientific Studies of Reading*, *5*, (2).

Definitions of Fluency

Which definition of fluency is most complete? Probably the second one. It states the important concept of "minimal rate to support understanding," rather than speed for its own sake.

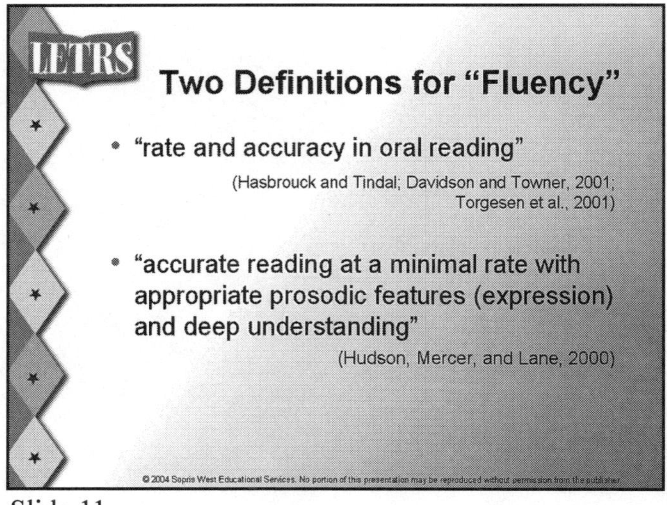

Slide 11

Some researchers who have studied fluency issues in reading use a simple definition: they equate fluency with speed and accuracy in oral reading because those variables are measurable. Others have attempted to capture the quality of fluent reading in their definition. Hudson, Mercer, and Lane (2000), for example, point out that speed of reading is not the issue in reading performance, but rather sufficient speed to allow comprehension to occur. A proficient reader communicates the author's intent to a listener by phrasing the syntax, placing emphasis, adding vocal contour, and reacting vocally to the message in the text.

You can tell by listening to someone read whether they are understanding as they go. Their vocal intonation and phrasing gives away the depth of their understanding.

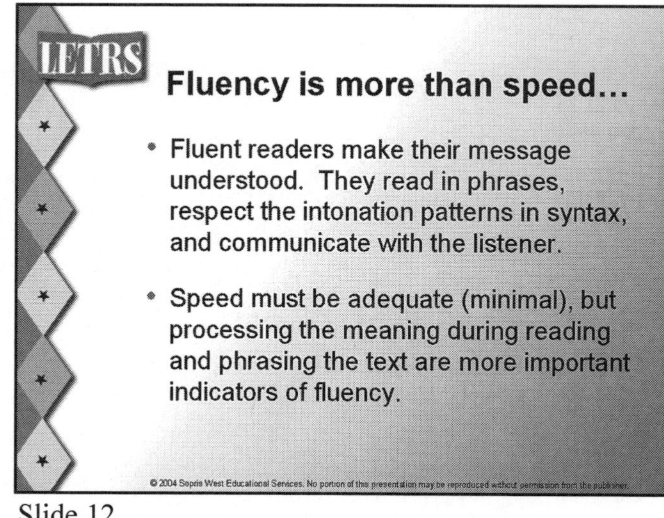

Slide 12

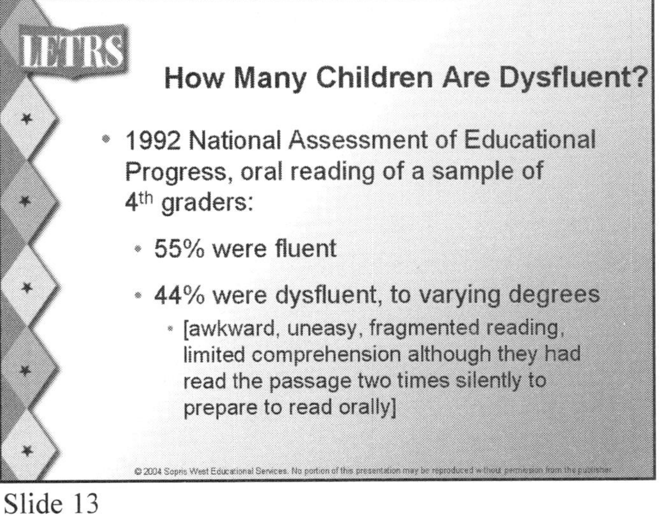

Slide 13

The NAEP study included oral reading from a sample of fourth grade children. Children were allowed to read a passage twice silently before reading aloud. The researchers also used a qualitative rating scale to characterize how the oral reading sounded.

The National Assessment of Educational Progress in 1992 included oral passage reading in its testing of a representative sample of fourth graders.[2] NAEP's data included both measures of oral passage reading fluency and accuracy, and scores on a qualitative scale of oral reading proficiency. The dysfluent readers, 44% of the fourth grade population, were slow, choppy, readers whose reading was difficult for a listener to comprehend. Students differed much more on their rate of reading than their accuracy.

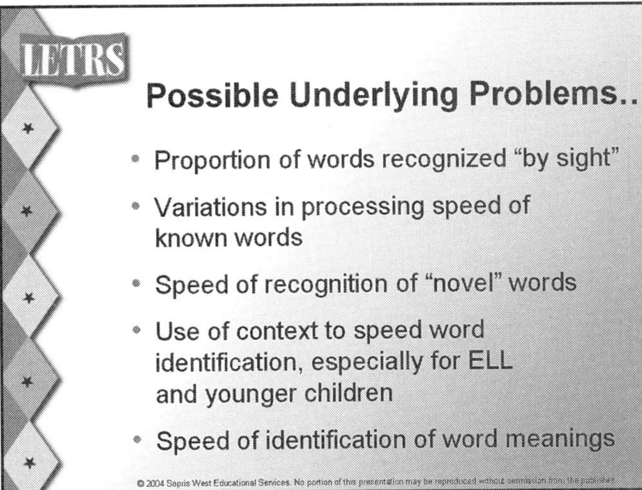

Slide 14

All or some of these factors could be the underlying reasons why students are dysfluent.

When we talk about recognizing words "by sight," we mean as a whole unit that has been decoded accurately. "By sight" does NOT mean that the word has been learned by configuration or as a logograph; "sight word" recognition is facilitated when sound-symbol association is accurate and automatic. Recognizing a word by sight is usually the consequence of being aware of its sound-symbol correspondences. (Linnea Ehri has done monumental work on the nature of word recognition that unravels these causal relationships.)

2   Pinnell, Pikulski, Wixson, Campbell, Gough, Beatty (1995), *Listening to Children Read Aloud: Data from NAEP's Integrated Reading Performance Record (IRPR) at Grade 4*. Report No. 23-FR-04. Washington, DC: National Center for Education Statistics, Office of Educational Research and Improvement, US Department of Education.

What Are the Causes of Dysfluent Reading?

Slow reading is a symptom with multiple causes. One type of slow reader has not automatized some or all of the subskills that support accurate and fluent word recognition. Those component subskills include:

- "sight" recognition of words as wholes, after one or more exposures to those words

- adequate processing speed for known words

- employment of phonic knowledge in sounding out novel or new words

- use of context to facilitate or to confirm accurate word recognition

- knowledge of vocabulary and access to word meanings in memory

Children who read text too slowly include many who are not yet accurate and fluent in the underlying skills, including phoneme awareness, phonic knowledge, sound blending for decoding, and sight word recognition. Some of these have simply not been taught and will respond well to intervention. A smaller subgroup will be those who have constitutionally based problems with phonological processing (typical dyslexia) that require a very structured, systematic, explicit approach to language remediation.

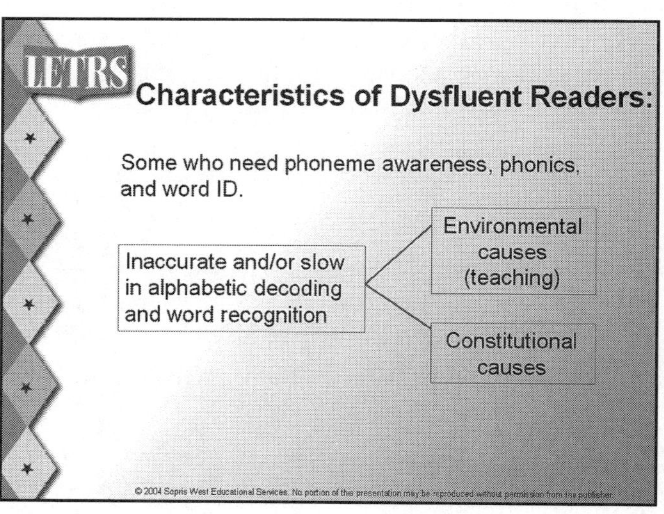

Slide 15

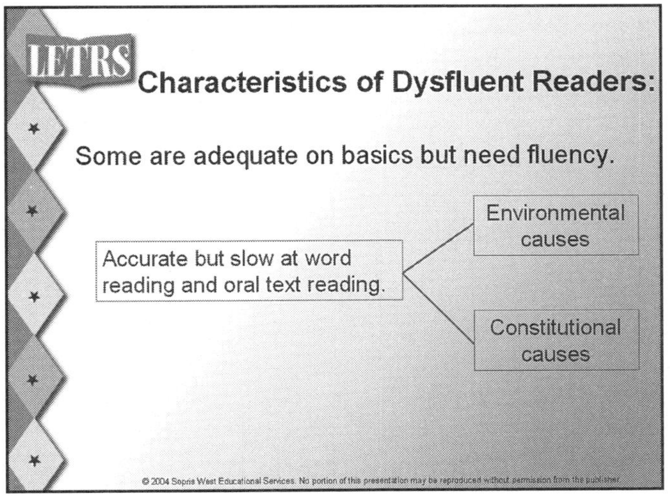

Slide 16

Some students know phonic correspondences and are able to decode accurately. They have not developed the ability to recognize words quickly or read at a satisfactory minimum speed. This fluency problem is common in students who have been taught phonics but whose instruction did not provide sufficient practice applying phonic correspondences during decoding and text reading. Also, many children have simply not practiced reading every day and will gain fluency quickly with the strategies in this module.

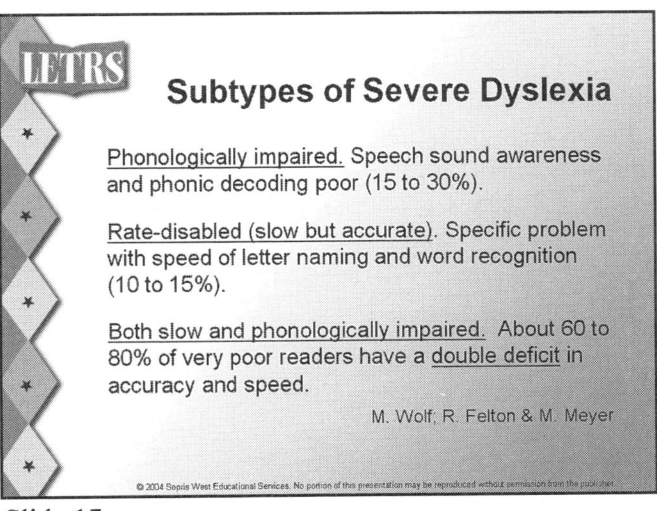

Slide 17

Children with serious reading disabilities—estimated to be between 5 and 15 % depending on the criteria used—are not all alike. The majority have phonological processing problems. A few have specific weaknesses in letter and number naming speed that are reflected in simple tests of rapid automatic naming of letters, numbers, objects, and colors.

Slow reading rate is most often an indicator of deficits in basic underlying reading skills (Type 1). These might include alphabet recognition, letter naming, phonological awareness, or sound-symbol association (phonics). From a developmental perspective, these students are stuck at the very beginning stages of reading and cannot move beyond them until the prerequisite skills are mastered. Some of these children have not been taught and will respond readily to good instruction. They lack reading experience and do not know how to read the print.

Other children whose problems are less severe and easier to remediate (Type 2) are lacking in reading experience and practice. They have intact phonological skills and can sound words out reasonably well. Motivation, experience, and instruction often play a role with this type of poor reader. They need many more hours of guided oral reading practice and the techniques described later in this module, but they will not have to have as much work on basic underlying skills as Type 1 poor readers.

Both groups of poor readers include some who present a constitutional or biological difference in either phonological skill or in reading rate. Constitutional deficits are those that should be classified as learning disabilities or dyslexia. Often it is impossible to tell if a student lacks practice or if he will be slow even if inordinate amounts of practice occur. Children's response to instruction and remediation is often the only way to be sure who is constitutionally afflicted with a learning disability and who is not.

Who Remains a Slow Reader?

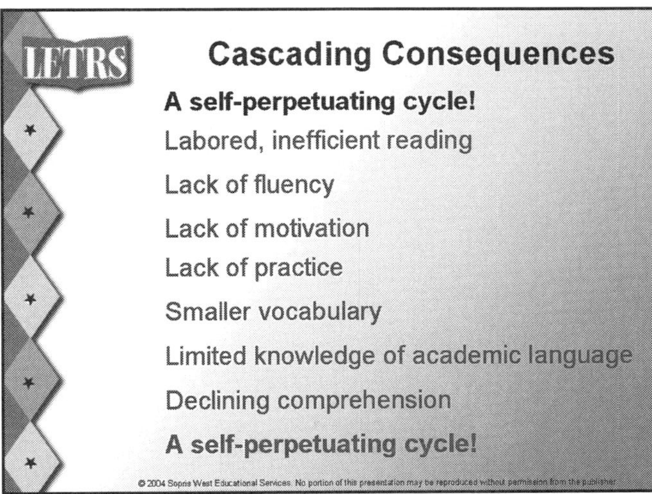

Slide 18

The "rich get richer and poor get poorer" saying is true of those who are good and poor readers; as with other aspects of reading, fluency is related to development of vocabulary and proficiency with academic language.

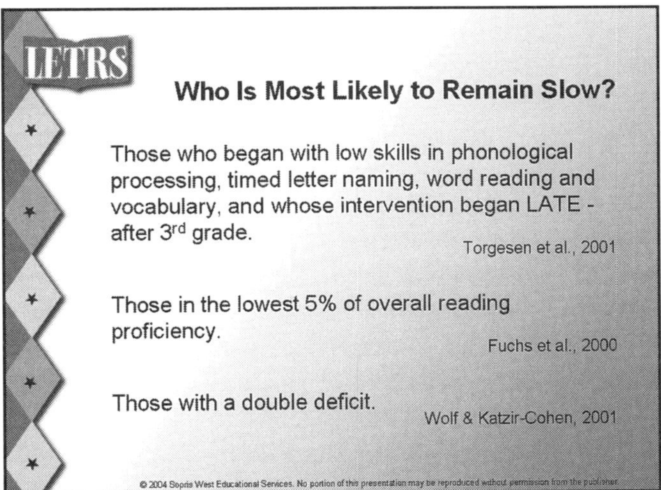

Slide 19

The later we identify children who are struggling with basic reading skills, the more likely it is that they will remain slow readers. Torgesen and his colleagues (2001) have shown that children whose remediation begins in third grade or beyond are far less likely to achieve satisfactory reading fluency than children who are identified and helped in first grade. Other researchers, including Meyer and Felton (1999), Wolf and Katzir-Cohen (2001), and Fuchs (2001) have shown that children with the most intractable reading problems almost always remain significantly slower than their age-mates. Again, the labored, inaccurate reading is associated with comparatively little reading practice because the children cannot tolerate sustained oral or silent reading. The lack of practice in turn is associated with diminished vocabulary and declining language comprehension in relation to age-mates.

Measurement of Reading Fluency

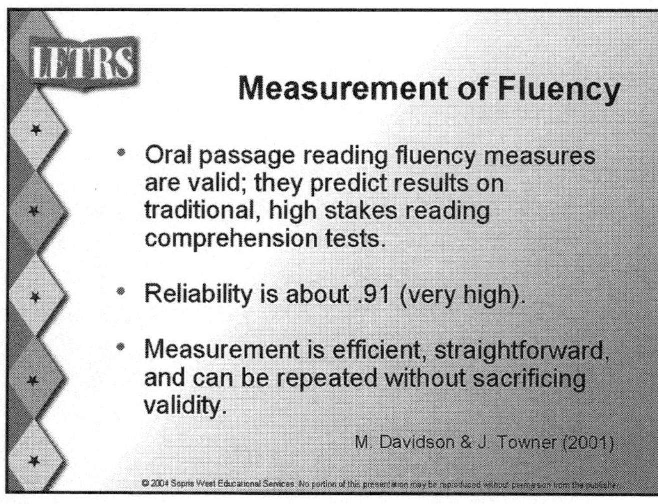

Slide 21

We need efficient, meaningful indicators of fluency. Researchers have shown many times that one minute timed readings of passages yield scores that predict with high accuracy who is at risk for being below grade level on high stakes outcome measures such as the Stanford 9.

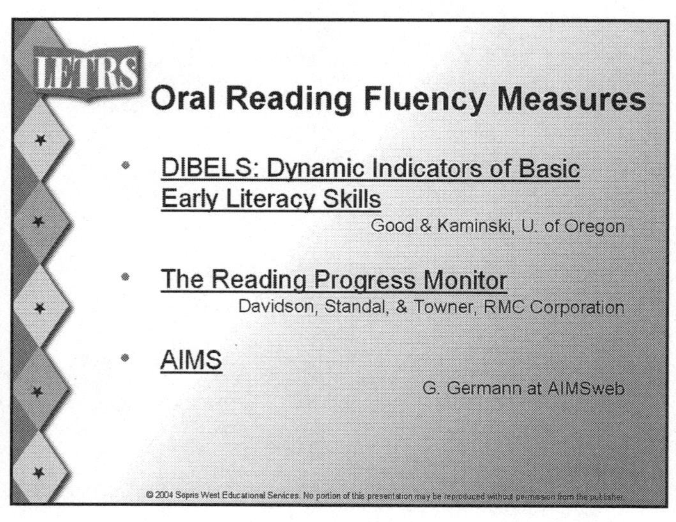

Slide 22

Others have been validated, including the fluency assessments on the Texas Primary Reading Inventory.

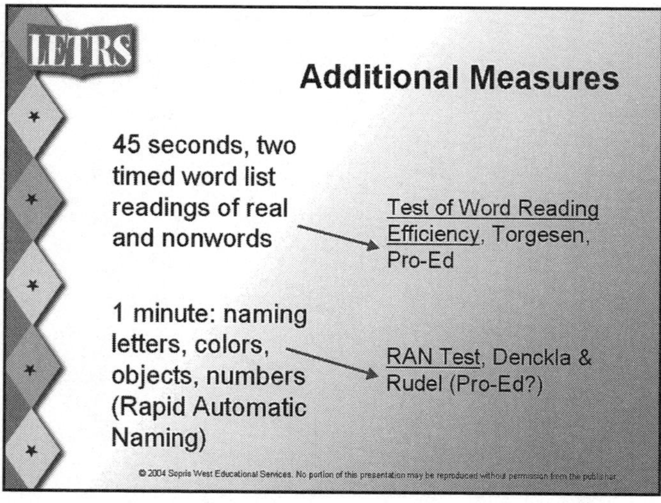

Slide 23

Other major short tests of fluency are published by Pro-Ed.

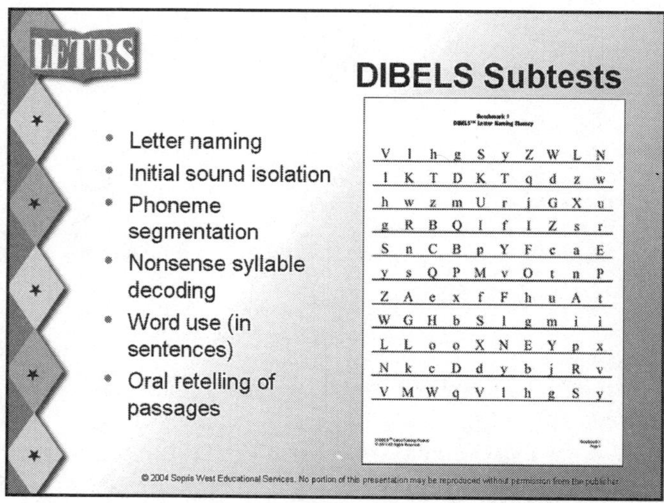

Slide 24

Fluency-based assessment is efficient, reliable, and valid for predicting longer term outcomes. Many diagnostic tests do not have a fluency component and therefore do not reflect this important aspect of reading.

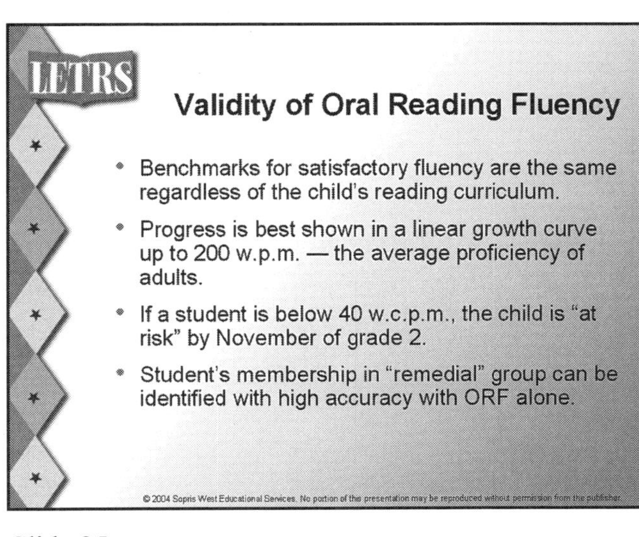

Slide 25

Why do fluency-based assessment?

Expectations for satisfactory oral reading rates extend across reading programs.

We know where we are aiming, we know what levels are satisfactory, we know who needs help on the basis of simple and economical measures.

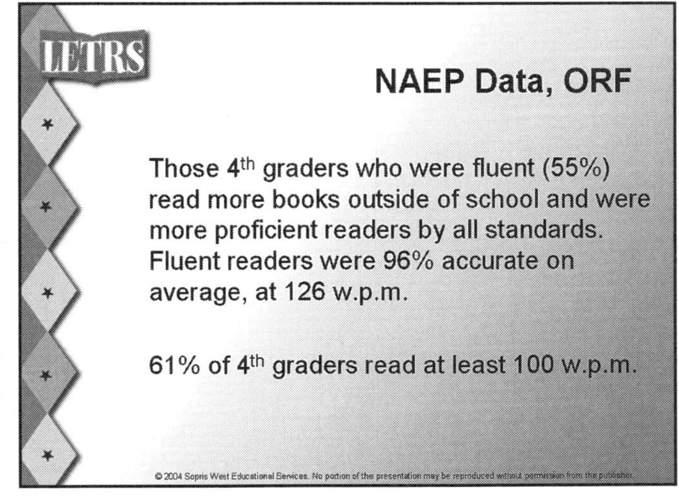

Slide 26

This fluency data was published as a separate study within the National Assessment of Educational Progress in 1992.

Fluent readers were more likely to read on their own and outside of school. Fluency and proficiency in overall reading skill went hand in hand.

100 w.p.m. by fourth grade was a minimal standard for grade level reading proficiency.

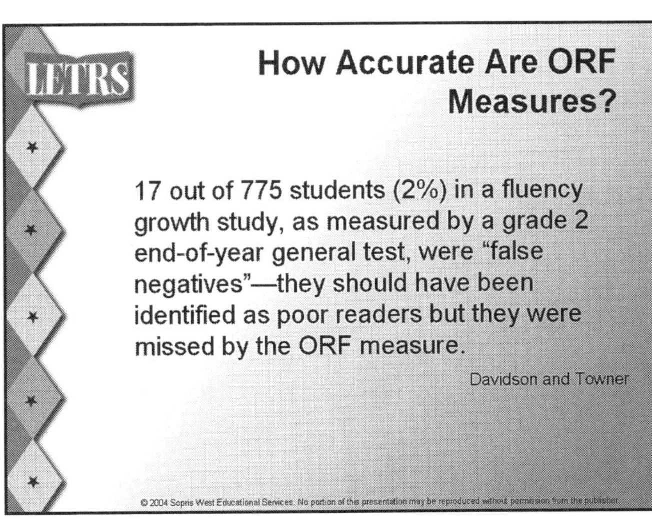

Slide 27

Oral reading fluency (words per minute correct) represents a high degree of predictive accuracy for knowing who is "at risk" and who needs help.

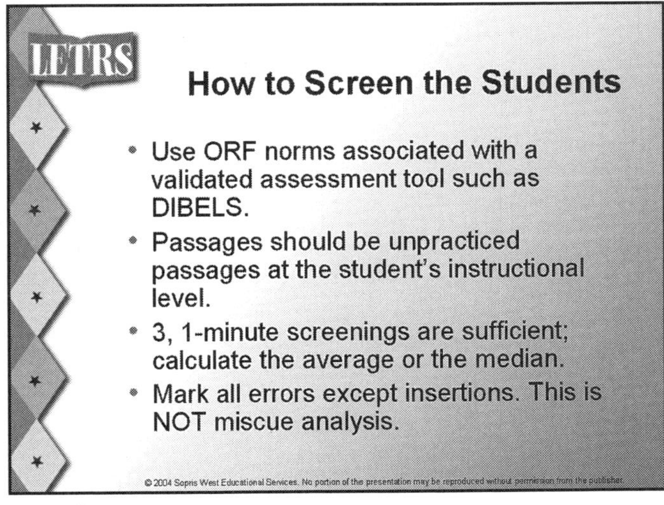

Slide 28

Unpracticed passages at the right level of difficulty are best for oral reading fluency measures. Three passages averaged yield a reliable estimate of the child's "true" score of words correct per minute. There are rules for counting errors. Children don't get credit for giving a substitute word that would make sense in the passage. Words must be accurately read.

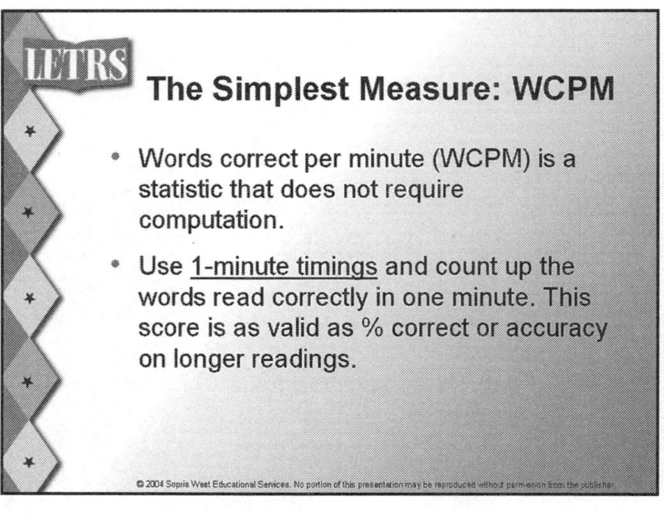

Slide 29

If you want a simple, easy method of measurement, you can do this with no trouble. Count the number of words read correctly in one minute.

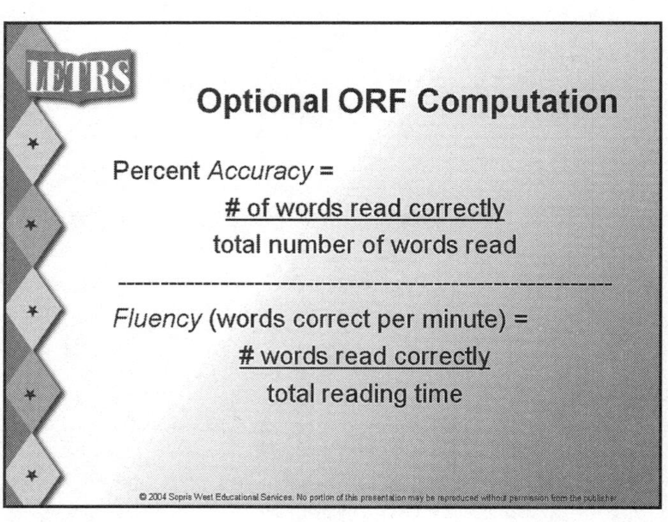

Slide 30

This approach can be used when the student reads on for longer than a minute. It isn't necessary to know how to do this calculation; we include the method because it has been used a lot in curriculum-based assessment. [read the formula]

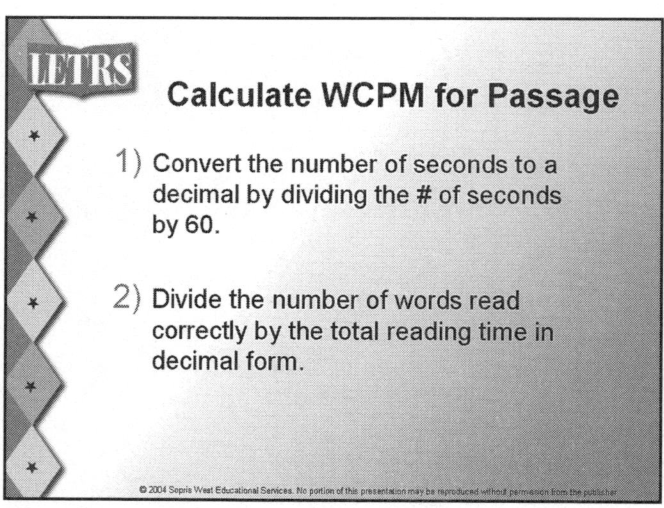

Slide 31

Converting seconds to a decimal: for example, if a student read 81 words correct in 55 seconds, what would the words correct per minute be?

Divide 55/60 = .9
Divide 81 by .9 = 90 wcpm

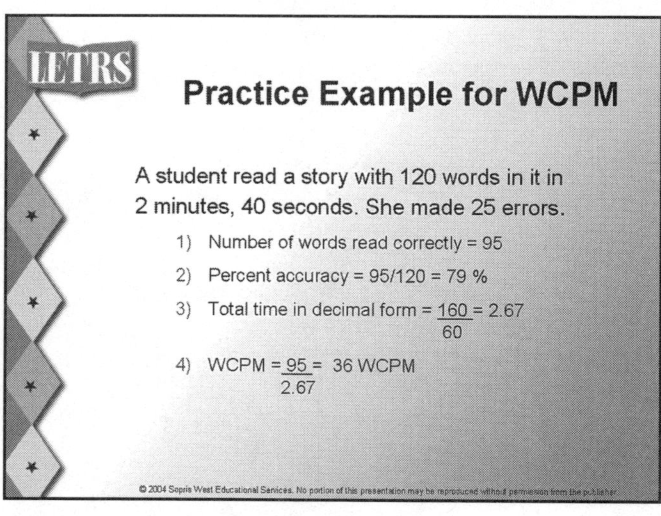

Slide 32

Talk the group through this computation, step by step, with reference to the formulas in slide #30.

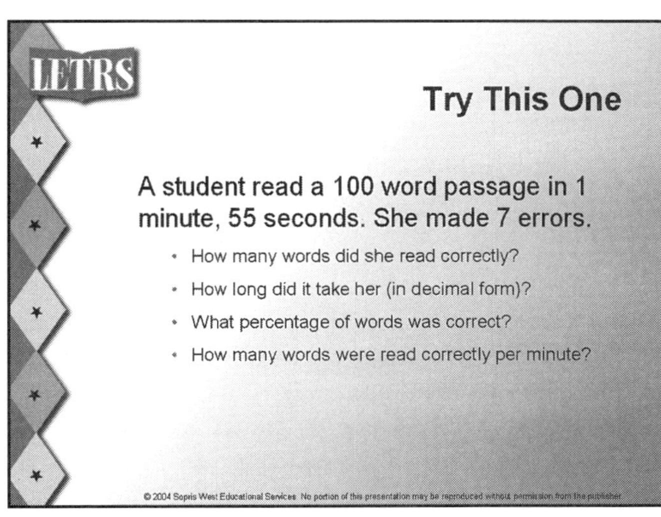

Slide 33

Give participants a couple of minutes to figure this out. Then ask for a volunteer to share her results. Walk through the computations.

Words read correctly = 100-7 = 93.
Time in decimal form = 115/60 = 1.9
% of words read correctly = 93/100 = 93%
WCPM = 93/1.9 = 49

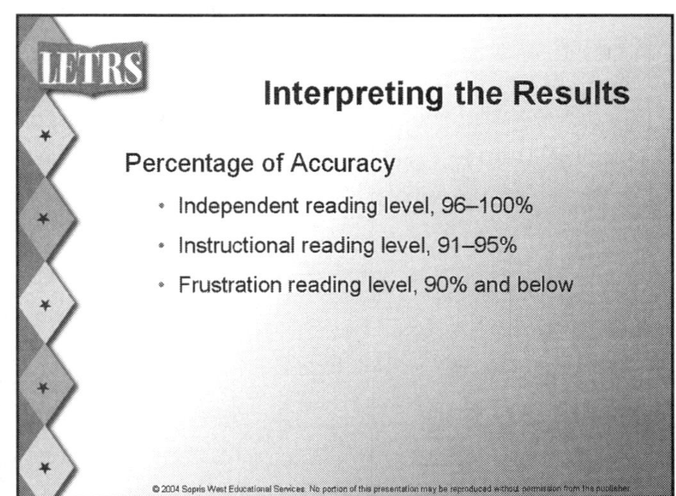

Slide 34

The % read correct is an indicator of the passage's level of difficulty for an individual child. These estimates are traditional in reading instruction. If the child reads with only one error in 20 words, the passage is easy enough for them to read independently. If the child misses one word out of ten, the passage is useful for reading with the support of instruction. If the child is missing more than one word out of ten, the passage is too difficult.

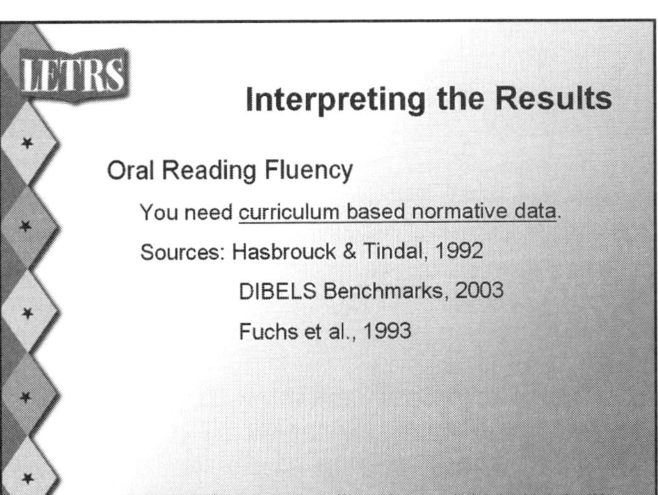

Slide 35

Normative data are necessary to know what level of fluency to aim for and to identify who is falling behind and who needs intervention. Several sources for these norms are available and are in good agreement with one another.

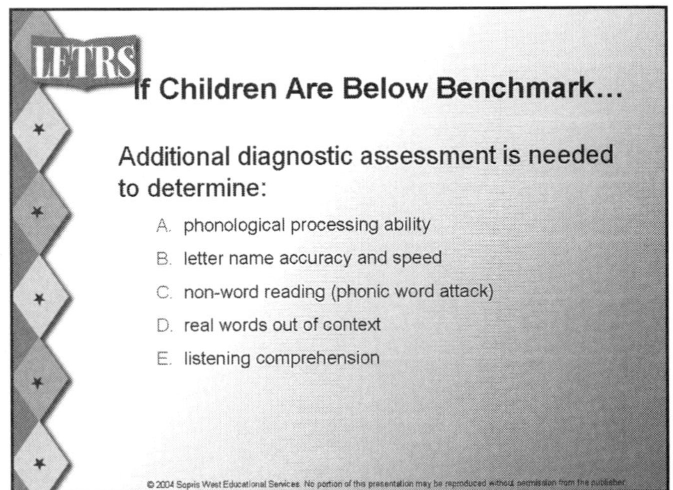

Slide 36

Exercise #3: Contemplate the benchmarks in the chart on fluency norms. Ask participants what they observe about the benchmarks and if any of them are surprising.

Point out that additional diagnostic testing in each of the skill areas named will help the teacher focus instruction on the student's needs. Fluency-based assessment in each domain will help determine the level at which intervention should occur and where the reading process is breaking down.

Exercise #3: Review Benchmarks

Review the following benchmarks for oral reading fluency.
How many children in your class are likely to meet the benchmark criteria?
Have you ever measured fluency? With what method?

Benchmarks for oral reading fluency are quoted from Hasbrouck and Tindal, 1992. Words correct per minute (w.c.p.m.) equals the number of words read correctly in one minute from unpracticed, grade level material. This number should be derived from the average of three readings. Grade 1 students should finish the year reading at least 40 w.c.p.m. in connected text.

Grade	%ile	Fall w.c.p.m.	Winter w.c.p.m.	Spring w.c.p.m.
2	75	82	102	124
	50	53	78	94
	25	23	46	65
3	75	107	123	142
	50	79	93	114
	25	65	70	87
4	75	125	133	143
	50	99	112	118
	25	72	89	92
5	75	126	143	151
	50	105	118	128
	25	77	93	100

Reprinted with permission

After grade 5, students at the 50th percentile read about 125 to 150 w.c.p.m. in oral text reading at grade level. Fluent adults read about 200 w.c.p.m. on oral passage reading; average silent reading is about 300 w.c.p.m.

Principles of Fluency Instruction

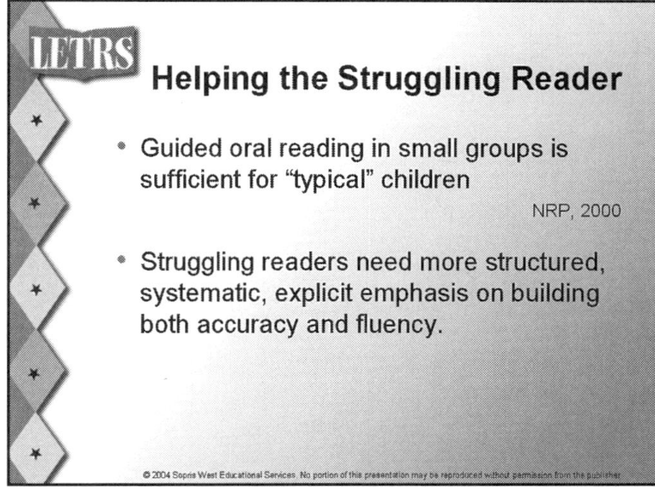

Slide 37

The techniques we will be exploring should never become the whole reading curriculum. They are techniques to be used with selected children who need structured practice building reading fluency. The amount of reading practice that normally progressing children get during guided oral reading of an anthology and library books is sufficient to increase fluency, and they may not need techniques such as repeated readings.

The National Reading Panel (2000) evaluated research concerning the most effective ways for students to practice reading in order to achieve fluency. Two major approaches have been studied: (1) oral reading with guidance and feedback (repeated reading, assisted reading, paired reading) and (2) independent silent reading (e.g., Accelerated Reader, Sustained Silent Reading, Drop Everything and Read). Based on the review of current research, the National Reading Panel reached the following conclusions:

♦ Multiple readings of continuous text (Repeated Reading) can lead to improvements in reading speed, accuracy, comprehension, and expression. This is true for normally progressing readers as well as students with reading problems.

♦ Insufficient research has been carried out to determine the effectiveness of independent, silent reading experiences during school instructional time. There is no evidence as yet that practices such as "Drop Everything and Read" (DEAR) lead to improved reading achievement in students who are slow readers. Students who most need feedback and instruction often do not use DEAR time productively.

Avoid conveying to children that speed alone is the goal. Passages that are read to build fluency still need to be summarized and discussed.

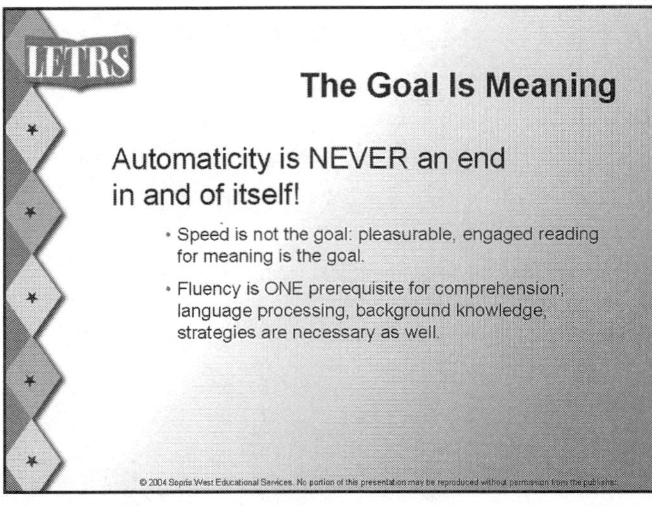

Slide 38

These three techniques have the most consistent record of success in reading research. Alternate or simultaneous oral reading involves the child reading with an adult or peer partner; repeated readings involve the child rereading a text, sometimes with a tape recorded version of the text, in order to improve w.c.p.m. over a baseline or "cold" reading of the text. When students chart their own results, they usually see progress and are very motivated by that.

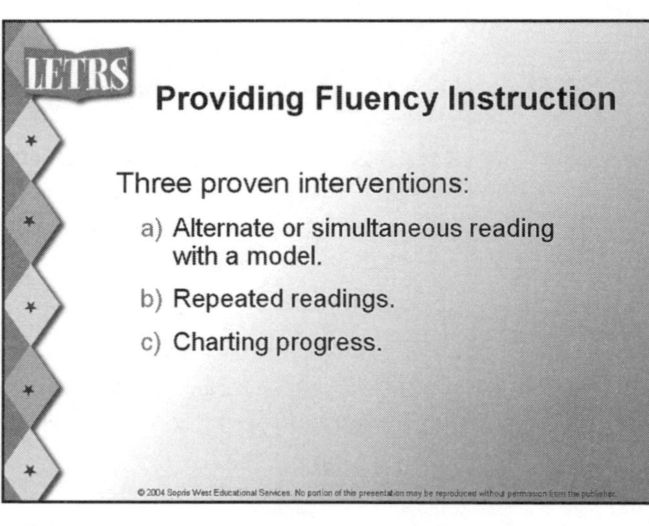

Slide 39

Developmental Approaches to Fluency Improvement

The following methods are termed "developmental" because they are helpful with most children with typical delays in achievement of reading fluency. Once children have learned phonic decoding and are able to read accurately, they are readily engaged in fluency-building activities within a comprehensive reading program. The remediation of severe reading disabilities will necessitate individualized intervention beyond these techniques, but many children in the low average range will improve their overall reading proficiency significantly if they have straightforward practice with alternate, simultaneous, and repeated reading.

Again, these techniques are most productive with students whose reading fluency is not yet developed to the benchmark level (established with a screening test) that will support independent reading for comprehension. They do not replace the reading instruction curriculum and are best done in brief sessions a few minutes per day.

General Guidelines for Oral Reading Fluency Practice

♦ Students should read materials that can be read accurately (90 to 95 percent accuracy). Material should be carefully selected so that the student is able to read the passage without undue frustration.

♦ Repeated practice on weak subskills, such as word lists, syllables or spelling chunks, or letter names may help increase fluency.

♦ Measures of rate and accuracy are both important benchmarks of improvements in reading fluency.

♦ Comprehension checks should be a routine part of any work on fluency.

♦ Specific strategies for multiple readings should take individual student characteristics into account. For more impaired readers, provide more adult guidance during reading; use more decodable texts as reading materials; practice on words and phrases from the text before reading the text; practice reading short passages; model expressive reading.

♦ Frequent, brief, distributed practice (spaced out over successive days) is better than concentrated practice.

♦ Let the child chart his or her own progress.

Alternate Oral Reading With a Model or Peer

In alternate oral reading, the "lead" or #1 reader is the stronger one. Reader #2 benefits from the modeling of reader #1.

Read through the procedures in the text for pairing up readers within a class.

Then have the participants pair up and do the role-play (Exercise #4). Assign each member of a pair the role of reader #1 and reader #2. Ask partners to try sitting right shoulder to right shoulder, facing different directions.

Role-play and reflection should take about 8-10 minutes.

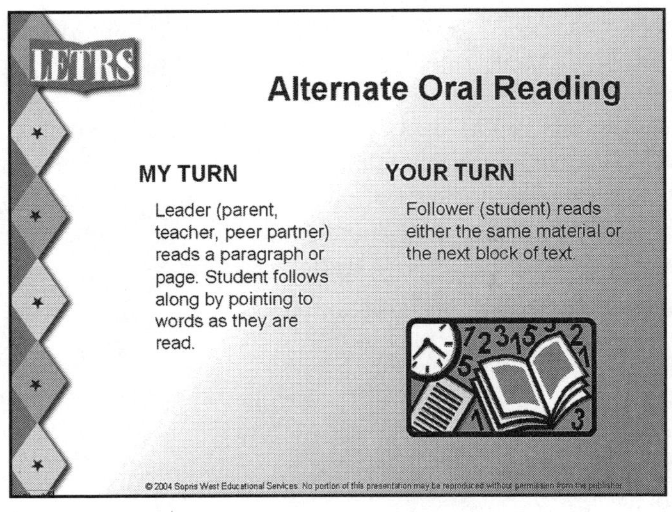

Slide 40

Enlist parents, volunteers, or peer tutors to help. If peers are paired up for alternate oral reading practice, establish the pairings by following these steps:[3]

1. Rank the class according to reading ability.

2. Divide the class list in half.

3. Assign pairs by matching the top reader of the top half of the class with the top reader of the bottom half of the class and so forth. These pairings are likely to be close enough in reading ability that they can work well together.

4. Check the pairings and change any that might not be compatible.

5. Be careful about peer assignments for children with exceptional needs, for example highly gifted readers or children with learning disabilities or emotional handicaps.

6. Use a text or story that the class has practiced or that is familiar. Tell students to read a section—a page or a paragraph—when it is their turn to read.

7. Reader #1 is the stronger reader and should read first while reader #2 listens and follows the text.

[3] Detailed guidelines for peer-assisted instruction can be found in Mathes, P. *PALS (Peer-Assissted Learning Strategies)* Longmont, CO: Sopris West.

8. Reader #2 then picks up when reader #1 stops reading.

9. Emphasize the importance of comfortable speed, reading with expression, and understanding what is read.

10. Direct children to go back and question each other about what they read after the reading is finished. "What was this part about?"

11. Reinforce appropriate behavior by keeping lists of books read, and giving points for following and listening well. Ask each pair to share with another what they read about.

Exercise #4: Role-Play

Role-play alternate oral reading with a partner, following the steps above.
Use *Little Bear Lost* in the text anthology for this purpose.

Simultaneous Oral Reading

Simultaneous oral reading involves the student reading a text along with the better reader—usually an adult. Various degrees of preparation and support are possible.

Read through the procedures in the text, then have the participants role-play as the exercise indicates. Be sure that the partners take turns being reader #1 for the role-play (Exercise #5). The lead reader should sit behind the right shoulder of reader #2, reading just ahead of reader #2's pace.

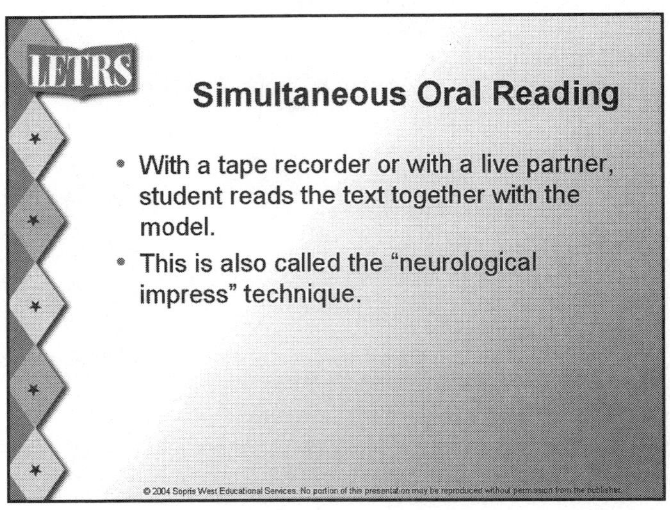

Slide 41

Simultaneous oral reading is also embodied in the "neurological impress technique," as it is called in older reading textbooks. When a fluent reader reads along with the weaker reader, the weaker reader hears better phrasing and experiences the sense of fluency that the model provides.

Select a short story or passage that student can read accurately. Before launching into the SOR exercise, preview the story by discussing the topic, illustrations, or titles. Preview any challenging vocabulary that the reader will encounter.

Then, the adult reads a portion of the text aloud using good expression while the student looks at words being read and follows the text with a finger or pencil eraser. Next, the adult model and the student read the text segment aloud together, trying to read with one voice. This step can be repeated two or three times, until the student is ready to read the selection independently. The student may be encouraged to practice reading the text silently as well.

Finally, the student reads aloud to the adult and the adult helps the child record time and errors on a simple graph.

Exercise #5: Role-Play

Practice simultaneous oral reading with a partner. Use a text you have already read or previewed, such as *Alice in Wonderland*.

Repeated Readings

Slide 42

Programs such as Great Leaps and Read Naturally use the technique of repeated readings, but it can be used with any text that is the right level of difficulty. The student should be reading a text in which at least 90% of the words are known. If the text is too easy, the student is not likely to make gains with repeated readings.

Slide 43

Repeated readings can occur with words, phrases, and passages.

Students who are less capable readers or less confident readers may need support and scaffolding during repeated reading exercises. Key words can be previewed; the content can be introduced; parts of the text can be read ahead of time; or the student can scan the text before reading. All these activities increase the likelihood of more accurate and fluent reading.

Slide 44

Three to four rereadings of a text, with the students graphing their own progress on successive days, is a powerful form of practice for many slow readers. Practice of this kind can occur in small groups as well as with peer partners and adult-child pairings.

The teacher ensures that the reading material is at the right level of difficulty (95 percent accuracy). Teacher previews the vocabulary, the main ideas, and the "hard parts" with the student so the student is well prepared.

Students then get ready to read the text orally while the teacher uses a one-minute or two-minute timer. [In order to encourage students to read a whole text through, the teacher may say "mark your paper" at the one-minute juncture but allow students to keep on reading until they reach a good stopping point. Then words correct per minute (w.c.p.m.) can be calculated when the reading is completed.] Student graphs the number of words read correctly in one minute on that passage.

Within the next day or two, the student practices reading the text with a tape recorder or to an adult. The timing procedure is then repeated. The student graphs his or her own progress. If the student gains about 10 percent or better in words read correctly per minute, the text can be changed. Again, it is not productive to memorize text, to read as fast as possible for the sake of speed, or to repeat a reading more than four times.

Phrase-Cued Reading

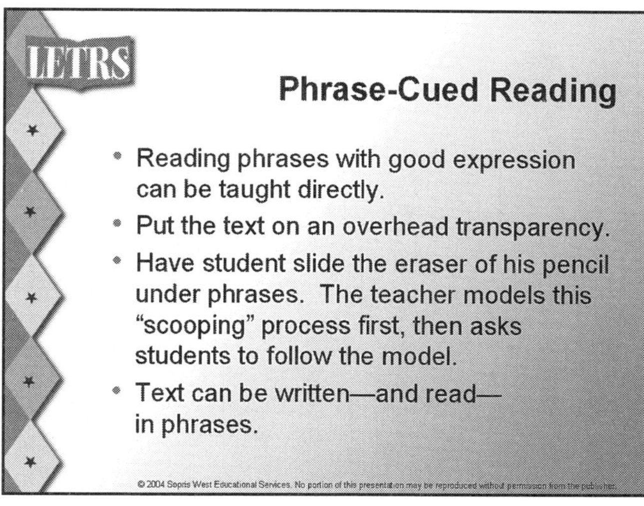

Slide 45

Exercise #6: Demonstrate phrase-cued reading by putting "Alice" on the overhead projector and reading aloud as you scoop under the phrases of the first few lines. Then ask the participants to repeat what you did. Then ask participants to model the process for each other, one reading aloud and the other following with the eraser end of the pencil.

The phrasing that characterizes good readers can be modeled and taught directly. With the class or small group, the teacher puts a text on an overhead projector. With an individual, the teacher uses one copy of text that both teacher and student can read.

The teacher models reading in phrases. Using the eraser end of a pencil, or a marker on the transparency, the teacher scoops under phrases as they are read. Then the student follows the model.

Some fluency-building programs, such as *Read Naturally* and *Great Leaps*, include direct practice in phrase reading. Phrases can be practiced out of and within the context of a sentence.

up the tree	if you can
why we are going	all around town
when he asked	could have been
in back of the house	away from everyone
more and more	not on your life

Exercise # 6: Phrase-Cued Reading

Find a partner. Read *Alice in Wonderland* alternately, taking turns as the Model. Scoop under phrases with the eraser of your pencil as you read.

Cumulative and Generalizable Gains

One reason why it is productive to read a passage 3 to 4 times and then move on to another is that there is a cumulative effect of increased fluency. Each baseline or first reading on a passage is likely to be a little bit better than the first reading of the passage before.

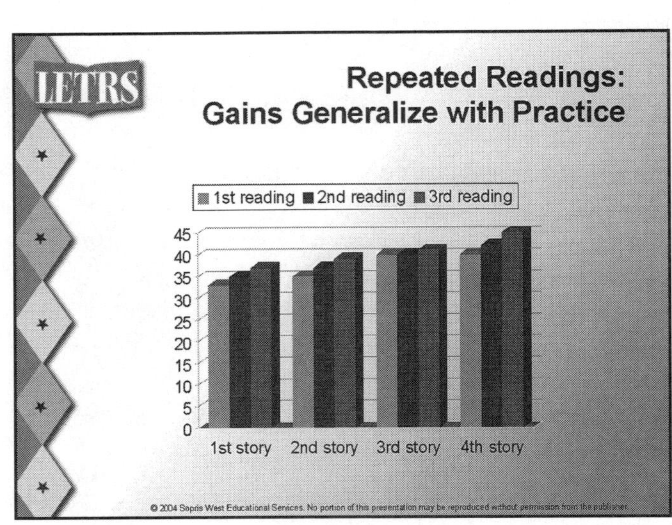

Slide 46

Over eight to ten weeks of frequent, distributed practice, a student's average weekly score should improve. The benefits of repeated readings of any specific text usually generalize to the readings of new texts. That is why there is no additional "pay off" for reading one text over and over.

Caveats: Less Effective Practices

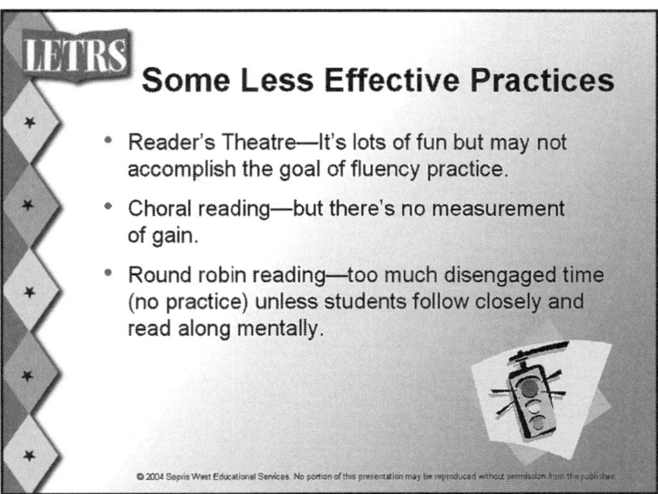

Slide 47

Examples of reader's theatre scripts taken off the internet are in the book. Reader's theatre is a great example of a classroom activity that appeals to teachers and students alike that may not have an effect on fluency. It is often cited as a way to improve fluency, but be sure participants understand that a more direct path to the goal is timed readings with charting.

Exercise #7 is optional.

Reader's Theatre is a highly motivating classroom activity that is currently very popular. Enjoyable, dramatic and poetic texts are parsed into segments, assigned to specific children, and then performed by that group of children for an audience. Reading aloud involves alternate and choral reading parts that are often read with dramatic flare. To learn their part, children must read, reread, and often memorize their "lines." The performance aspect of Reader's Theatre is entertaining, engaging, and adaptable to many kinds and levels of text.

If the goal of an intervention is fluency-building, however, the teacher must be careful to measure the effect and benefit of Reader's Theatre activities for the specific children they are designed to help. Children may memorize their parts without reading, may not actually receive much reading practice, or may not get the benefit of direct feedback about their own reading rate.

Exercise #7: A Reader's Theatre Activity

Break into small groups and prepare a reading of either *The Billy Goats Gruff* or *The Little Red Hen.* Perform for your peers.

Charting Fluency Data

Charting progress is almost always highly motivating to students. They need the concrete indication of gain. Very small improvements will show on the chart. The goal should be a % of gain over the baseline that will keep the student on the aim line—the path to benchmark proficiency levels.

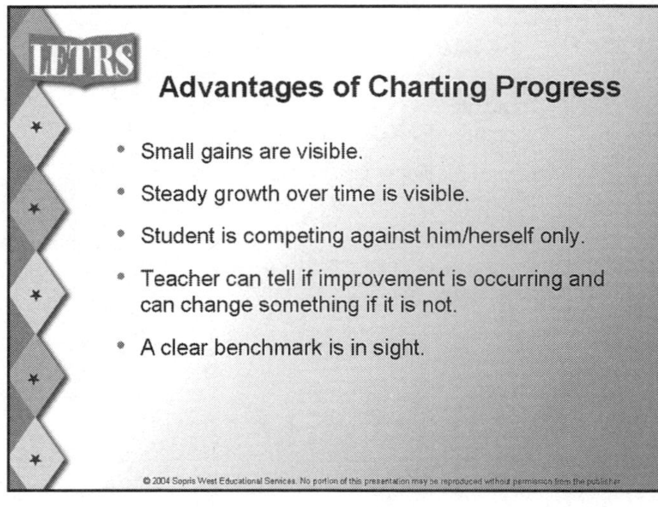

Slide 48

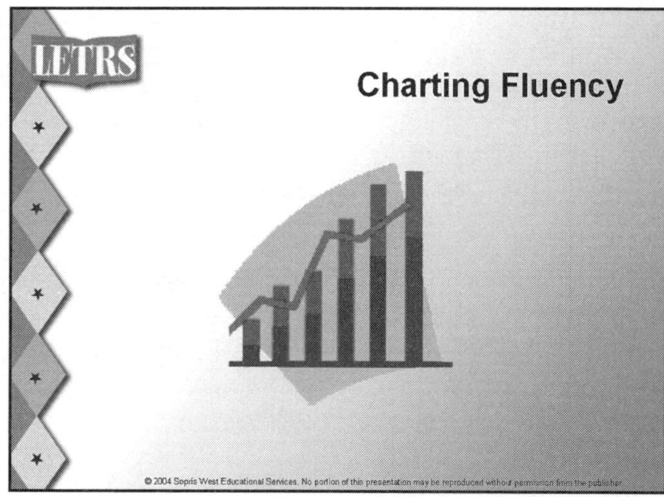

Slide 49

Slide 50

Exercise #8: Use the blank chart and the data on one child's reading to demonstrate how this would be done. First, let participants represent the given data on the chart. Then, show your completed chart for participants to compare their charts. Discuss ideas the participants had while doing this. Usually several people in the group have had experience using charts of progress in reading fluency and are willing to share reflections.

Exercise #8: Chart Data

Use the *Chart It* graph from *LANGUAGE !* Show how you would record the following oral reading data:

Date	Text	w.p.m. (1 min)	# Errors
10/2	Like the Birds	43	5
10/4	Like the Birds	55	4
10/6	Like the Birds	62	3
10/10	Too Close to the Sun	50	5
10/12	Too Close/Sun	57	3
10/14	Too Close/Sun	65	2
10/17	Hot Air Balloons	59	3
10/18	Hot Air Balloon	67	2

~~~ **Chart It** ~~~

Student: _______________ Date: _______________

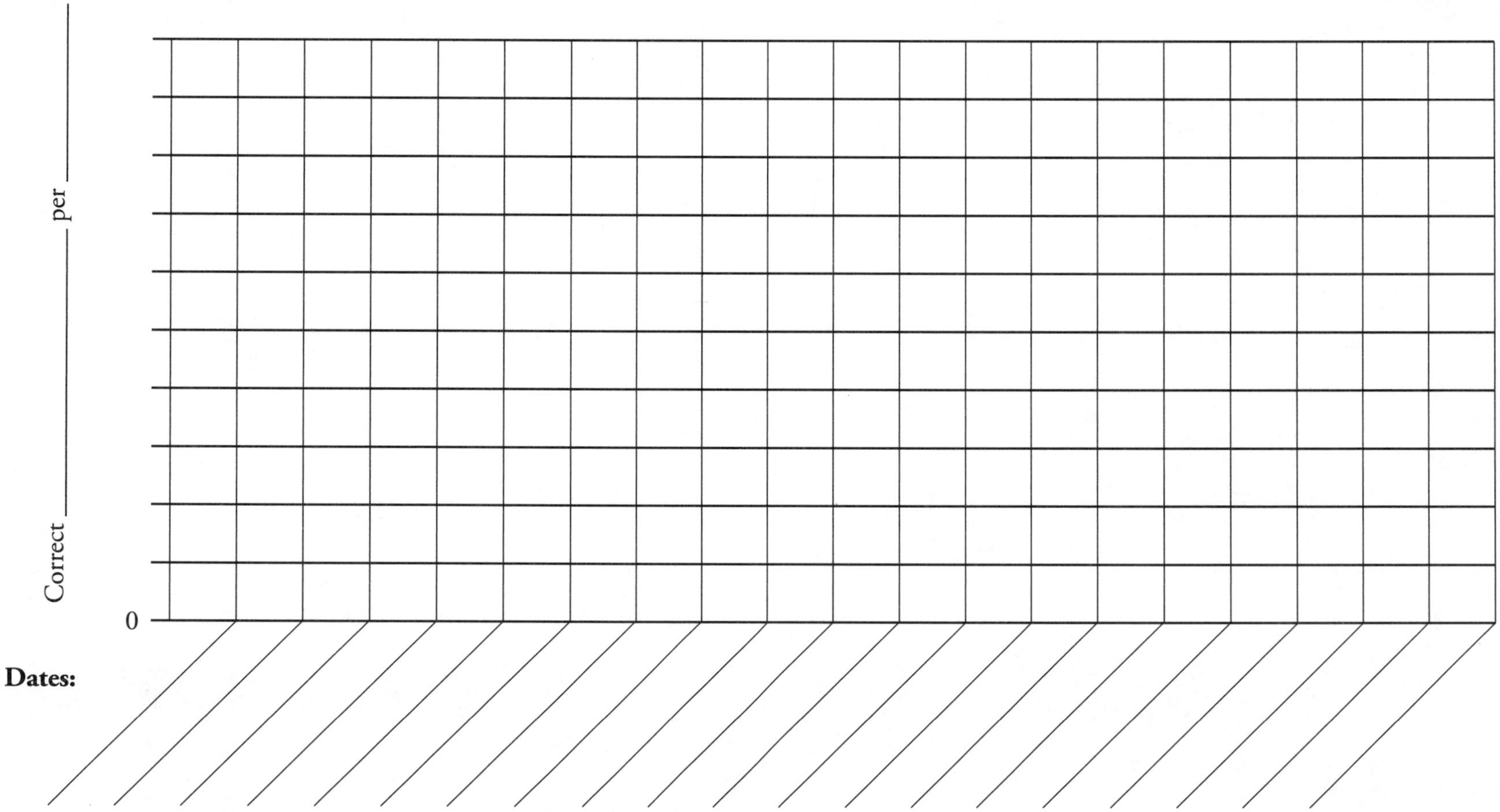

Correct _______________ per _______________

Dates: _______________

Target Skill(s) or Content: _______________

Getting Up To Speed: Developing Fluency

~~~ **Chart It** ~~~

Student: __________

Date: __________

Correct

per

0

Dates: __________

Target Skill(s) or Content: __________
~~~

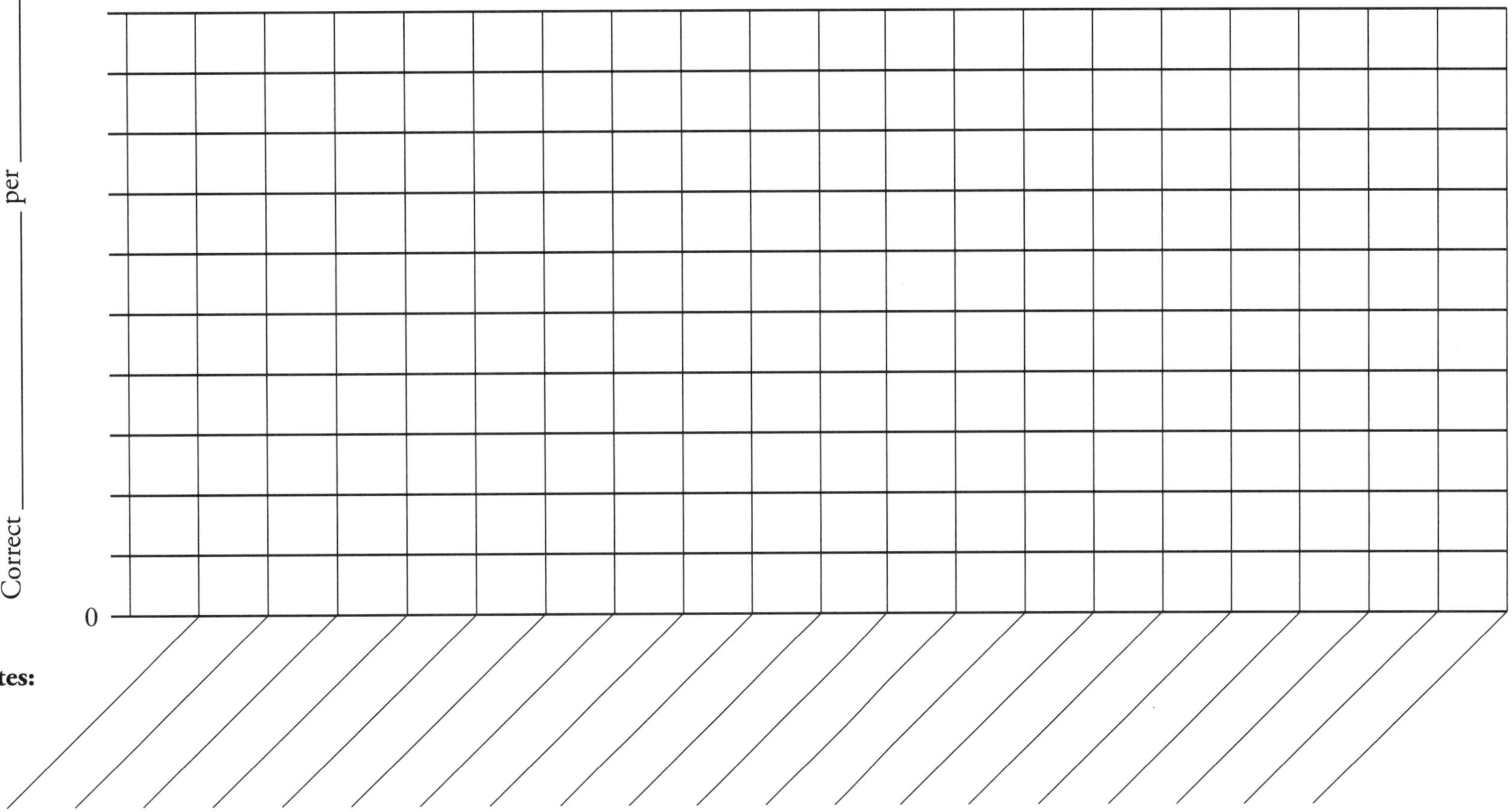

Make It Fluent: Fluency Builder Progress Chart

Unit: ______ Student: ________________________________ Date: ____________

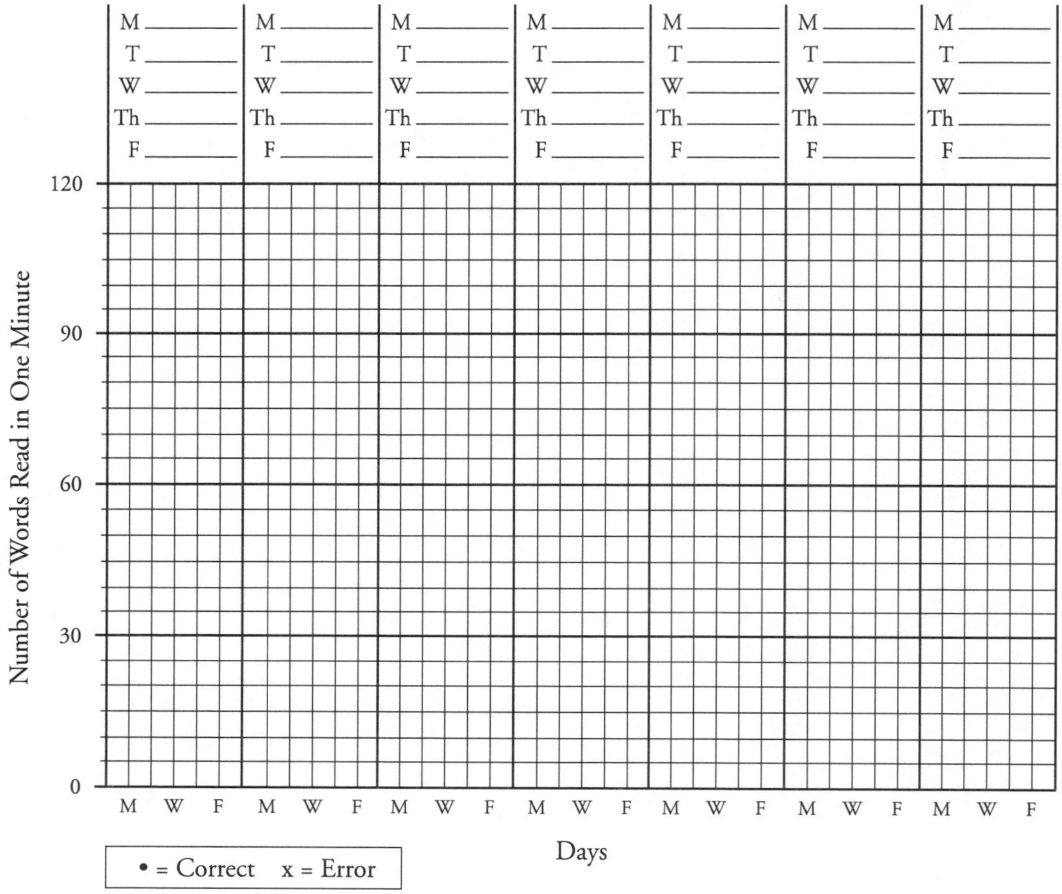
M
T
W
Th
F
120
90
60
30
0
Number of Words Read in One Minute
M W F M W F M W F M W F M W F M W F M W F
Days
• = Correct x = Error

Week 1						Week 2						Week 3					
Date	M	T	W	Th	F	**Date**	M	T	W	Th	F	**Date**	M	T	W	Th	F

Week 4						Week 5						Week 6					
Date	M	T	W	Th	F	**Date**	M	T	W	Th	F	**Date**	M	T	W	Th	F

Week 7						Week 8						Week 9					
Date	M	T	W	Th	F	**Date**	M	T	W	Th	F	**Date**	M	T	W	Th	F

Week 10					
Date	M	T	W	Th	F

~~~~ Make It Fluent: Fluency Builder Score Sheet ~~~~

Unit: _______   Student: _________________________________   Date: ____________

Date	Unit #	Sheet #	Number Correct	Number of Errors

Comments:

More Interventions for Children With Persistent Fluency Problems[4]

Practice at the level of letters and letter-sound correspondence. Before they can develop speed in text reading, students must first become automatic in their ability to recognize letters and associate letters with sounds for reading and writing. In the initial stages of developing accuracy in letter-sound associations, cues (such as picture cues, objects, gestures, and key words) are used. In the later stages, the cues are dropped. Cues may be necessary for vowels long after they are necessary for consonants. The teacher presents selected letters and spellings on cards and the students respond with the correct sounds. This drill is helpful even after students are developing text reading fluency.

Practice at the word level. After accuracy for a particular type of syllable or word (e.g., closed syllables with consonant digraphs) is established, students record their individual baseline times (units correct per minute) on appropriate word lists. Students must be encouraged to compete against themselves, not against each other. The teacher must be sure to create an atmosphere of trust, support, and patience.

After students have developed automaticity in single syllables or words, units can be combined into two-syllable words or compound words.[5] For example, students can be given sets of words containing contrasting spelling patterns such as closed versus silent-e syllables (can versus cane). First, the students should look at the print and mark the vowels as long or short. Then, the students go back and read them aloud. Students can also be asked to scan a page of words or syllables and locate those with a specific characteristic, such as a vowel combination. Whatever the specific strategy, the purpose is to focus the student's attention on the print, the sounds, and the connections between them. For variety, students can read the words by saying the vowel sound first. After the patterns have been marked and practiced, the students are then timed on reading the set of words to establish a baseline. Then the set is practiced until mastered.

Practice with phrases and text. Phrases that include both decodable and irregular sight words (e.g., on the mat; up a tree) can also be practiced in the same way. The teacher should select the phrases to practice and emphasize those that include words and patterns already taught. The poorer the student's skill level, the more important it is that they practice what they have been taught with decodable text. After students become proficient in reading a core set of irregular words and have mastered basic decoding skills it is appropriate to

---

[4] These techniques are elaborated in Meyer and Felton's (1999) comprehensive review of remedial practices with very poor readers.

[5] Phyllis Fischer's *Speed Drills* are an especially well developed set of practice exercises at this level.

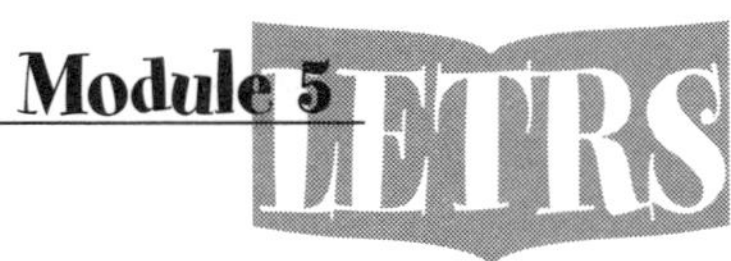

select non-decodable texts for fluency practice. Books for this purpose should be "leveled"—that is, their readability should be designated by the Lexile rating system or other similar readability index. Text for practice must be easy for the child to read—that is, the text can be read with 95 percent accuracy or better.

Exercise #9: Attempt Speed Drills

Attempt the sample fluency drills from the collection in Appendix B. Letter, word, and text drills are from Fischer's *Concept Phonics*; Beck et al.'s *Basic Skill Builders* program (Sopris West); and *Spellography* (Moats and Rosow, Sopris West).

Summary

As with any complex skill, reading fluency develops as a consequence of extensive practice, both with a set of subskills and with the integration of those skills in the service of purposeful reading. First, students must be accurate to be automatic at word recognition. To be accurate, they need to know letters, sounds, and decoding strategies. If those skills are strong, they are more likely to recognize a large number of words without having to sound them out. Students have automatic word reading skills when the mind effortlessly and accurately connects the print with speech.

Reading print with automaticity gives the mind more "desk space" to devote to comprehension. Listening to a good reader, one can tell if the reader understands what he or she is reading because the phrasing, emphasis, and voice contour convey the meaning of the language. Fluency is the achievement of adequate reading speed to support text comprehension. Those who are fluent are more likely to be avid readers outside of school and to experience the benefit of substantial text exposure.

Simple measures of reading fluency—both of critical subskills in reading and text reading itself—are among the best screening, progress monitoring, and outcome measures available to the field. If students are not fluent text readers, it is highly likely that their overall reading achievement, as measured on summative tests of silent passage reading, will be inadequate to sustain grade level performance. Fluency-based measurement of reading skill is efficient, accurate, and valid.

When children lack sufficient fluency, the cause may be lack of basic or advanced decoding skill, lack of automatic processing capabilities, or insufficient reading practice. Diagnostic tests are sometimes needed to determine the cause of dysfluent reading before an intervention plan can be designed.

Most students develop fluency as a consequence of guided oral reading practice and silent independent reading of books at the right level of difficulty. Slow readers with persistent fluency problems respond to several types of validated interventions. The poorest readers need continuing instruction in the basics as well as text reading practice. Those who have the basics need more emphasis on techniques such as partner reading, repeated readings, and simultaneous oral reading. Not all fluency problems have the same cause or respond to the same treatment.

Finally, not all students need deliberate work on reading fluency. Those who will benefit should be identified with a good screening tool such as the Dynamic Indicators of Basic Early Literacy Skills (DIBELS). The goal of intervention is never to "read faster"—it's to be able to read smoothly, with comprehension, and a sense of enjoyment. It's to experience the intrinsic rewards of access to written language.

Summarize the main points with the participants. Ask them to contribute any insights or main ideas they will take away from these exercises.

If time permits, video of a fluency-based instructional program in action is a useful addition to the module.

Slide 51

Instructional Resources for Development of Reading Fluency

Basic Skill Builders—Beck, R., Conrad, D., & Anderson, P. (1997) Longmont, CO: Sopris West.

Degrees of Reading Power (DRP). Book Link. Sopris West 800-547-6747. Index to 12,500 classic literature titles with their readability levels.

Great Leaps—Kenneth Campbell and Cecil Mercer. Diarmuid, Inc., P.O. Box 138, Micanapy, FL 32667. Provides word lists, phrases, and short selections graded for elementary, middle grade, and high school readers.

Practices for Developing Accuracy and Fluency. Neuhaus Center, Houston, Texas.

Read Naturally—2329 Kressin Avenue, St. Paul, Minnesota 55120 (1-800-788-4085). www.readnaturally.com Selections of graded texts to be used with tape-recorded models of reading accuracy and prosody.

Speed Drills from Concept Phonics—Phyllis Fischer, Oxton House Publishers, Farmington, ME 1-800-788-4085. Word, phrase, and text readings sequentially organized to complement most structured, sequential reading programs.

References

Beck, R. (1979). *Report for the office of education joint dissemination review panel.* Great Falls, MT: Precision Teaching Project.

Beck, R. & Clement, R. (1991). The Great Falls precision teaching project: An historical review. *Journal of Precision Teaching*, *8* (2), 8-12.

Carreker, S. (2001). Teaching reading: Accurate decoding and fluency in J. Birsh (ed.), *Multisensory Teaching of Basic Language Skills*, Baltimore: MD: Brookes Publishing.

Davidson, M., Blake, G., & Towner, J. (1999). *Findings from the second grade reading testing pilot program.* Bellingham, WA: Applied Research and Development Center, Western Washington University.

Davidson, M., Stage, S., & Towner, J. (1999). *Second grade testing follow-up study.* Bellingham, WA: Applied Research and Development Center, Western Washington University.

Davidson, M. R., Standal, T. C., & Towner, J.C. (2002). *The reading fluency monitor: Technical manual.* RMC Research Corporation, 1000 Market Street, Portsmouth, New Hampshire, 03801. 800-258-0802.

Davidson, M. & Towner, J. (2001). *The reliability, validity, and applications of oral reading fluency measures.* Paper presented at the meeting of the Society for the Scientific Study of Reading, Boulder, Colorado.

Eden, G.F., & Moats, L.C. (2002). The role of neuroscience in the remediation of students with dyslexia. *Nature Neuroscience*, *5*, 1080-1084.

Fuchs, D., Fuchs, L.S., Mathes, P., Libsey, M., & Roberts, P.H. (2001). *Is "learning disabilities" just a fancy term for low achievement? A meta-analysis of reading differences between low achievers with and without the label.* Washington, DC: Office of Special Education Programs, United States Department of Education.

Fuchs, L.S., Fuchs, D., Hamlett, C. L., Walz, L., & Germann, G. (1993). Formative evaluation of academic progress: How much growth can we expect? *School Psychology Review*, *22* (1), 27-48.

Good, R.H., Simmons, D.C., Kame'enui, E.J. (2001). The importance and decision-making utility of a continuum of fluency-based indicators of foundational reading skills for third-grade, high stakes outcomes. *Scientific Studies of Reading*, *5* (3), 257-288.

Hasbrouck, J. E. & Tindal, G. (1992). Curriculum-based reading fluency norms for students in grades 2-5. *Teaching Exceptional Children*, 41-44.

Hasbrouck, J.E., Woldbeck, T., Ihnot, C., & Parker, R.I. (1999). One teacher's use of curriculum-based measurement: A changed opinion. *Learning Disabilities: Research & Practice*, *14*, 118-126.

Hudson, R., Mercer, C.D., & Lane, H. (2000). *Exploring reading fluency: A paradigmatic overview.* Unpublished manuscript, University of Florida, Gainesville,

Kame'enui, E. & Simmons, D. (Eds.) (2001). The role of fluency in reading competence, assessment, and instruction: Fluency at the intersection of accuracy and speed. *Special Issue, Scientific Studies of Reading*, *5*(3).

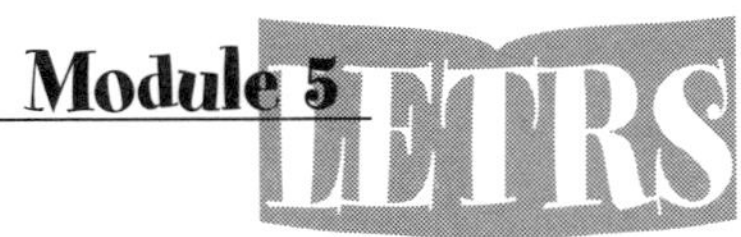

Kemper, L.W. (2001). Advanced decoding and fluency. In S. Brody (ed.), *Teaching reading: Language, letters, and thought*. Milford, NH: LARC Publishing.

Kuhn, M.R. & Stahl, S.A. (2000). Fluency: A review of developmental and remedial practices. CIERA Report #2-008. Center for the Improvement of Early Reading Instruction, University of Michigan, Ann Arbor.

Lyon, G.R. & Moats, L.C. (1997). Critical conceptual and methodological considerations in reading intervention research. *Journal of Learning Disabilities*, *30*, 578-588.

Meyer, M.S., & Felton, R. H. (1999). Repeated reading to enhance fluency: Old approaches and new directions. *Annals of Dyslexia*, *49*, 293-306.

National Reading Panel (2000). *Teaching children to read: An evidence-based assessment of scientific research literature on reading and its implications for reading instruction*. Bethesda, MD: National Institutes of Health.

Pinnell, G.S., Pikulski, J.J., Wixson, K. K., Campbell, J.R., Gough, P.B., & Beatty, A.S. (1995), *Listening to children read aloud: Data from NAEP's integrated reading performance record (IRPR) at grade 4*. Report No. 23-FR-04. Washington, DC: National Center for Education Statistics, Office of Educational Research and Improvement, US Department of Education.

Samuels, S.J. (1997). The method of repeated readings. *The Reading Teacher*, *50*, 76-81.

Shinn, M. R. (Ed.) (1989). *Curriculum-based measurement: Assessing special children*. New York: Guilford.

Tyler, B. & Chard, D.J. (2000). Using readers theatre to foster fluency in struggling readers: A twist on the repeated reading strategy. *Reading and Writing Quarterly*, *16*, 163-168.

Wolf, M. (2003). *RAVE-O: A curriculum for the development of skills in retrieval rate, automaticity, vocabulary elaboration, and orthography*. Medford, MA: Tufts University, Center for Reading and Language Research.

Wolf, M. (Ed.) (2001). *Dyslexia, fluency, and the brain*. Baltimore: York Press.

Wolf, M. & Bowers, P. (2000). Special series: The double-deficit hypothesis. *Journal of Learning Disabilities*, *33* (4).

Wolf, M. & Katzir-Cohen, T. (2001). Reading fluency and its intervention. *Scientific Studies of Reading*, *5*(3), 211-239.

Worthy, J. & Prater, K. (2002). I thought about it all night: Readers theatre for reading fluency and motivation. *The Reading Teacher*, *56* (3), 294-297.

Appendix A:
Reader's Theatre

See http://raven.jmu.edu/~ramseyil/redhen.htm and http://raven.jmu.edu/~ramseyil/billygoat.htm.

Little Red Hen

Characters:

Narrator
Little Red Hen
Cow
Pig
Dog

Setting:

A farm

Scene I.

Narrator: The Little Red Hen found a sack of wheat seed and rushed to tell her friends. Perhaps they would help her plant the seeds.

Little Red Hen: "Cow, will you help me plant my seeds?"

Cow: "Not I, not I. It is too hot to do such work."

Little Red Hen: "Pig, will you help me plant my seeds?"

Pig: "Not I, not I. it is too hot to do such work."

Little Red Hen: "Dog, will you help me plant my seeds?"

Dog: "Not I, not I. It is too hot to do such work."

Narrator: So the Little Red Hen planted the seeds all by herself.

Scene II.

Narrator: Several weeks went by and the seeds began to grow. The Little Red Hen decided to ask her friends to help her tend and weed the garden.

Little Red Hen: "Cow, will you help me weed the garden?"

Cow: "Not I, not I. The shade is too cool to leave."

Little Red Hen: "Pig, will you help me weed the garden?"

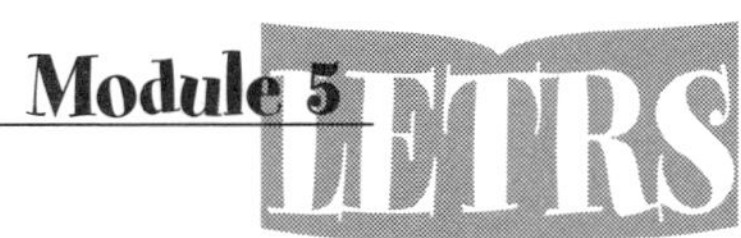

(continued) **Little Red Hen**

Pig: "Not I, not I. The mud is too cool to leave."

Little Red Hen: "Dog, will you help me weed the garden?"

Dog: "Not I, not I. The doghouse is too cool to leave."

Narrator: So the Little Red Hen weeded and tended the garden all by herself.

Scene III.

Narrator: As the weeks went by, the sun ripened the wheat until it was ready to harvest. So the Little Red Hen decided to ask her friends to help her harvest the wheat.

Little Red Hen: "Cow, will you help me harvest the wheat?"

Cow: "Not I, not I. It is too hot today."

Little Red Hen: "Pig, will you help me harvest the wheat?"

Pig: "Not I, not I. It is too hot today."

Little Red Hen: "Dog, will you help me harvest the wheat?"

Dog: "Not I, not I. It is too hot today."

Narrator: Once again the Little Red Hen had to do all the work herself. She harvested the wheat. When she was finished, she asked her friends to help her grind the wheat into flour.

Little Red Hen: "Cow, will you help me grind the wheat into flour?"

Cow: "Not I, not I. It is too close to milking time."

Little Red Hen: "Pig, will you help me grind the wheat into flour?"

Pig: "Not I, not I. It is too close to supper time."

Little Red Hen: "Dog, will you help me grind the wheat into flour?"

Dog: "Not I, not I. It is too close to supper time."

Narrator: So the Little Red Hen ground the wheat into flour all by herself.

Scene IV. The next day

Narrator: The Little Red Hen decided to bake her flour into bread. She decided to give her friends another chance to help her.

Little Red Hen: "Cow, will you help me bake this flour into bread?"

Cow: "Not I, not I. It is too hot to bake."

(continued) **Little Red Hen**

Little Red Hen: "Pig, will you help me bake this flour into bread?"

Pig: "Not I, not I. It is too hot to bake."

Little Red Hen: "Dog, will you help me bake this flour into bread?"

Dog: "Not I, not I. It is too hot to bake."

Narrator: The Little Red Hen baked the bread all by herself. When it was done, she let it cool for awhile. Before she knew it, the time came to cut and eat the bread. Looking around, she didn't see anyone.

Little Red Hen: "Hum, I wonder who will help me eat this bread?"

Cow: (rushing up) "I will!"

Pig: (rushing up) "I will!"

Dog: (rushing up) "I will!"

Little Red Hen: "No, you won't. I did all the work. I get the rewards of that work...this bread."

(The cow, the pig, and the dog all hang their heads.)

Narrator: The Little Red Hen enjoyed the rewards of her hard work very much.

The End

Three Billy Goats Gruff

This script is designed for use with elementary school students. Reader's Theater is a tool for developing children's reading comprehension skills. Teachers will need to provide direction in oral interpretation. Interpretation note: The goats' voices and trip, trap sounds as they cross the bridge should become louder with the size progression of the billy goats.

Characters:

Narrator
Little Billy Goat Gruff = Little BG
Middle-Size Billy Goat Gruff = Middle BG
Big Billy Goat Gruff = Big BG
Troll
Bridge

Narrator: "Welcome to our show. The play is The Three Billy Goats Gruff."

SCENE I

Narrator: Little Billy Goat Gruff sees a rickety, old bridge. On the other side of the bridge is a meadow with green, green grass and apple trees.

Little BG: "I'm the littlest billy goat. I have two big brothers. I want to go across this bridge to eat some green, green grass and apples so that I can be big like my two brothers."

Narrator: Little Billy Goat Gruff starts across the bridge.

Bridge: "Trip, trap, trip, trap, trip, trap."

Narrator: Just as the Little Billy Goat Gruff came to the middle of the bridge, an old troll popped up from under the bridge.

Troll: "Who is that walking on my bridge?"

Little BG: "It is I, Little Billy Goat Gruff."

Troll: "I'm a big, bad troll and you are on my bridge. I'm going to eat you for my lunch."

Little BG: "I just want to eat some green, green grass and apples in the meadow. Please don't eat me. I'm just a little billy goat. Wait until my brother comes along. He is much bigger than I am."

Troll: "I guess I will. Go ahead and cross the bridge."

Little BG: "Thank you very much, you ugly troll."

Troll: "What did you call me? Come back here!"

Little BG: "Bye!"

Bridge: "Trip, trap, trip, trap, trip, trap."

(continued) **Three Billy Goats Gruff**

Narrator: Little Billy Goat Gruff ran across the bridge. He ate the green, green grass and apples. The troll went back under his bridge and went to sleep.

SCENE II

Narrator: Middle-Size Billy Goat Gruff walks up to the rickety, old bridge. He too sees the meadow with the green, green grass and apple trees.

Middle BG: "I'm the middle-size billy goat. I have a big brother and a little brother. I want to go across this bridge to eat some green, green grass and apples so that I can be big like my brother."

Narrator: Middle-Size Billy Goat Gruff starts across the bridge.

Bridge: "Trip, trap, trip, trap, trip, trap."

Narrator: Just as the Middle-Size Billy Goat Gruff came to the middle of the bridge, an old troll popped up from under the bridge.

Troll: "Who is that walking on my bridge?"

Middle BG: "It is I, Middle-Size Billy Goat Gruff."

Troll: "I'm a big, bad troll and your are on my bridge. I'm going to eat you for my lunch."

Middle BG: "I just want to eat some green, green grass and apples in the meadow. Please don't eat me. I'm just a middle-size billy goat. Wait until my brother comes along. He is much bigger than I am."

Troll: "I guess I will. Go ahead and cross the bridge."

Middle BG: "Thank you very much, you ugly troll."

Troll: "What did you call me? Come back here!"

Middle BG: "Bye!"

Bridge: "Trip, trap, trip, trap, trip, trap."

Narrator: Middle-Size Billy Goat Gruff ran across the bridge. He ate the green, green grass and apples. The troll went back under his bridge and went to sleep.

SCENE III

Narrator: Big Billy Goat Gruff sees the rickety, old bridge. On the other side of the bridge is a meadow with green, green grass and apple trees.

Big BG: "I'm the biggest billy goat. I have two brothers. I want to go across this bridge to eat some green, green grass and apples so I can get even bigger."

Narrator: Big Billy Goat Gruff starts across the bridge.

(continued) **Three Billy Goats Gruff**

Bridge: "Trip, trap, trip, trap, trip, trap."

Narrator: Just as the Big Billy Goat Gruff came to the middle of the bridge, an old troll popped up from under the bridge.

Troll: "Who is that walking on my bridge?"

Big BG: "It is I, Big Billy Goat Gruff."

Troll: "I'm a big, bad troll and you are on my bridge. I'm going to eat your for my lunch."

Big BG: "Come on and make my day! If you come up here, you will be going, going, gone!"

Narrator: The troll climbs onto the bridge. Big Billy Goat Gruff lowers his head and charges the troll! Big Billy Goat Gruff knocks the troll off the bridge!

Big BG: "That bully won't bother us again. I have done my job. Now, I'm going to eat that green, green grass and apples."

Bridge: "Trip, trap, trip, trap, trip, trap."

Narrator: Big Billy Goat Gruff ran across the bridge. He ate the green, green grass and apples. That mean old troll never came back to the bridge. He learned that being mean never pays.

Appendix B:
Speed Drills

Excerpts used by permission from:

Phyllis Fischer's *Concept Phonics Program* (Oxton House)
Beck, Conrad, and Anderson's *Basic Skill Builders* (Sopris West)
L. Moats and B. Rosow's *Spellography* (Sopris West)

Sample Fischer Speed Drill

rid   hid   hide   kit   kite   ride   hide   rid   hid   kit

ride   hid   kite   ride   rid   kit   hide   hid   ride   kit   rid

hide   hid   kit   rid   kite   ride   hid   kite   kit   ride   rid

hid   hide   kite   rid   hid   hide   kite   hid   ride   kit   hid

ride   hid   kit   rid   ride   kite   kit   hide   hid   kit   kite

ride   hid   kit   hide   rid   kit   kite   rid   hid   ride   hide

(12 lines)

SPEED DRILL RECORDING SHEET

Dates: 10/11 - 11/14 '89   NAME: J. E.

DATES / TITLE OF DRILL:	the h was were what	saysaid says has are	of from some come one	do done does don't anymany		at fat sat am him	cape came late game name	jam zap yam tax at	if im is it his him	ace face race age rage rage	at ate fat fate hat hate
GOAL:	60	60									
10/11	29					23					
10/12	32					26					
10/13	30					24					
10/16	38					30	31				
10/17	44	27				32	34				
10/18	46	36				35	40				
10/19	54	39				41	39	21			
10/23	57	40				43	42	29			
10/24	60	46	34			47	46	32	36	32	
10/25	59	53	33			45	48	30	43	36	
10/26	62	49	38			48	51	37	47	37	
10/27	61	57	41			50	53	38	52	41	
10/30	63	60	41			53	50	42	53	49	
10/31		62	50	22		57	54	46	52	50	
11/1		59	56			54	59	44	57	49	29
11/2		64	61	28		61	60	47	63	54	28

Sample Fischer Drills

Training the Orthographic Processor

MARKING THE VOWEL IN CLOSED AND MAGIC-E SYLLABLES

1. **If the word is a closed syllable, mark the vowel short:** ˘
2. **If the word is a magic-e syllable, mark the vowel long:** ¯

Example: take   hunt   clasp   sole   ice   set

· ·

nine   hop   wish   lake   us   tone   clash   flute   rest

rule   eke   egg   same   step   at   choke   lane   pat

ate   trump   time   ace   slop   set   use   broke   drape

loft   tame   class   prune   whip   odd   kite   tint   bone

left   stretch   eke   trust   plate   stone   flute   punt

Linking the Orthographic and Phonological Processors

Contrast Card: PRACTICING THE SOUNDS OF A IN CL & ME SYLLABLES

<table>
<tr><td colspan="10">Say /ă/ or /ā/ for each word:</td></tr>
<tr><td>mat</td><td>lamp</td><td>ate</td><td>bake</td><td>cash</td><td>fact</td><td>ace</td><td>trade</td><td>Jane</td><td>fast</td></tr>
<tr><td>map</td><td>age</td><td>sang</td><td>stake</td><td>at</td><td>scratch</td><td>name</td><td>tank</td><td>an</td><td>sage</td></tr>
<tr><td>ask</td><td>fate</td><td>flake</td><td>tag</td><td>ad</td><td>same</td><td>bank</td><td>page</td><td>phrase</td><td>rap</td></tr>
<tr><td>band</td><td>pace</td><td>rag</td><td>crate</td><td>tax</td><td>cap</td><td>date</td><td>camp</td><td>flame</td><td>ape</td></tr>
</table>

B A S I C

Skill Builders

SEE TO SAY

Lower Case Letters—Random

Directions: Say each letter.

	Correct	Error
First Try		
Second Try		

b	g	a	j	p	c	u	x	q
n	k	v	z	d	s	y	i	r
f	t	o	h	m	e	w	l	m
k	e	r	y	f	w	q	x	a
o	b	j	v	d	p	s	h	t
n	g	z	l	i	u	c	a	k

(9)
(18)
(27)
(36)
(45)
(54)

BASIC Skill Builders

SEE TO WRITE

	Correct	Error
First Try		
Second Try		

Beginning and Ending Sounds

Directions: Write the letter representing each beginning and ending sound for the picture.

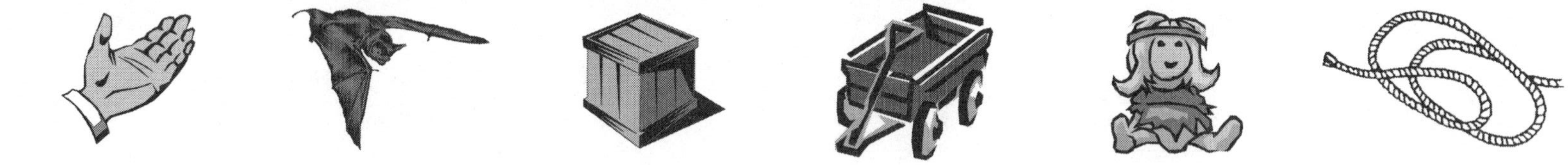

(12)

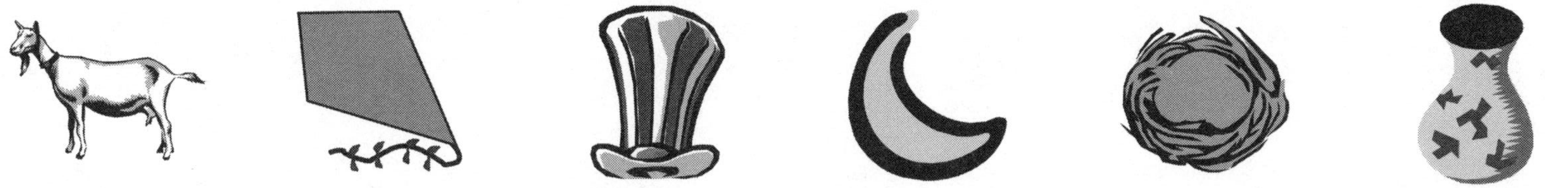

(24)

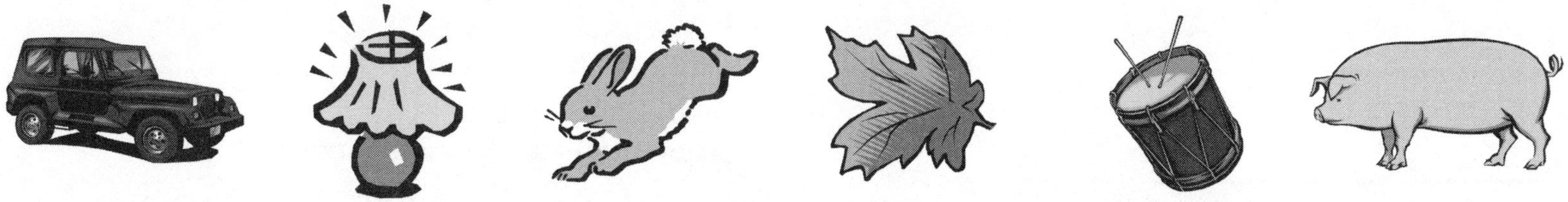

(36)

BASIC Skill Builders

SEE TO SAY

	Correct	Error
First Try		
Second Try		

Vowel Sounds—Short and Long Vowels (ā - stay, a - apple)

Directions: Say each vowel.

i	ā	o	i	ē	u	a	e	ō	u	i	ā	o	ī	ē	(15)
ē	ū	a	o	a	ī	e	ī	o	ū	e	u	ā	o	ā	(30)
e	ī	u	ō	i	ā	u	a	ē	o	e	ī	u	ō	i	(45)
ū	o	ē	a	u	e	ī	o	a	ī	u	o	i	ē	i	(60)
u	ō	i	ē	i	ā	o	a	ū	e	o	ē	a	u	ō	(75)
ī	a	ō	i	ē	u	a	ē	o	u	ē	u	ā	o	a	(90)
ē	u	a	ō	a	ī	e	i	ō	u	e	ū	a	ō	a	(105)
e	ī	u	o	ī	a	u	ā	e	o	ē	i	u	ō	i	(120)
ī	a	ō	i	ē	u	a	e	ō	u	i	ā	o	i	ē	(135)
e	ū	a	o	a	ī	e	i	o	ū	e	u	ā	o	a	(150)
ī	a	ō	i	e	ū	a	ē	o	u	e	u	a	ō	ā	(165)
ē	i	u	ō	i	ā	u	a	e	ō	o	e	ī	u	o	i	(180)

SEE TO SAY

	Correct	Error
First Try		
Second Try		

Blending Sounds with Short Vowel Sounds

Directions: Say each sound.

bac	ded	ris	wol	tuv	pug	man	bac	ded	(9)
lem	hik	vop	jox	fuh	nam	set	lem	hik	(18)
kid	rim	gog	zuz	bad	sek	cak	did	rim	(27)
def	wic	zot	tub	kux	hag	mez	def	wic	(36)
nip	dom	sod	lus	pab	wet	tik	nip	dom	(45)
vig	ron	hut	gqf	jel	bon	zix	vig	ron	(54)
coz	muc	fat	gad	reb	dit	hob	coz	muc	(63)
fuf	bul	sas	ned	lid	mok	roc	fuf	bul	(72)
cum	kah	teg	dif	fin	goz	vux	cum	kah	(81)
zat	pep	wem	bik	top	hud	cac	zat	pep	(90)
dal	beb	niz	job	sux	sut	gap	dal	beb	(99)
fes	rib	kot	mol	luv	tad	sel	fes	rib	(108)

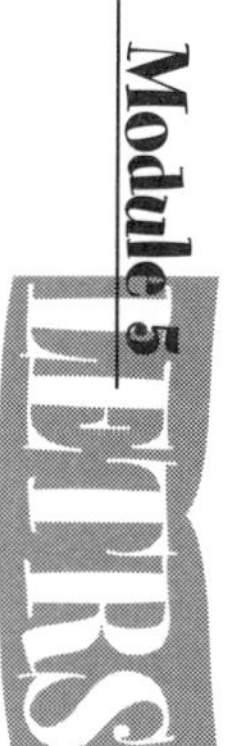

SEE TO SAY

	Correct	Error
First Try		
Second Try		

Blending Sounds with Both Long and Short Vowels

Directions: Say each sound.

shud	nane	flib	cate	phude	claf	chet	brin	phode	(9)
whote	plime	blox	twile	brug	theme	rollo	clak	drask	(18)
glape	snat	crend	tompt	blep	rosk	kine	quip	bode	(27)
frodo	ship	silo	stos	chike	slone	base	tite	pove	(36)
mump	tast	thrud	flisp	stete	shape	splam	lipe	frew	(45)
shas	dife	phob	cuse	brik	spile	clift	nint	wile	(54)
theck	grun	pleb	quit	zone	frust	goke	phig	glid	(63)
dasp	cril	fruf	stut	snim	whave	thas	chez	mote	(72)
spip	rime	thit	frak	dresk	phono	crump	pano	whes	(81)
glish	draf	bine	vamp	chip	fune	slap	tefe	snop	(90)
phat	fluft	crend	presk	blosp	thap	whipe	glape	spift	(99)
blox	slimp	vepe	bufe	quile	rame	blep	chasp	blox	(108)

PS1-9

SEE TO SAY

Dolch Words—1

	Correct	Error
First Try		
Second Try		

Directions: Say each word.

a	and	my	run	can	three	look	help	in	for	(10)
down	we	big	here	it	away	me	to	said	one	(20)
where	is	yellow	blue	you	go	two	the	up	see	(30)
play	funny	make	red	come	jump	not	find	little	I	(40)
a	down	where	play	and	we	is	funny	my	big	(50)
yellow	make	run	here	blue	red	can	it	you	come	(60)
three	away	go	jump	we	look	me	two	not	help	(70)
to	the	find	in	said	up	little	for	one	see	(80)
I	a	and	my	run	can	three	look	help	in	(90)
for	down	we	big	here	you	go	me	away	to	(100)

BASIC
Skill Builders

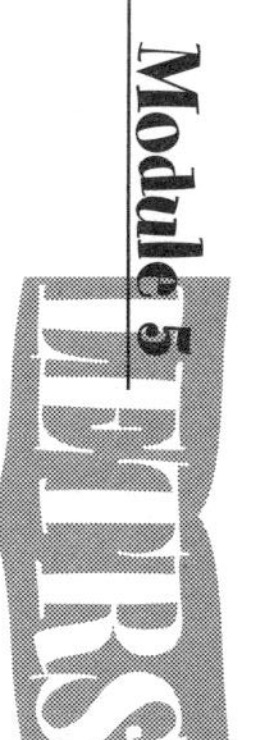

SEE TO SAY

	Correct	Error
First Try		
Second Try		

Dolch Phrases—5

Directions: Say each phrase.

the little chickens   then he came   if you wish   as he did   to the farm   as he said   (18)

when you come   as I do   the small boat   the new doll   the little pig   the white duck   (36)

in the water   I may get   did not fall   the little dog   what I say   has come back   (54)

if I must   to the house   in the barn   he would try   down the street   I will come   (72)

in the window   the funny man   from the tree   a big house   the red cow   from the farm   (90)

when you know   when you come   as he said   to the farm   as he did   if you wish   (108)

then he came   the little chickens   I may get   in the water   the white duck   as I do   (126)

in the barn   to the house   if I must   has come back   what I say   the little dog   (144)

did not fail   the funny man   in the window   I will go   I will come   down the street   (162)

he would try   when you come   from the farm   when you know   the red cow   a big house   (180)

from the tree   I may get   the little chickens   then he came   if you wish   as he did   (198)

in the barn   as I do   the small boat   the new doll   the little pig   the white duck   (216)

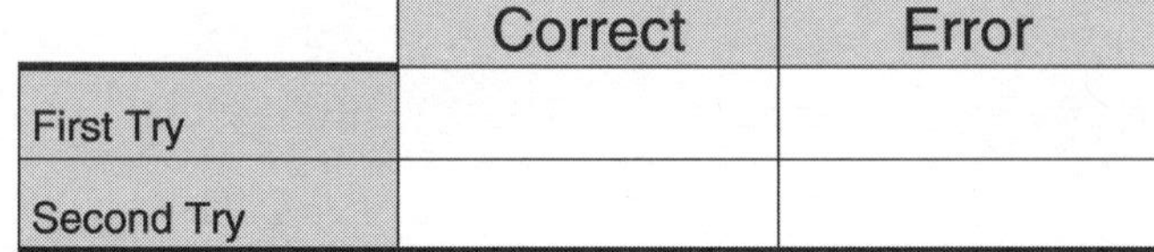

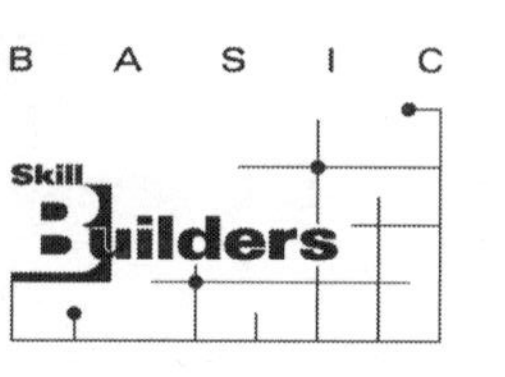

SEE TO SAY

	Correct	Error
First Try		
Second Try		

Passages—2-2 (Second Grade, Second Semester) #8

Directions: Say each word.

"I want a place of my own," thought Evan. He climbed up the steps to his apartment. Soon his three (20)

sisters and two brothers would be home. "Mighty lot of family," Evan thought. "And no place to call just (39)

mine." He put the key in the door. He was surprised to see his mother home early. "There are eight of (60)

us," said his mother. "That means each one of us can have a corner of our own." Evan had the first (81)

choice. One corner had a rug and another had a wall with a crack in it. Evan choose the one with a (103)

small window. He ate his dinner and his dessert in his corner. Then he watched two pigeons who cooed (122)

on the window ledge. He enjoyed wasting his time this way. "What shall I do in my corner?" asked Adam. (142)

"Whatever you like," said Evan. Evan hung a picture in his corner. He took his toothbrush glass and put (161)

some lacy flowers in it. He put his flowers on the window sill. Then an idea struck him. He went to the (183)

pet store and saw some baby green turtles scrambling all over each other. One clumsy turtle took a dive (202)

off a rock. One turtle swam to the edge of the bowl. The turtles cost fifty cents. Evan worked at the (223)

supermarket to earn fifty cents. He worked hard carrying bags. He gasped for air as he eased a heavy (242)

bag into a lady's car. He proudly gave the man at the pet store his dimes. "This is my pet," boasted Evan. (264)

Exercise 13

Speed Read Time yourself on three different days reading these columns of words out loud from top to bottom. Record your errors, too.

fur	par	burr	herd	lord
far	purr	bore	hard	lard
for	pore	bar	harden	lured
	port	barred	hardly	
art				sir
tart	form	ark	ore	fir
start	dorm	park	pore	first
smart	storm	spark	port	thirst
smarter	stormy	sparkle	import	thirsty
smartest	stormed	sparkled	imported	

Day 1	Day 2	Day 3
Time: ________	Time: ________	Time: ________
Errors: ________	Errors: ________	Errors: ________

Finally: Take the Posttest, and record your score here.   **Number Correct:** ____________

Exercise 13

Speed Read Time yourself reading these words out loud on at least three different days. Read each line across (left to right), and record your times and errors.

ridge	bridge	edge	hedge	ledge	pledge
cringe	fringe	ledge	sedge	sledge	pledge
urge	merge	verge	large	barge	charge
forge	gorge	George	sarge	barge	Marge
tinge	singe	hinge	hinged	unhinged	
binge	budge	nudge	judge	grudge	trudge
jolly	golly	junk	gunk	jet	got
gent	gents	gentle	gently	gentlemen	
jack-in-the-box		jackpot	jackrabbit	jack-o'-lantern	
jump	jumpy	jump shot	jump-start	jumping jack	

Day 1	**Day 2**	**Day 3**
Time: ______	Time: ______	Time: ______
Errors: ______	Errors: ______	Errors: ______

Finally: Take the Posttest, and record your score here. **Number Correct:** ___________

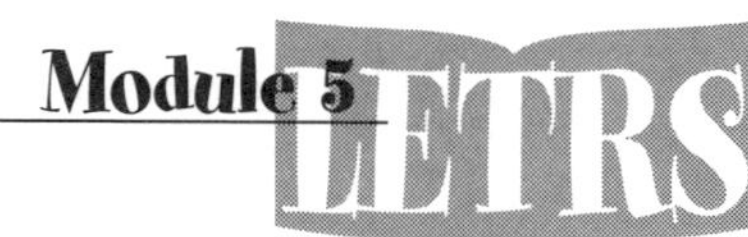

Professor Thunker thought that he could get rich by writing a soap opera set in the early days of the Paleo Era, which occurred about 12,000 years ago. Thankfully, this project went the way of the Paleo people—although this prehysteric draft was mysteriously found inside a woolly mammoth horn, half-buried near the entrance to the Shelburne Museum. Time yourself reading this passage on three different days. Record your time and errors.

The Lives of the First Thunkers

Way back before computers or nose-hair clippers—at the birth of history—there lived a muscular brute named Urrg and his charming partner, Cora. Together they shared a sparse cave overlooking a sandbar by the Champlain Sea. Each morning, Urrg and Cora would carefully sharpen barbs on their harpoons before going forth to the sea to spar with the fierce beasts therein. Returning with swordfish, shark, or marlin, they would sear the fish in strips over sparking flames. Beside the dark waters, under sparks and stars, Urrg and Cora would pass a birch bark bowl—steaming with morsels of charred fish—back and forth. Later, keeping warm under thick furs, Urrg and Cora would stare past the flames and sparks to the stars and worship the spirits that brought them together and kept them from harm.

Day 1	Day 2	Day 3
Time:	Time:	Time:
___	___	___
Errors:	Errors:	Errors:
___	___	___

Challenge Activity
Underline all of the **v + -r** combinations in this reading. How many did you find? _67_

Finally: Take the Posttest, and record your score here. **Number Correct:** __________

Exercise #12: Speed Read Time yourself on three different occasions reading out loud Thunker's infamous account of the demise of the oyster hoister, Roy Doyle.

Roy Doyle, Oyster Hoister

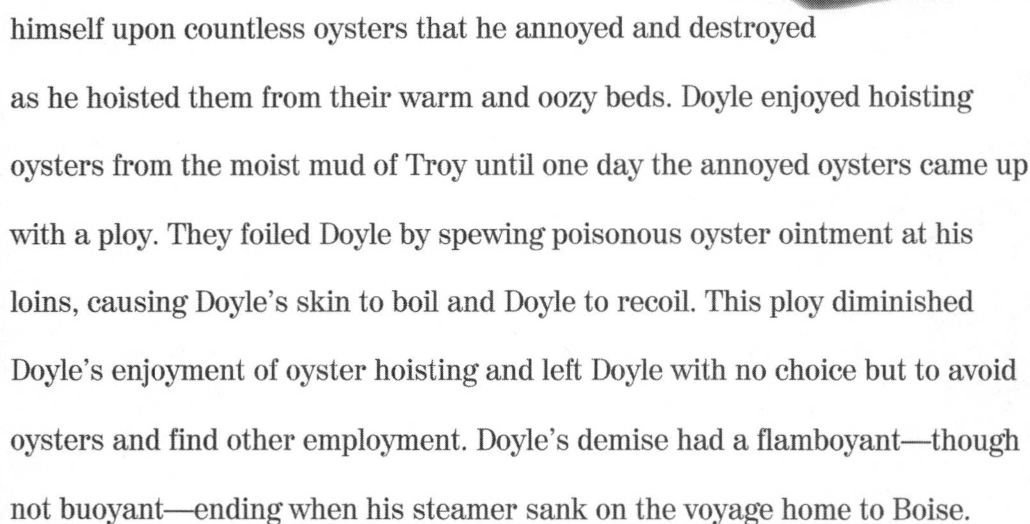

Roy Doyle was an oyster hoister employed by the Royal Oyster and Cracker Crumb Company. In his oilcloth slicker and soiled boots, Doyle toiled in the moist mud flats of Troy. There, he foisted himself upon countless oysters that he annoyed and destroyed as he hoisted them from their warm and oozy beds. Doyle enjoyed hoisting oysters from the moist mud of Troy until one day the annoyed oysters came up with a ploy. They foiled Doyle by spewing poisonous oyster ointment at his loins, causing Doyle's skin to boil and Doyle to recoil. This ploy diminished Doyle's enjoyment of oyster hoisting and left Doyle with no choice but to avoid oysters and find other employment. Doyle's demise had a flamboyant—though not buoyant—ending when his steamer sank on the voyage home to Boise.

Day 1	Day 2	Day 3
Time:	Time:	Time:
____	____	____
Errors:	Errors:	Errors:
____	____	____

Challenge Activity

1. How many /oi/ spellings are there in Roy's story? _56_

Finally: Take the Posttest, and record your score here. **Number Correct:** __________

Speed Read This is the last time—OK, the last three times—you will be asked to suffer through reading a Thunker clunker out loud. (Record your times and errors after each reading.) He hopes it leaves a lasting impression on you—three times over!

Last Licks

Thunker and Bess heard rowdies go
squeaking and whopping, squawking and screeching
through the fields and meadow below.

"Fleas and roaches! What encroaches?" wondered Thunker.

Into view did spew a rowdy crew,
led by Stupor Stu and others Thunker knew.

"Mumble, grumble!" grumbled Thunker.
"Why is that hodgepodge marching to my bunker?"

"We're here," replied the aged Sage Page,
"because your students have reached this stage."

"Each of them did what it took
to be ousted from this spelling book."

At that, Chunky Chucky struck a gong
and started chanting enchanted ranting
(which sounded to Thunker like chickens panting).

The singing vowel cats joined the jam,
along with Clem the fisherman.

The nose vowels hummed, the **-r** vowels rumbled,
Strange Georgia shook her rump and stumbled.

Urrg and Cora, Chip, Thor, and Mack
jittered up and down with Cracker Jack.

The Royal Oyster and Cracker Crumb Company sent oyster stew,
and the Moody Moose added special pickle and prune goo
(which he purchased while moaning about Sue in Peru).

While a rooster and an emu were heard to argue
over which was better, the stew or the goo.

And everyone made such a hullabaloo,
because they all were—and are—so proud of you!

Day 1	Day 2	Day 3
Time:	Time:	Time:
————	————	————
Errors:	Errors:	Errors:
————	————	————

125

Module 6

Digging for Meaning:
Teaching Text Comprehension

Contents for Module 6

Content of LETRS: The Language-Literacy Connection

Components of Comprehensive Reading Instruction	Organization of Language						
	Phonology	Morphology	Orthography	Semantics	Syntax	Discourse and Pragmatics	Etymology
Phonological Awareness	2	2					
Phonics, Spelling, and Word Study	3, 7	3, 7, 10	3, 7, 10				3, 10
Fluency	5		5	5	5		
Vocabulary	4	4	4	4	4		4
Text Comprehension		6		6	6	6, 11	
Written Expression			9, 11	9, 11	9, 11	9, 11	
Assessment	8, 12	8, 12	8, 12	8, 12	8, 12	8, 12	

Slide 3

These are the "big ideas" of the module – the ones we hope participants will take away. The module will end with a small group study of text, lesson outline based on that text, and sharing of ideas among the participants. Time permitting, it will also involve close examination of the teacher's manual of the adopted core reading program in use in the state or district.

Goals for Teacher Participants

♦ Understand the major factors that influence comprehension.

♦ Elaborate how the text itself, the context in which reading occurs, the reader's characteristics, and the specific task can determine how well a student comprehends.

♦ Explore the challenges of "academic language" at the phrase, sentence, and discourse level, and become familiar with techniques for teaching sentences and text structure directly.

♦ Differentiate among the instructional strategies most useful before a text is read, during text reading, and after text reading.

♦ Summarize important research findings on comprehension strategy instruction.

♦ Prepare to teach a text by reading it, segmenting it into major sections, summarizing the meanings to be taught, generating questions to ask during reading, and planning specific activities that would enhance children's comprehension of the text.

♦ Evaluate the reading comprehension instruction in your own adopted reading program.

Comprehension: What Can Be Taught?

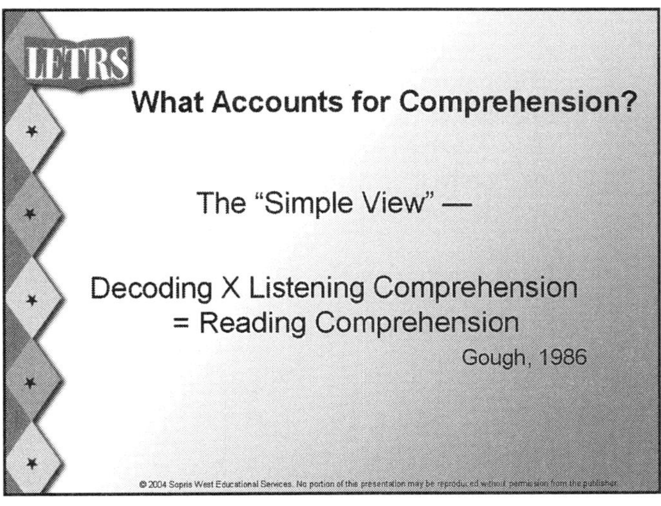

Slide 4

Reading comprehension is the product of decoding and listening comprehension. It is more than the sum of decoding and listening comprehension, because these two parts of reading interact with and influence one another.

Listening comprehension is measured without reading; the student listens to a passage and then answers questions about it or summarizes it orally.

Decoding is the ability to "sound out" new words; decoding ability underlies or facilitates the ability to recognize words quickly as wholes.

The "simple view" gives us a model for understanding various kinds of reading profiles.

Reading: The Product of Decoding and Comprehension

In the "simple view" of reading (Gough & Tunmer, 1986), the ability to read is described as the product of decoding (the ability to read the words accurately) and comprehension (the ability to interpret what is read). Comprehension, moreover, is verbal reasoning itself. Readers' comprehension of a written text should be roughly equivalent to their ability to comprehend what is read to them or said to them. This idea, in turn, suggests that some individuals have trouble comprehending because they cannot read the words accurately or efficiently, and others do not bring good reading comprehension skills and strategies. Subtypes of good and poor readers can thus be classified in this way:[1]

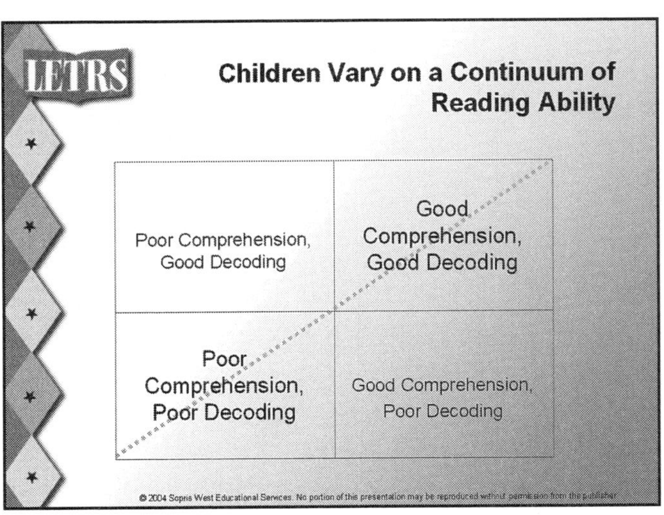

Slide 5

The dotted line going on the diagonal would represent a continuum of perfect correlation between decoding and comprehension. We could predict one from knowing the other with 100% accuracy if decoding and comprehension were perfectly correlated.

So the question is, to what extent are decoding and comprehension related to one another? Are there children who are poor at comprehension and good at decoding? Good at comprehension and poor at decoding? Many studies have addressed these questions; some of the best are done through the Haskins Laboratory and Yale University with a sample of several hundred children who were followed from kindergarten through college.

---

[1] See Shankweiler et al. (1999) for discussion of subtypes and frequency of subtypes in the population of children with reading difficulties (below the 30th percentile).

Comprehension Ability

<table>
<tr><td></td><td colspan="2">POOR ▬▬▬▬▬▬▬▬▬▬▬ GOOD</td></tr>
<tr><td rowspan="2">**Word Recognition** GOOD</td><td>Good word recognition with specific language comprehension problems.</td><td>Accurate, fluent reader with comprehension commensurate with verbal ability</td></tr>
<tr><td>Weak comprehension and poor word recognition.</td><td>Inaccurate and/or slow word identification with good comprehension.</td></tr>
<tr><td>POOR</td><td></td><td></td></tr>
</table>

The decoding (word recognition) and comprehension components of reading are not so separate as this chart might suggest. Although these components are often measured independently on tests and can be differentiated, the most common type of poor reader is a child who has trouble with both decoding and comprehension. Such problems exist on a continuum, of course, with a few children having specific and significant problems in one domain or another, but many children who are between the low average and average ranges need coherent, coordinated instruction that teaches them to read the words *and* comprehend the text once it is decoded.[2]

The correlation between decoding and comprehension is high but not perfect. For the majority of children, poor decoding is associated with poor comprehension, and good decoding is associated with good comprehension. Scores are distributed normally along the diagonal line of the graph.

To some extent, however, these two parts of reading are dissociated. Some children (about 10% of poor readers) are better at decoding than they are at comprehension. These children can read the words but don't get what they mean. About 20% of poor readers have much better comprehension than decoding. They are the "classic dyslexic" children whose verbal comprehension is much better than their decoding and word recognition.

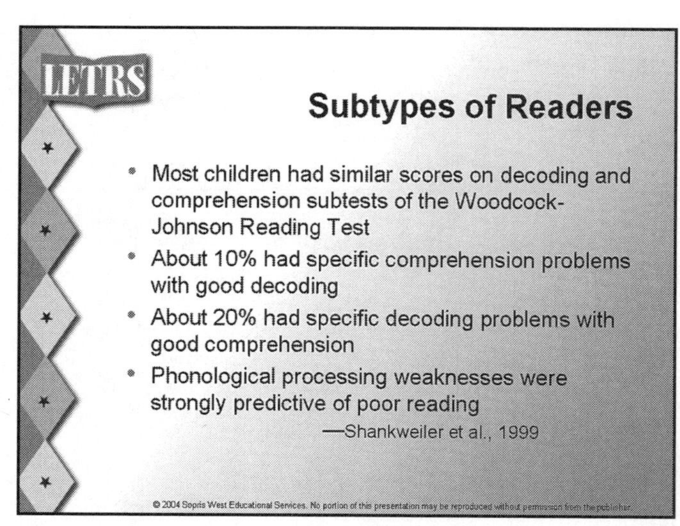

Slide 6

[2] See Catts et al. (1999), Perfetti et al. (1996), and Shankweiler et al. (1999) for reviews of the evidence.

Slide 7

Listening comprehension sets an upper limit. That means that a student with vocabulary and verbal learning ability at the 35th percentile, as measured by listening and verbal reasoning tests, may not develop reading comprehension skill much beyond that level.

Children who have prominent weaknesses in reading comprehension in spite of good word recognition often have global problems with verbal reasoning or mastery of standard English. Learners with limited vocabulary, background knowledge, or familiarity with academic language, may have even more difficulty comprehending written language than they have decoding it.[3] Other common limitations on comprehension include reading too slowly to piece the text meanings together, reading passively and superficially, or simply not knowing the meanings of the words (vocabulary). English language learners who face all of these problems need instruction in all levels of language that extends to listening, speaking, reading, and writing.

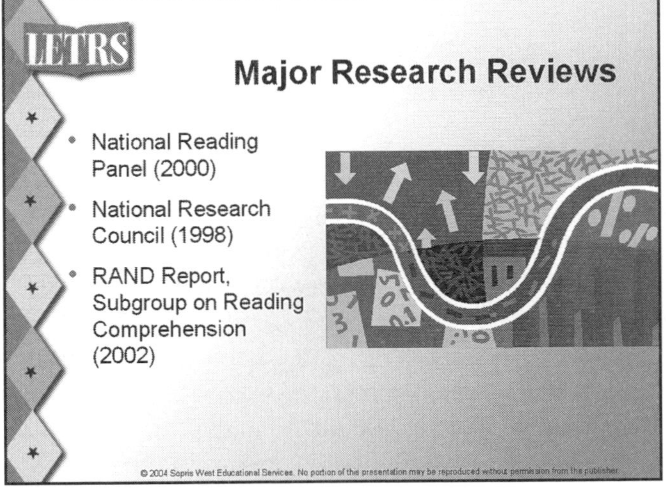

Slide 8

The National Reading Panel did not go so far as to set a research agenda for the study of comprehension, so the RAND corporation recruited a study group for that purpose. Catherine Snow headed the task force and the resulting report is a very thorough summary of what we know about reading comprehension development and instruction.

---

[3] See Catts et al. (1999) for a comprehensive update on the relationship between various language abilities and the development of reading skill.

Although the National Reading Panel (2000) summarized the findings of several hundred studies on teaching reading comprehension, many questions remained about the nature of comprehension and how to improve comprehension in young readers after their report was issued. Consequently, another "blue ribbon" study group was convened (RAND Reading Study Group, 2002) to define the next frontier of reading comprehension research. This panel summarized what we do and don't know about comprehension and proposed an extensive program of research to address many unanswered questions. Progress is urgently needed, said the report, in order to help large numbers of children who, for various reasons, lack the reading comprehension ability to meet state standards, pass high-stakes tests, experience academic success, or perform reading required in the workplace.

One fact that reading researchers agree on is that comprehension will improve if certain skills and strategies are well taught. In many classrooms, however, comprehension is simply expected and is not taught. Traditionally, teachers use questions to TEST comprehension rather than to TEACH comprehension (Durkin's findings).

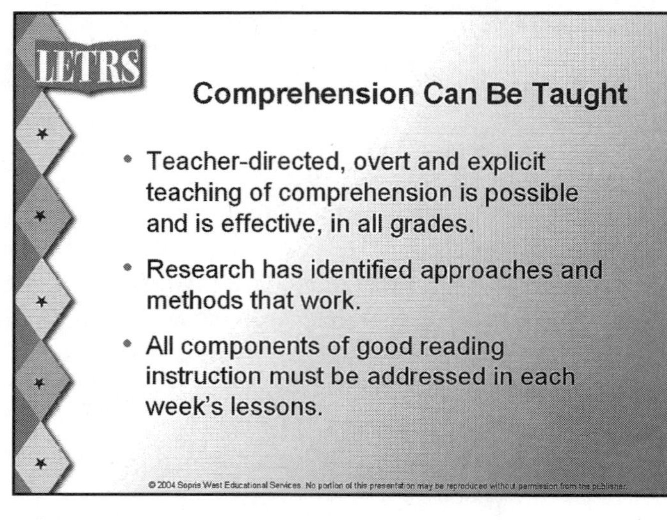

Slide 9

Even if students learn to read by third grade, instruction in reading comprehension is necessary for students who read at "basic" levels to reach "proficient" and "advanced" levels.

Reading comprehension instruction should use modeling, thinking aloud, questioning, and other techniques to promote active construction of meaning. Children often must be taught comprehension skills; encouragement to silently read trade books or to read independently will be insufficient to engender the language awareness and underlying mental habits that are characteristic of proficient readers. Research supports the effectiveness of teacher-directed, overt and explicit instruction in comprehension skills and strategies, in addition to instruction in word recognition that builds reading fluency. This module gives teachers the opportunity to review, understand, and practice components of comprehension instruction that will help students become thoughtful, eager readers.

Dimensions of Comprehension: Text, Reader, Task, and Context

What factors or variables influence comprehension? A simple conceptual model suggests that there are many factors that enhance or undermine comprehension. The conceptual model below conveys the complexity and multi-faceted nature of reading for meaning.[4] Comprehension occurs as a consequence of the interaction between the person who is reading, the text the reader is reading, the specific task the reader is trying to accomplish, and the circumstances under which the reading is done (the context).

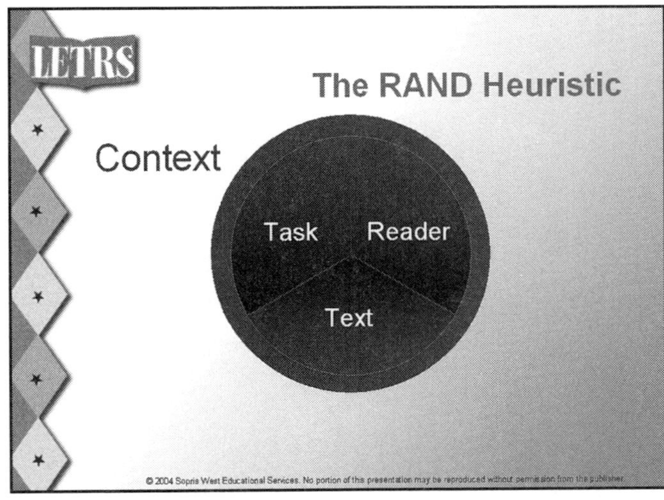

Slide 10

This diagram of the major factors contributing to comprehension was the basis for organizing the RAND report. Let's stop and consider the many factors that can influence whether or not the reader understands the meanings that were intended by the author of a text.

Use this model as a brainstorming springboard. Put this model on the transparency projector and jot notes as you and the participants brainstorm the factors that influence how well a reader understands what they read. As the discussion ensues, ask participants to take notes on the page of text with this model. After a free ranging brainstorm and discussion of about 5-10 minutes, review the next slides to summarize the main points about each area of influence.

---

[4] This heuristic is used by the RAND Study Group on Reading in their 2002 report.

Exercise #1: The Dimensions of Reading Comprehension

Take notes on this simple schematic diagram regarding the factors that contribute to reading comprehension. As each component is discussed, elaborate the conceptual map in your own way by adding detail, examples, or dynamic indicators of the way these factors interact. After the discussion, you will be asked to summarize your notes orally to a colleague.

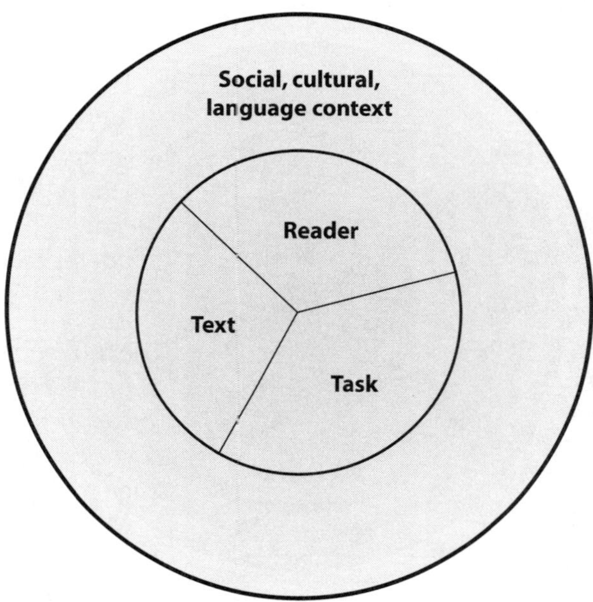

What Matters in the Text Itself

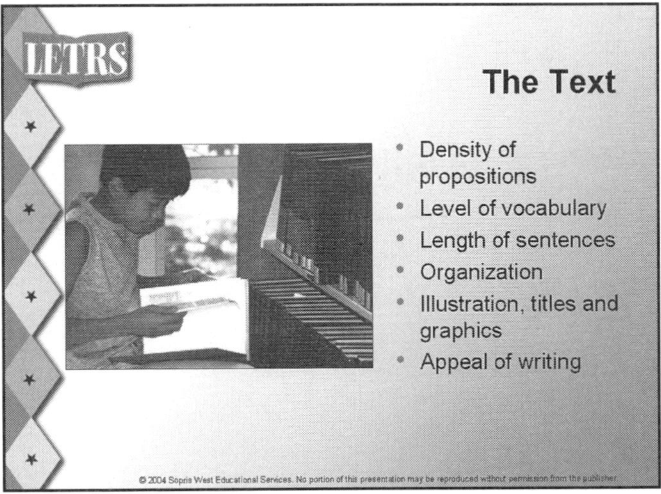

Slide 11

Density of propositions refers to the number of ideas that are embodied in each sentence. Number of ideas is not the same as number of words. For example, "This creek flows into the east fork of the north fork of the Upper Wood river" has about five ideas in it: The river; flows; there are four streams/rivers: the creek, the east fork, the north fork, the Upper Wood main river.

Level of vocabulary would be the frequency of rare words.

Length of sentences would also suggest their syntactic complexity.

Organization refers to how clearly the text follows a known or expected pattern, such as compare/contrast, and these patterns are culture-specific. Hispanic writers, for example, may not write in as linear a progression as Anglo writers.

Friendly texts offer much support from illustrations, lists, diagrams, and subtitles.

Author's style makes the text appealing or unappealing.

What makes a text easier or harder to read? What characteristics of texts affect how they are ranked in difficulty or "leveled"?

Text embodies not only the words we read, but the underlying knowledge structures or mental models (schemas) that a reader must understand to take away the meanings. Further, the words themselves represent idea units in the text base—the thoughts or meanings that each word, phrase, and sentence represents. The degree to which the surface representation—the language— conveys the underlying ideas and their relationship with one another—the propositions—has much to do with whether the text is understandable.

Texts vary by genre: a **narrative** tells a story, an **expository** text explains or gives factual information. Other genres such as letters, poetry, and dramatic dialogues also have distinctive forms and conventions. Texts vary in their proposition density; textbooks usually contain a high number of new ideas or propositions per sentence, while narratives may have a lower concentration of new or distinct ideas and thus can be easier to understand. Texts may vary in the number of unfamiliar or unusual words, the length of the sentences, the connectedness of those sentences and the figures of speech used to express ideas. Some texts are "reader friendly" because they are clearly organized, complete, explicit, and visually easy to scan, while others are harder to navigate. For example, a text with an introduction, subtitles, illustrations, and repetition of main ideas in summary passages or lists is easier to manage than one in which those text organizers are lacking. All of these factors may influence how well the reader comprehends.

The measurement of text readability is a sub-discipline in reading psychology. Readability quotients allow publishers to assign grade levels to children's reading material. Formulas for calculating readability often do not agree with one another because they are, of course, imprecise and depend on which text descriptors are put into the readability quotient. Nevertheless, classic

approaches that researchers and publishers use typically rely on ratios of unusual or lengthy words to common words and the length of idea units within sentences, or syntactic complexity. The Spache formula, for example, was used to calculate the difficulty and equivalence of passages on the DIBELS assessment.[5]

What Does the Reader Bring?

Much of the variation in comprehension ability resides within the reader, the person doing the reading. Knowledge of words and the background necessary to read the text is critical. Attention, persistence, abstract reasoning ability all are factors. But also the readers' conscious or habitual use of adaptive strategies can make a big difference in their comprehension. If they don't comprehend, what do they do about it?

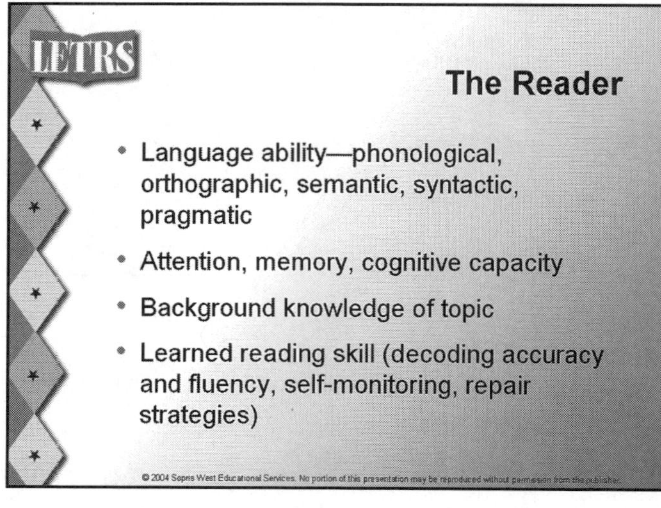

Slide 12

To any reading task, the reader brings unique cognitive, experiential, and linguistic capacities. The reader's attentional resources, memory, insight, ability to make inferences, and capacity for constructing visual images, affect both listening and reading comprehension. The reader brings knowledge of the world, mental models of topical content, and a unique background through which any reading experience is filtered. The reader also brings a set of learned reading skills that are both linguistic and meta-cognitive. These include the ability to identify the names of the words on the page; knowledge of word and phrase meanings; the ability to read phrases and sentences with sufficient fluency to support comprehension; short term and working memory capacity to keep ideas on the "cognitive desktop" as meaning is being constructed; the ability to integrate new information into existing mental models (schemata) and extract main ideas; capacity for emotional response to the text; and the active search for connections between what is in the text and what the reader already knows or wants to know.

Whew! No wonder a class of students can interpret a text very differently from one another, from what the author intended, and from what the teacher wants the students to interpret.

---

[5] *Dynamic Indicators of Basic Early Literacy Skills*, Roland Good and Ruth Kaminski, University of Oregon; test materials published by Sopris West Educational Services. *DIBELS* is introduced in Module 8 of *LETRS*.

© The New Yorker Collection 2001 by Mike Twohy. Reprinted with permission.

"It's funny how two intelligent people can have such opposite interpretations of the tax code!"

The Nature and Purpose of the Reading Task

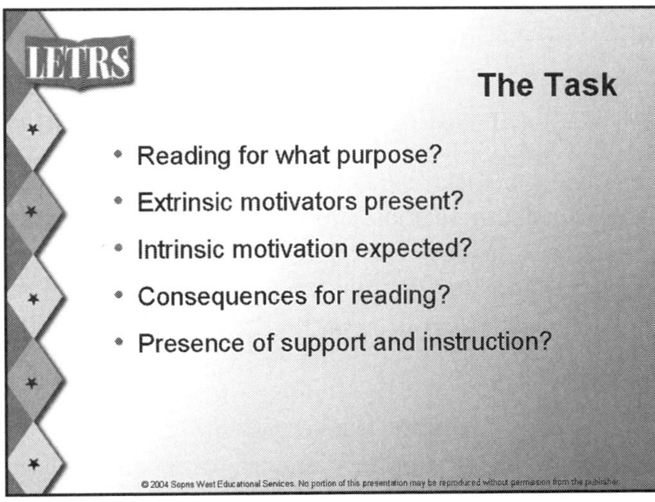

Slide 13

Reading is undertaken in a context and for a purpose. If we are scanning for a specific bit of information, we read in one way. If we are scanning for the gist, we read another. If we are doing critical analysis of literary devices, we read in another way. If there are consequences for understanding – such as passing a class and taking an exam, we may read more carefully than we would otherwise. Reading for pleasure and for self-education is characteristic of a minority of people in our culture.

The task is what the reader is supposed to do or intends to do with the text. Is the text to be read superficially or deeply? Is it to supply information, to amuse, or to direct? Is the reading task imposed or selected? All of these circumstances may affect motivation to persist with reading for meaning.

Reading for a specific purpose may also be linked with a specific consequence. Extrinsically imposed consequences for reading may include test scores, grades, or products that will be judged by others. Intrinsic consequences include satisfaction, frustration, enlightenment, amusement, or access to information necessary for some ancillary purpose.

The purpose or motivation with which one reads can affect many aspects of reading itself. The purpose of the reading can affect the strategies selected during and after reading and the pace of reading. If a task is viewed as unimportant, irrelevant, or impossible to understand, then reading is likely to be superficial and comprehension is likely to suffer.

In What Context Does Reading Occur?

The reading habits of those in our linguistic community influence us. If everyone is reading something, we might want to read it too out of curiosity. Think of Oprah's book club and how that influenced the public's reading habits. If no one reads in our household, we are less likely to read ourselves.

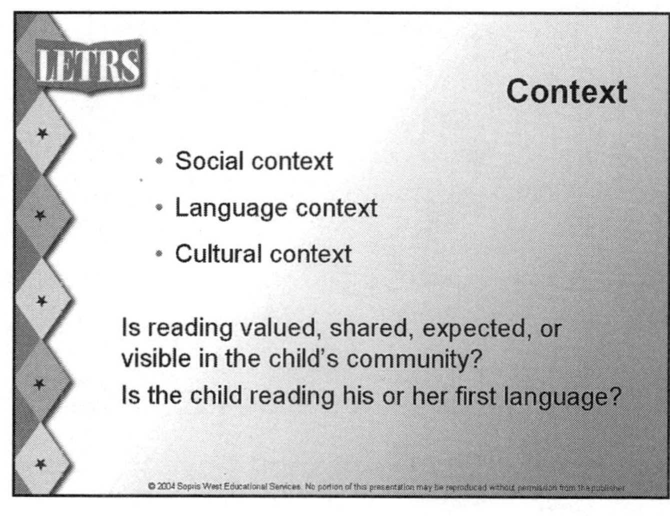

Slide 14

How much assistance is available to the reader if something is not understood? Is the reading a social experience or an individual experience? Are there time constraints? Can ideas be shared with others for whom understanding is important? In a supportive context, students are more likely to persist with challenging material and to grapple with challenges to their understanding. Support can be emotional or cognitive. Support can model and encourage strategic, persistent reading or it can provide interpretive information that the reader may have missed. The scaffolding process can include summarizing, clarifying, answering specific questions, or tying information to what is known or what will be found out. Peer partners, parents, small groups, teacher leaders, or computers can give such support.

All of these factors and others will determine how well a student comprehends. If the text is highly interesting and compelling, the reader is more likely to persist. If the reading is well prepared for, is shared in a group, and is supported and guided by a teacher, students are more likely to comprehend at a deeper level than if they are reading on their own. If a student is part of a group that values and enjoys sharing the experience of reading, he or she is more likely to value and enjoy reading. The habit of independent reading is less likely if reading sets the student apart from a peer group or family group or if there is no opportunity for the student to communicate with others about the experience. Home, community, and social contexts do help determine if students will become good readers.

Exercise #2: Summarize

Now refer back to your graphic organizer notes from the previous discussion. Verbally summarize the main points about the causes and influences on students' reading comprehension.

Comprehension is determined by a number of factors. It is influenced by the text itself, the verbal ability and background knowledge of the reader, the circumstances under which reading is done, and the purpose and nature of the reading assignment. To be understood, the text must be within the range of difficulty that the reader can handle, typically with 90% or more of the words recognized. Word meanings must be familiar and the text must be organized so that inferences are facilitated. The reader must have sufficient decoding ability and reading fluency to attend to the meanings in the text. The reader must be able to follow a logical structure and make inferences of many kinds. The reader must bring background knowledge to the task and connect to experiences beyond the text in order to fully comprehend. Finally, the environment in which reading takes place and the purpose of the reading task will influence how deeply and intentionally the reader reads.

The Challenge of "Book" Language

We have reviewed these ideas in other modules, but they are again important here. Academic language is not simply "harder"; it has properties and constructions that are different from conversational language, and thus they must be taught to children explicitly, just as we would teach a second language explicitly.

Using the chart, review these properties by asking the participants to reflect and feed back as you write on a transparency.

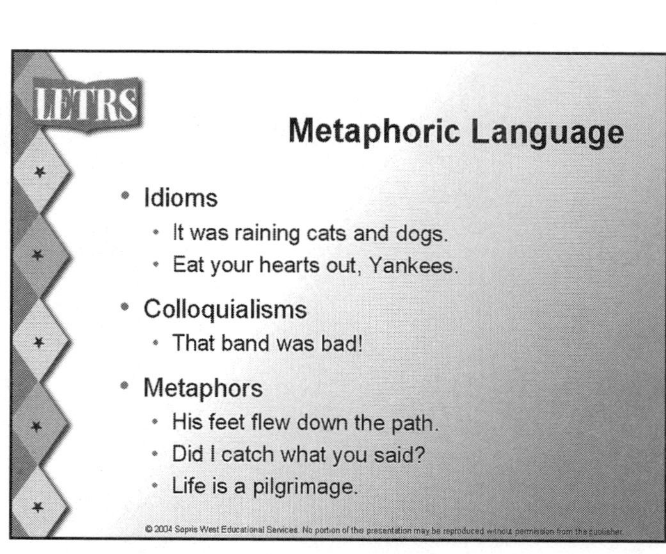

Slide 15

Those who comprehend well while they are reading are making sense of language at many levels. They are integrating information in the text with what they already know, extending beyond the text in their imaginations, actively summarizing and questioning as they go, and changing their strategy if they are not making sense of what they read. They are interpreting the meanings of the individual words used in specific contexts, the syntax in which those words occur, and the text structure itself. This section brings into focus those aspects of language that students often need help deciphering.

Idioms, Metaphors, Figures of Speech, and Colloquial Expressions

Literary language tends to have more figurative language. The term "metaphoric" here is used to mean "figurative"—or language that has meaning other than that typically conveyed by a word. Feet don't fly; hearts don't sing; girls are not tigers.

Children who are concrete thinkers may misinterpret such language until it is directly explained to them.

Slide 16

Language is by nature metaphorical. The words often do not mean exactly what they say. Words and phrases often embody special meanings; moreover, those meanings evolve continuously in a language community. When children are concrete thinkers, second language learners, or verbally limited, they may misinterpret abstract words and phrases. They may only process the concrete or literal meaning of a phrase without understanding what it refers to. For example, the phrases and sentences below can easily be misunderstood by young children, new users of English, or older students with global comprehension difficulties:

Idioms

The thrill of *pushing the envelope* is addictive for an extreme athlete.

It's a good plan, but where's the *fly in the ointment*?

Metaphors

Her *heart froze* when she realized her brother was lost.

The horse was a *lamb*, compliant and good-tempered.

Time flies.

Colloquial Expressions

Easy come, easy go.

Mark my words, something's up.

He went out on a date with a *real dog*.

Her *emotional baggage* interferes with her relationships.

Such idiomatic and figurative uses of language are learned from multiple examples in context. Children who think concretely, however, such as the boy who thought that "emotional baggage" was carried in a suitcase, benefit from direct explanation. Idiomatic phrases can be selected for review before reading, revisited after reading, or commented upon during reading. Every few days, a new saying, expression, or idiom can be taught, interpreted in context, reviewed, and catalogued for future reference in the classroom.

Exercise #3: Locating Figurative and Idiomatic Language

Locate the metaphorical and idiomatic expressions in any one of the accompanying texts. Pick one figurative or idiomatic expression. How would you explain the meaning of the expression to young students?

Mansion for a Mollusk

"if danger comes knocking"

Little Bear Lost

Blue Cloud felt her heart sink.
Something that made her heart freeze in fear...
Her [mother's] anger lasted for many moons.

How the Whale Got His Throat

He was a man of infinite resource and sagacity...
The 'stute fish [astute fish] ...
Once upon a time, O my best beloved

His mother had "given him leave to trail his toes in the water"

Sentence Comprehension

Most speakers acquire knowledge of sentence structure or syntax by hearing sentence patterns spoken by others in their language community. The sentence structure of academic texts and other reading matter, however, can be unfamiliar and challenging to young readers, ELL students, dialect speakers, or verbally challenged older students. Although syntactic knowledge is largely implicit, or learned without direct instruction, children's capacity to interpret the special language of written text can be improved with explicit practice. Again, written language is different from oral language, and many of its characteristics must be formally studied to be learned.

Good readers and good writers are more aware of sentence structure than poor readers and writers. They can think about and consciously manipulate the parts of a sentence to interpret it or make it sound better. While writing, they can choose the structure of their sentences deliberately. They have a good "ear" for what sounds right, and they can also identify what is not well expressed. They treat words as tokens or movable objects that can be rearranged, recombined, deleted, added, or substituted. Similarly, good readers can deconstruct a long sentence and find the kernel ideas.

Syntactic awareness, or consciousness of sentence structure, helps a reader notice and correct errors of word recognition. Once he makes an error of decoding, a child with good syntactic awareness will try to repair the error spontaneously. In addition, syntactic awareness enables proofreading and editing of one's own writing.

Poor readers or those who struggle with comprehension may not process the meanings of sentences for several reasons. One reason may be lack of experience with or exposure to the longer, more embedded, more formally constructed sentences found in written material. Children who do not read well do less reading and are therefore less likely to practice reading longer, complex sentences. Another reason for miscomprehension is that the working

Lengthy syntax places a heavier demand on working memory. A compound subject or compound predicate adds complexity. Here the subject noun "Marvel" has to be linked to five verbs in a row in this sentence.

Slide 17

memory capacity of students may not be sufficient to hold a whole sentence on the cognitive desktop until its core meanings are extracted. Finally, children with weaker language abilities simply find that certain types of sentences are very difficult to interpret.

Sentences that are the most challenging have structures that diverge from the most common patterns of word order. Even simple sentences, with one independent clause, can be challenging if they include any of the following constructions:

Research on these linguistic challenges is summarized in the Carlisle and Rice book on reading comprehension. Language researchers such as Elizabeth Wiig have known for many years that the constructions listed here present processing challenges to developing readers.

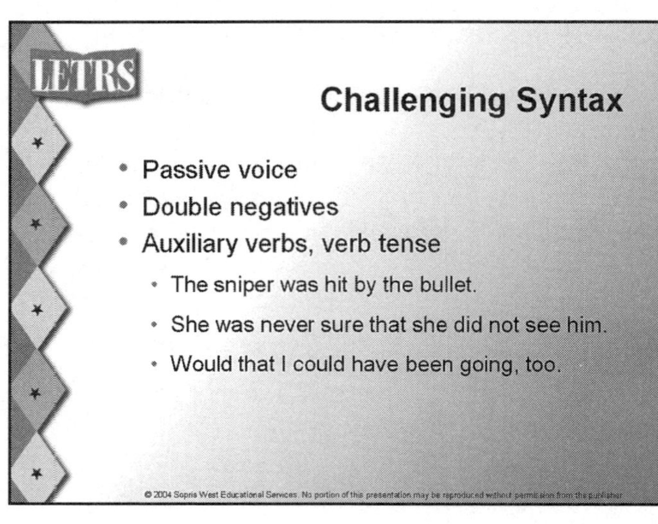

Slide 18

Problematic Sentence Structures

a. **Passive voice.**

Summer clothes *are to be replaced* by winter clothes.

New ideas *are often misunderstood* by those with firmly held biases.

The white mini-van *was hit* head-on by the motorcycle.

b. **Double negative.**

We had *no* reason to think she was *un*stable.

There was *no* evidence that the suspect was *not* at home as he had claimed on the night of the robbery.

It was *not* true that he *dis*liked the gift.

I did *not* advise him *never* to reveal his intentions to her.

c. **Verb tenses and auxiliaries.**

Under orders, *we were to be patient* for hours.

Would it not have been easier to say "yes"?

What would he be doing if he were here?

d. **Prepositions and articles.**

He put the paper *aside* to read the book.

He put the paper *beside* the book.

He put the paper *inside* the book.

This is *the* major problem.

This is *a* major problem.

e. **Ambiguous phrases, word order, and placement of phrases.**

Folding diapers would be expensive.

Hanging plants would require light.

They will understand only this.

Only they will understand this.

The drunken driver with the VW struck the woman.

The drunken driver struck the woman with the VW.

Compound and Complex Sentence Structures

If compound sentences are joined by a conjunction more complex than "and," students may struggle to comprehend the logical relationship. "Although" is not readily understood by many students until 5th grade or so.

"The manager selected Tim for the team, although he did not make good plays at the tryouts."

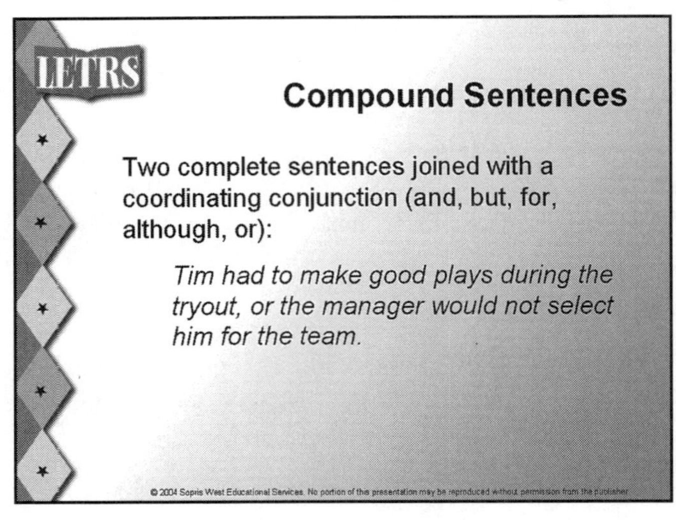

Slide 19

Simple sentences can have compound subjects (nouns), objects (nouns), or predicates (verbs). Each of these can be elaborated with phrases or modifiers.

Compound subject	*Our hero and his friends* trudged on.
	Mickey, Minnie, and Melissa all favored chocolate ice cream.
Compound predicate	Jerry *hung up* his coat, *strode* down the hall, and *marched* boldly into the room.
Compound object	There he found some *ink*, a *pen*, some *paper*, and *directions* for filling out the form.
Elaborated subject	Our *bold, intrepid* hero trudged on.
Elaborated predicate	Jerry strode *down the hall, into the room*, and *up to the platform where he began to give his speech.*

A variety of clauses and phrases can either introduce or be embedded into a simple or compound sentence to create a complex sentence. Here are some examples:[6]

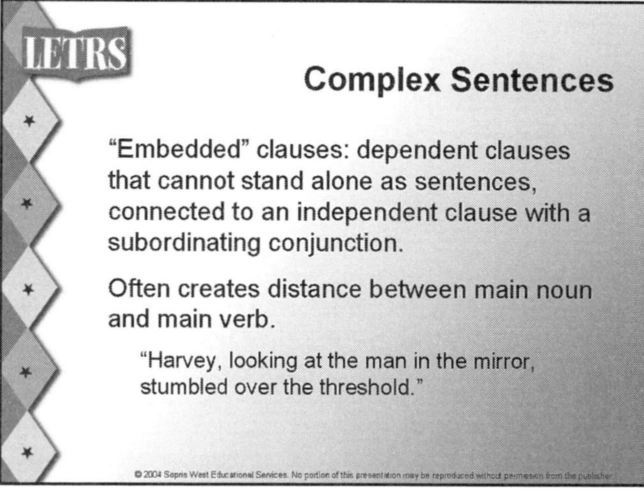

Slide 20

Read the example sentence aloud; ask for other sentences with clauses introduced by subordinating conjunctions.

"Harvey, who stumbled over the threshold, continued to stare at the man in the mirror."

Appositive	Stuart, *a shy character*, spoke quietly.
Elaborated subject	Every problem, *including some of the toughest in our history*, was eventually solved.
Prepositional phrase	*Over the fields* and *through the woods*, we ran as fast as possible.
	Those *without big packs* made better time.
Participial phrase	*Knowing that he was right all along*, the candidate stuck to his position.
Relative clause	The residents *who welcomed new neighbors* were friendly.
	News *that television broadcasts* is often sensational.
Infinitive phrase	*To feel as if one cannot keep up* produces anxiety.
Adjectives or participles	*Exhausted and bleeding*, the soldier pleaded for help.

[6] Types derived from Carlisle and Rice (2002), p. 121.

In complex, compound, or complex-compound sentences, the reader must apprehend the meaning of several ideas in a logical relationship to one another. The logical relationships are often expressed in the coordinating or subordinating conjunction that joins the clauses. The reader must process truth relationships such as causation (*because, so*), time sequence (*then, now*), reversal (*but, although*), and conditionality (*if-then; unless*) to interpret longer sentences in text. Children understand the additive conjunction (*and*) as preschoolers, but they need many years to master the interpretation of complex logical relationships that entail reversal or conditionality (*even though, although, if-then*). Comprehension of reversal and conditional relationships in syntax develops much later than understanding of addition, causation, or sequence. Therefore, before fourth grade or so, teachers should expect that children will not understand the more abstract and difficult logic in some complex and compound sentences. It is desirable, however, to expose children to these language patterns by reading aloud so that children are familiar with the structures.

Apprehension of meaning is generally more challenging in sentences whose main subject is separated from its main verb by a clause or phrase. Such sentences can leave the reader asking, "Who or what did the action?" For example:

> *Benjamin, knowing that many hours would be required to prepare the picture for Elaine, began early in the day.*

Even middle grade students commonly misinterpret such sentences or need to go back and locate the subject. Good readers, however, learn to reread to check their construction of the meaning of embedded sentences if they have lost track of the subject.

Alice in Wonderland provides many examples of lengthy, complex syntax.

Slide 21

Exercise #4: Anticipating Comprehension Problems at the Sentence Level

Locate three complex or compound sentences in the accompanying texts. Can you describe what may be difficult for a student to comprehend? Could the sentences be simplified, rearranged, or broken down in some way to facilitate comprehension? What strategies do you already use to build children's sense of the sentence?

[KIPLING] – But while the whale had been swimming, the Mariner, who was indeed a person of infinite resource and sagacity, had taken his jackknife and cut up the raft into a little square grating all running crisscross, and he had tied it firm with his suspenders (now you know why you were not to forget the suspenders!), and he dragged that grating good and tight into the whale's throat, and there it stuck!

But from that day on, the grating in his throat, which he could neither cough up nor swallow down, prevented him from eating anything except very, very small fish; and that is the reason why whales nowadays never eat men or boys or little girls.

Building Sentence Sense

Another reason to read aloud to children from books that are above their instructional reading level, is to help them hear the sentence patterns in literary text.

When children give short sentences in response to questions, the teacher can say, "Tell me more." "Tell me why." "Tell me who, why, and when."

Model sentence expansion; ask a participant to give you a short sentence, and you supply elaboration. Then ask the student to repeat what you said. Or, you can ask the speaker to tell you more about who, what, when, etc.

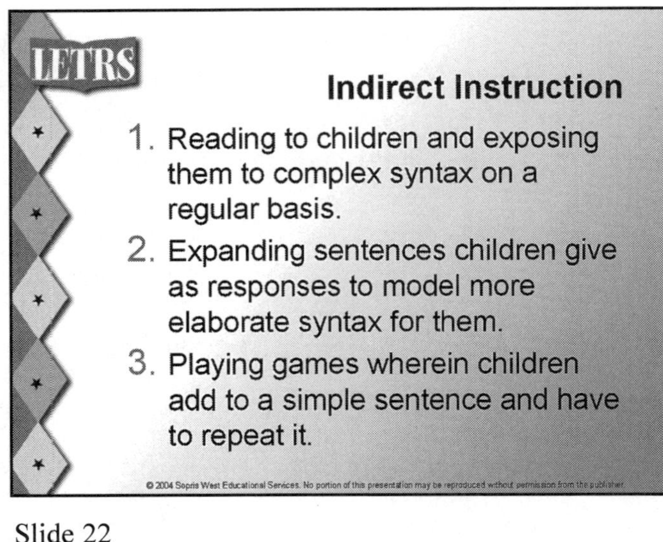

Slide 22

A variety of sentence manipulations can help children develop sentence sense. Language instruction each day can include a few minutes of sentence study. Writing, reading, and language instruction are complements of one another in sentence study.

Phyllis Weaver in 1979 found that students' reading comprehension improved if she gave them sentence manipulation activities, especially sentence anagrams.

In doing exercise #5, take about 10 minutes to have participants make up and try out a sentence anagram with a partner; then ask people to leave their anagram on the table and move about the room, trying at least 10 different anagrams. At the end, ask them to talk about the mental processes at work, such as looking for the subject and main verb, putting phrases together, remembering that some words have several grammatical roles.

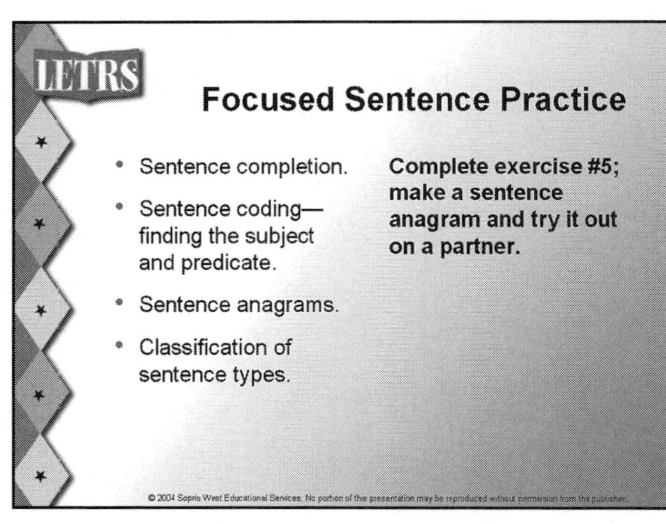

Slide 23

Structure the exercises so that children are manipulating sentence components and developing a sense of the functional parts of the sentence. The "who or what" part and the "doing" part can be identified right away as the essential parts of any sentence. The "subject" and "predicate" labels for these parts can be gradually introduced in second grade and beyond. The grammatical roles of words—noun, verb, adjective, adverb, preposition, conjunction, helping verb (auxiliary)—are taught to young children first by labeling the role of the words, phrases, and clauses in a complete, well-formed sentence, and then by substituting the formal terms one at a time until the concepts are learned.

1. **What's Missing?** Complete these sentences. When you see a triangle, the first letter of the word must be a capital letter.[7]

    [Who or What] ⟶ [Is/Was Doing?]
    Subject   **Predicate**

    a. Burt, the giant troll ___drooled___ .

    b. ▲ _Big Bertha_ buried the worms.

    c. After Myrtle ate, she ___burped___ .

    d. ▲ _The trained terriers_ juggled the tennis balls.

    e. Spider man, arms outstretched, _flopped over backwards_

    f. ▲ _Helicopters_ flew over the hayfields.

2. **Find** the subject; underline it with one line. Box the subject noun (person, place, thing, idea). Find the predicate; underline it with two lines. Put a wavy line under the main verb. Say whether the action of the verb is physical or mental.

    a. The first |restaurant| served big fat rich crabcakes.
        ~ physical verb

    b. |We| enjoyed a leisurely meal by the waterfront dock.
        ~ mental verb

    c. After we drove home, my |husband| asked for Alka Seltzer.
        ~ physical verb

---

[7] An elaborate sentence coding scheme that includes the beginning bump in the sentence frame for a capital letter is embodied in *Framing Your Thoughts*, Language Circle Enterprises, Bloomington, MN.

3. **Sentence anagrams.** Rearrange the words to make a complete sentence that sounds right. Start by finding the main action word (verb) and putting words together to make phrases.

<u>If the small fish senses danger it will hide.</u>

senses	it	if	fish	hide
danger	the	will	small	

Exercise #5: Sentence Anagrams

Use small post-it notes to create a sentence anagram for a partner to solve. Exchange several of these with other people. Which sentences are the most difficult to sequence?

---

4. **Recognize type of sentence.** Sentences may be statements, questions, commands (imperatives), or exclamations. Recognition of sentence type is necessary for understanding the role of end punctuation (period, exclamation point, question mark).

   a. Look out! <u>command</u>

   b. I can't believe it! <u>exclamation</u>

   c. Hush up! <u>command</u>

   d. Did you understand what I said? <u>question</u>

   e. That was a false alarm. <u>statement</u>

   f. Hurry! <u>command</u>

   g. We will be late. <u>statement or exclamation</u>

   h. Can't you move faster? <u>question</u>

5. **Complete sentences** that start with an unusual word or phrase:

   a. After awhile, _Margaret realized she had won._

   b. With a little more warning, _we could have found shelter._

   c. Suddenly, _it began to hail round stones._

   d. By hanging upside down, _I stretched my spine._

   e. Swallowing her pride, _she admitted her error._

6. **Systematic sentence elaboration** with simple diagramming added.[8] [See "Diagram It," from the *LANGUAGE !* curriculum].

   a. Create a kernel sentence with two essential parts: who did it, and what did the subject do?

      Herbert spat.

   b. Paint the predicate by saying how, when, where, and/or why the "doing" happened.

      Herbert spat at the visitors who came too close to his cage during his afternoon meal.

   c. Move the predicate painters.

      During his meal, Herbert spat at the zoo visitors who came too close to his cage.

   d. Paint the subject by saying more about which one, how many, or what kind.

      During his afternoon meal, Herbert the aging Orangutan spat at the zoo visitors who came too close to his cage.

   e. Substitute better words and add detail if necessary.

      Munching peacefully on a banana, Herbert the aging Orangutan spat at the curious visitors who approached his cage.

---

[8] These steps are followed in the Masterpiece Sentences component of the *LANGUAGE !* curriculum (J. Greene, Sopris West Educational Services).

Exercise #6: Sentence Elaboration

Follow the steps above for creating a Masterpiece Sentence. Then try diagramming the base subject, predicate, and modifiers.

This step-by-step process of sentence elaboration is a centerpiece of LANGUAGE !.

Walk participants through the steps several times.

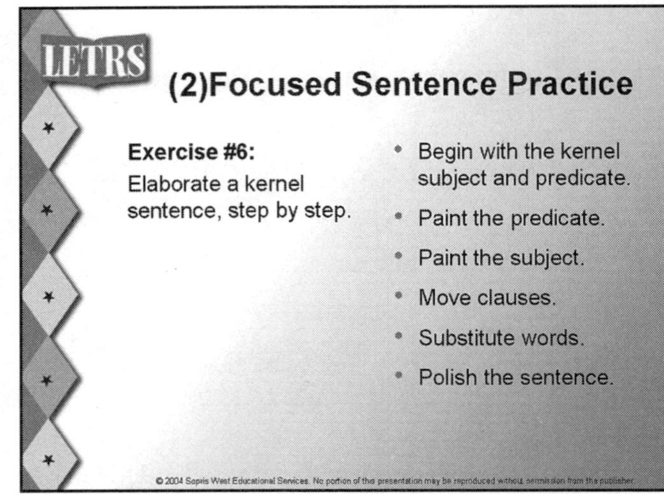

Slide 24

Slide 25

Deconstruction of a long, complex sentence may be necessary to identify all the propositions in it or to locate the main subject and main verb.

Sentence combining practice has a positive impact on reading comprehension and writing, if it is done in small doses within a comprehensive language arts program.

7. **Sentence deconstruction and paraphrase.** If a sentence is very long and embedded, break it down into several simpler thoughts expressed in simple sentences, using paraphrase if necessary.

I pledge allegiance to the flag of the United States of America and to the Republic for which it stands, one nation, under God, indivisible, with liberty and justice for all.

> *I promise loyalty to the United States.*

> *I also pledge loyalty to the Republic (free, representative government) that the flag stands for.*

> *The Republic, the United States, is one country that cannot be divided into several countries.*

8. **Sentence combining.** Simple sentences are combined into complex, compound, or complex-compound sentences.

Small fish provide an essential service.
They are specialized for cleaning others.
They feed on parasites.
They clean the gills and fins of larger fish.

> *Small fish that are specialized for cleaning others feed on parasites that live in the gills and fins of larger fish and thereby provide an essential ocean cleaning service.*

9. **Read aloud** text with more challenging sentence structures than children are used to hearing or reading. Children's syntactic processing systems will adjust to accommodate new sentence structures heard on a regular basis. **Reading aloud and reading challenging material with sufficient scaffolding is probably the most essential instructional strategy of all for enhancing children's ability to interpret complex syntax.**

Reference and Cohesive Ties

Explain the different types of referential relationships in text. The names of these are not as important as the idea that referential relationships are of several kinds and are found throughout connected text. Cohesion in a text results from the author's skillful use of reference.

Exercise #7 is instructive; show on the transparency what you intend the participants to do (draw lines between words that refer to one another). Then give them 3-5 minutes to complete the exercise. How many words are there for the same thing?

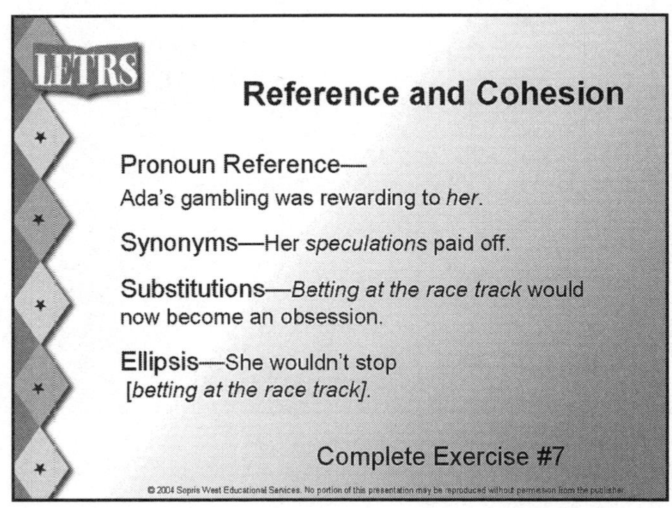

Slide 26

Cohesive devices bind a text together so that the reader can follow the progression of ideas within and between sentences. Well-written text is bound together in a number of ways. Carlisle and Rice (2002) summarize these devices as follows:

Reference

Reference is use of one word to refer to something else that has already been named. Personal pronouns (I, we), possessive pronouns (his, her, ours), demonstrative pronouns (there, here, these, those) and relative pronouns (who, that) are in this category. The entity to which a pronoun refers is called its referent. Students may forget what a pronoun refers to if it is separated from its referent by too many words. In addition, miscomprehension may occur if the pronoun referent is ambiguous.

– Sue and *I* met *her* brother at the show. *We* were on time.

– *He*, however, was late getting *there* and *we* missed the first scene.

Substitution

Substitution is renaming a person, place, thing, idea, or action with a word or phrase that means the same thing but that is not a pronoun. Synonyms used to avoid repeating the same words in a passage are a standard form of substitution that maintains reader interest without changing the subject. A writer who substitutes words and phrases for each other must have a broad vocabulary.

– The *verbal capacity* of a reader also determines comprehension. *Verbal reasoning* can be improved with practice.

– We enjoyed a *gourmet meal* for my daughter's birthday. Many *fine delicacies* were consumed at the party.

Digging for Meaning: Teaching Text Comprehension

Lexical Cohesion: The Ties That Bind

Lexical cohesion refers to the way ideas or propositions are linked within and across sentences. Cohesion is accomplished by repeating key ideas, such as the topic or subject of the paragraph, in successive sentences, or by use of alternative expressions for the same idea.

– The *mother dog* meets all of the puppies' needs herself. Her body *provides warmth*, *safety*, *food*, and *companionship*.

– The *mother dog* provides everything. *She* is the sole *care-taker* for about 8 weeks of the puppies' life.

Ellipsis

Words that name or refer to an entity already named in a previous sentence are assumed but not stated. The words must be processed as part of the unstated underlying sentence structure.

– I asked her to be prepared for the trip. She said that she would [be prepared].

– There were gorgeous antique carpets in the bazaar. I could afford none [of the carpets].

Exercise #7: Marking Cohesive Ties

Using arrows or other indicators, mark the pronoun referents, word substitutions, and cohesive ties that make this passage on forest fires hang together. Notice how much the reader must process as this text is read.

The heated air above a fire rises in a pillar of smoke and burnt gases, pulling fresh air in from the sides to replace it. Firefighters use this fact when they "fight fire with fire." They start a fire well in front of the one that they are fighting. Instead of traveling on in front of the inferno, the smaller fire is pulled back toward it by the updraft of the larger blaze. As it travels back to meet the large fire, the smaller backfire burns away the fuel that the forest fire needs to survive.

Even when a backfire has been well set, however, the fire may still win the struggle. The wind that firefighters used to help them may now become their enemy. When the backfire meets the main fire, before both die for lack of fuel, there is tremendous flame, great heat and turbulent winds. A strong gust may blow the fire into the treetops beyond the area, giving the fire new fuel and a new life.

Excerpt from "Fire is Fearsome," *The New Practice Readers*

Inferences

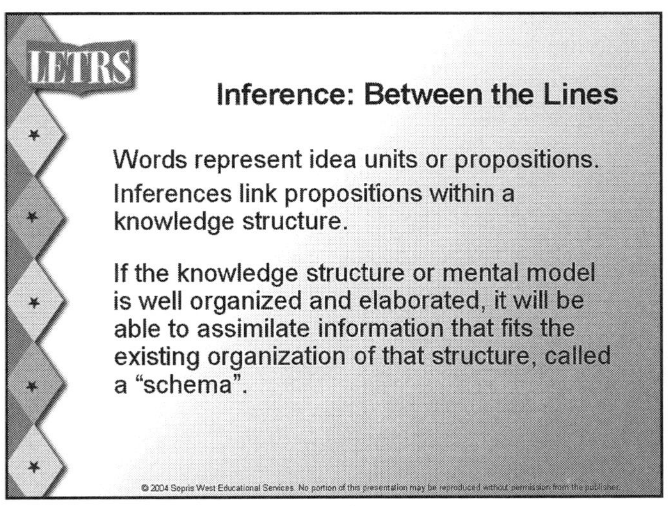

Slide 27

The terms "knowledge structure," "mental model," and "schema" are used interchangeably here. Talk about the idea of a mental model that has the potential to become filled out and elaborated as we gain new knowledge. The old knowledge determines in part how much new knowledge we can assimilate about a topic. Organized knowledge is easier to add on to than disorganized knowledge. The better the knowledge structure we bring to reading, the more easily we can make inferences.

Read the passage in the text and point out the places where inferences must be made. How does the child know that the treehopper is an insect and not a frog, for example?

Inference-making is required frequently when we read. The words on the page are the surface expression of messages about underlying ideas or propositions. Comprehension of text, then, entails more than the combination of individual word meanings. Comprehension resides in apprehension of the relationships among the ideas behind the words and the organization of ideas (schemata) in which individual ideas are embedded. Students may not easily read between the lines for inferences if they misread or misunderstand individual words, know too little about a subject, if too little is explained by the author of the text, if they have trouble reasoning abstractly, or they miss subtleties of language use such as the cohesive ties described above.

> *Most insects lay their eggs and leave them. Treehoppers, however, are better mothers. After laying eggs, the mother treehopper guards them. Lizards, birds, and grasshoppers are likely to go hungry around a treehopper nest, where the mother will stand on her hind legs and spread her wings to look as scary as possible.*

In this passage, the reader must know or infer that treehoppers are insects, that lizards, birds, and grasshoppers like to eat treehopper eggs, and that the mother insect is brave and successful at driving off much larger predators.

The necessity of inference-making to comprehension can also explain the origin of students' misunderstandings. If a student's existing knowledge structure about a subject is misinformed, then the student can easily make wrong inferences while reading between the lines of a passage. For example, if the student does not infer that the treehopper is an insect, he or she might believe that the passage is about a frog.

Inability to interpret the author's or a character's tone of voice or intent may also hamper inference-making. Sarcasm, irony, puns, and figures of speech are typically not well understood by young children or older students with language processing weaknesses who tend to take words at face value.

Text Structure

Stories or narratives usually follow a format that defines this genre. Narratives may be fiction or nonfiction; they may be written in the third person or first person. Nevertheless, they are organized around a central problem that the main character(s) must solve or resolve and the action moves forward toward that resolution.

At the most basic level, children can work with a story structure that conveys sequence of events. Later, the dynamic of rising action and tension (suspense) can be grasped.

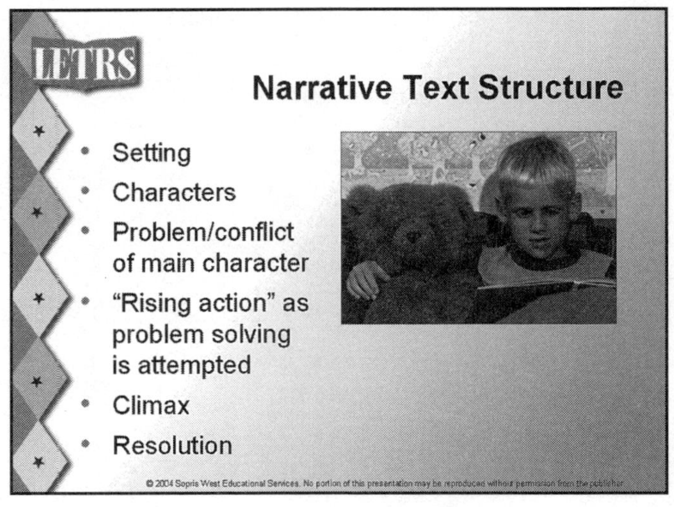

Slide 28

Well-written text follows an organizational structure that facilitates the reader's comprehension. It is organized into paragraphs, chapters, or a larger discourse structure that follows conventions of genre or type of text. Narrative text structure usually has a setting, characters who include the protagonist or main character, a problem that the main character is trying to solve, episodes or segments of action that lead toward a problem solution, a climax or reckoning that resolves the problem, and a conclusion in which loose ends are tied up. Expository text, on the other hand, explains or puts out information. Narrative text may be realistic, biographical, or fictional. Expository text is nonfiction. Many other genres with characteristic organizational structures exist as well, including poetry, drama, journalistic reporting, and cataloging.

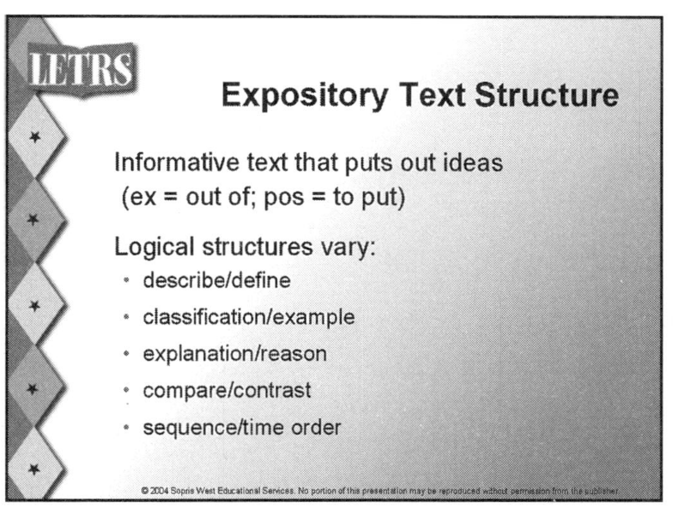

Slide 29

In young children's reading material, there is often not enough well-written expository text. One of the common problems with classroom and school libraries that reading experts suggest correcting is the imbalance of expository and narrative text.

Later in life, most people read informational text, usually in the workplace. Only a minority read fiction for pleasure or entertainment.

Children will benefit from direct teaching about these organizational structures. A good resource on paragraph types and expository structures is Joanne Carlisle's Reasoning and Reading (Educators Publishing Service).

Paragraph structure is especially relevant to the comprehension of expository text. A paragraph is much more than a series of sentences that begin with an indentation. It is about a single topic or idea; it is a cluster of sentences that explicate one main thought. The key idea resides in the topic sentence if the paragraph is well formed. The key idea is elaborated with supporting details that are often followed by a restatement or concluding sentence.

Within those basic guidelines, however, paragraphs differ considerably. Several kinds of logical relationships are embodied in expository paragraphs such as the ones children are likely to read in a science, social studies, or current events chapter.

Paragraph structures in authentic expository text are not always perfect examples of the following logical patterns. Nevertheless, the purpose for a paragraph will be related to its structure. Purposes may be to describe or define, to explain the reasons for a fact or assertion or to explain a cause-effect relationship, to compare and/or contrast ideas, or to tell an order of events. The topic sentence of the paragraph should indicate what information is to come and how the detail sentences might be related to the unifying idea.

Paragraph and overall text structure can be represented with graphic organizers. A graphic organizer is a visual representation of the logical relationships among ideas. Graphic organizers help many students understand how ideas are connected, especially those with good nonverbal, visual-spatial abilities. Other students have difficulty comprehending an abstract visual representation of information structure. Graphic organizers can be used to assist students in summarizing what they have read, in preparing to read about a new topic, and in preparing to write an informational piece.

Exercise #8: Paragraph Types and Graphic Organizers

With reference to the graphic organizers on the next few pages,[9] identify what structure is likely to go with each of the following topic sentences. Consider as well what signal words are most likely to appear in a paragraph of that type.

- Description or definition
- Class-example relationships
- Explanation of the reasons why something is true
- Compare and/or contrast
- Tell a sequence of events (time order)

1. Many events over ten years led up to the civil rights march on Washington, DC, in 1963.

2. A good cheerleader has many attributes beyond a pretty or handsome face.

3. Although we say that Mexican Americans and Spaniards both speak Spanish, the languages differ in many respects.

4. The class of working dogs includes those that hunt, herd, lead, carry, and protect.

5. Writing is the most difficult language skill that students must learn.

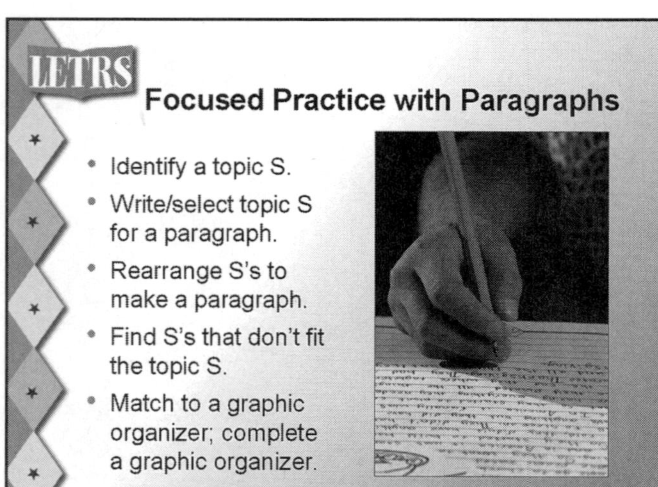

Complete exercise #8. Notice that the topic sentence suggests the style of the paragraph that could follow.

Look over the graphic organizers attached in the next section and select the ones that might best match the topic sentences in the exercise. Or, draw a new graphic organizer that would fit the topic indicated.

Slide 30

 [9] Greene, J. (2000). *LANGUAGE !* Longmont, Colorado: Sopris West. Used by permission.

In the intermediate grades, children can benefit from several kinds of practice with these paragraph structures so that they develop familiarity with the underlying organization of ideas in text and improve their ability to extract a main idea.[10] They can identify the topic sentence in a well-formed paragraph, write or select a topic sentence for a paragraph, rearrange sentences to make paragraphs, find sentences that do not fit into a given paragraph structure, and identify the logical structure of the information with the help of a graphic organizer.

Word Wheel (Semantic Relationships)*

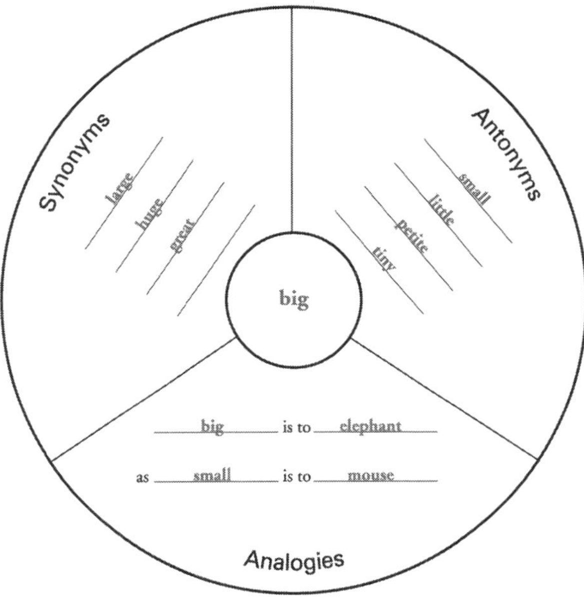

Write a sentence to show one of these relationships to the target word:

In contrast to small mammals such as mice,

elephants are not just big, they are huge.

---

[10] An excellent tool for this type of work with children is Joanne Carlisle's *Reasoning and Reading*, Cambridge, MA: Educators Publishing Service.

Example Map

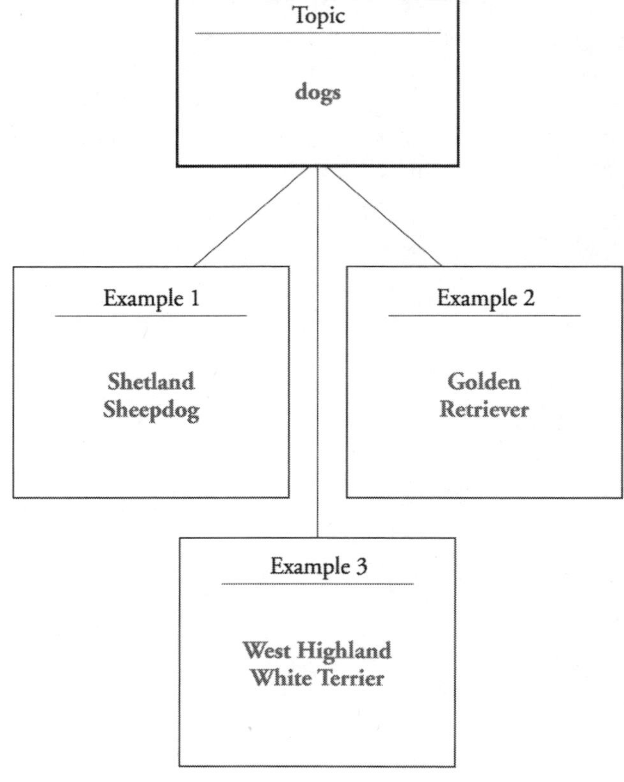

Process (Time Sequence) Map

Goal:	Write a research report
1st	Choose a topic
2nd (Next)	Conduct research
3rd (Next)	Create an outline
Last; finally	Write your paper
Result:	A well-constructed report

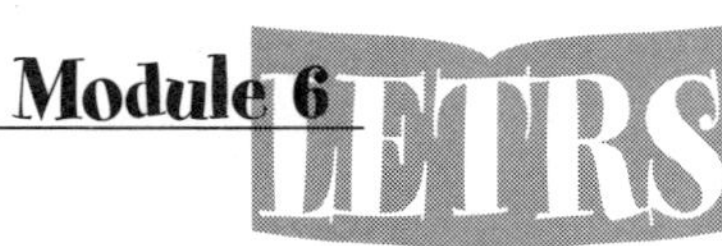

Reason (Explanation) Map

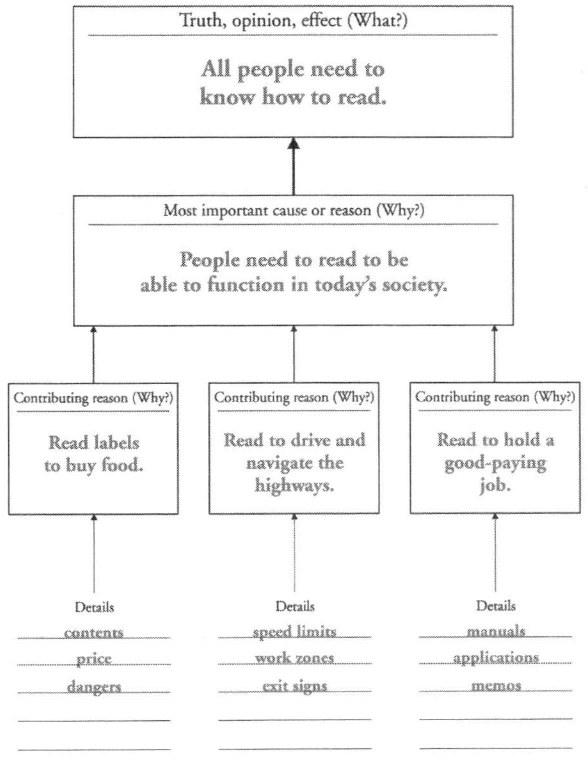

Classification Paragraph

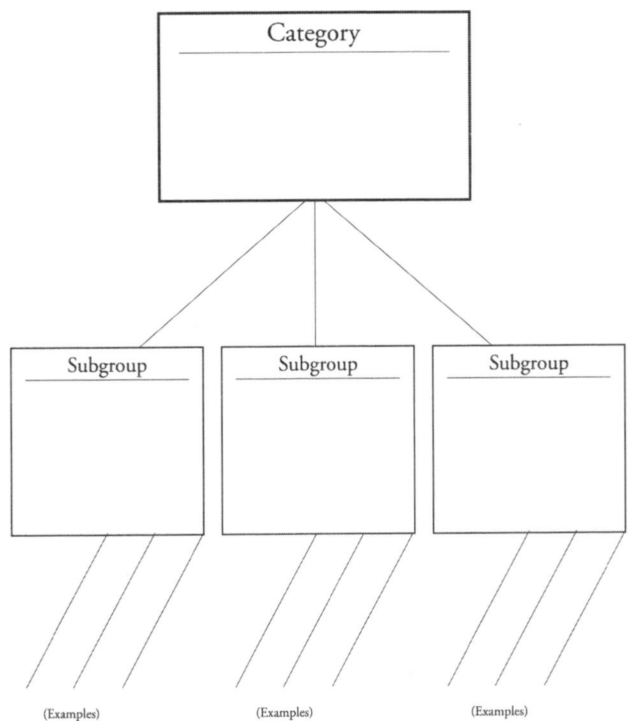

Main Idea Map

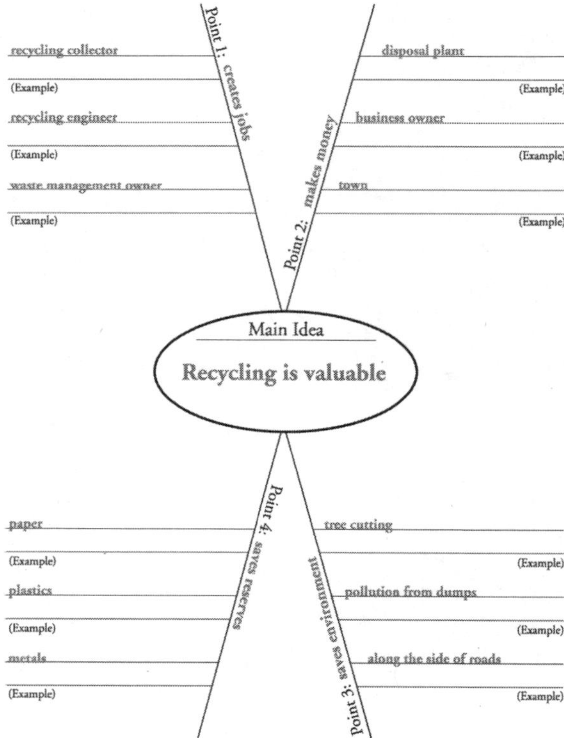

Compare-Contrast Essay

	Idea 1	(What?)	Idea 2
State	Golden Retrievers make good pets.		Shetland Sheepdogs make good pets.

	Similarities (both what?)
Compare	- dogs - long hair - working class - long noses - feathered tails

	Differences (1 is _______ but 2 is _______)
Contrast	- GR larger than SSD (appearance) - GR one color / SSD multicolor (appearance) - GR calm / SSD skittish (personality) - GR bred to retrieve / SSD bred to herd (work)

	Significance (Why important?)
Conclude	It is important to know the similarities and differences between dogs to select the best pet for your family.

Digging for Meaning: Teaching Text Comprehension

Story Recipe: Idea Generator

Characters
Who? Traits?

- Three little pigs - 2 carefree; 1 worker
- Big Bad Wolf - hungry, big eater

Setting
Where? When?

- In the country
- Once upon a time

Plot
What happened?

Beginning event: The three pigs each built a house.

Nature of problem: The wolf was hungry. The pigs had built two
weak houses and one strong house.

Character's action: The wolf chased the pigs into their houses. It
wanted to eat them.

What happened: The wolf huffed and puffed and blew the first two weak
houses down. The pigs ran for safety to the third house,
which the wolf did not blow down.

Consequence
Result at end? Meaning?

The pigs were safe at the end because of a strong house.
The moral: take time, plan, do the job well.

Story Structure Map

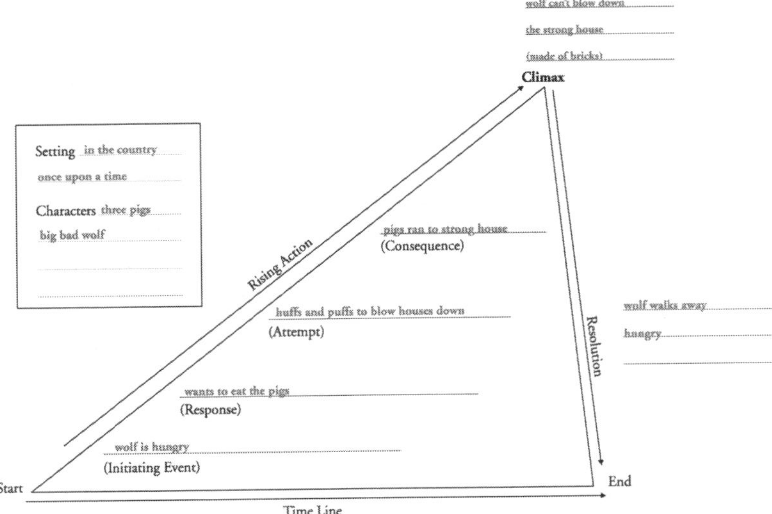

Reading Comprehension Strategies That Work

Before Reading Begins

The strategies employed for teaching children to comprehend a text can be grouped into those most useful before reading, during reading, and after reading.

Emphasize the importance of preparing children to read an unfamiliar text.

Reading the text aloud all the way through so that the flow is not lost; this is desirable either as a first or second reading.

Slide 31

Avoid plunging headlong into a text without preparing the children to read it! Time spent previewing a text will enhance students' eagerness to read the text, confidence that they can comprehend it, and depth of understanding.

Browsing or previewing activities should be brief (5-15 minutes) but should be aimed at acquainting students with key vocabulary, skimming the text as an orientation to the content, and connecting students' prior knowledge to what they will be reading. Prediction or looking ahead creates what is called "anticipatory set" or receptiveness to what will be discovered by reading. Previewing activities are most effective when they involve an active search for what is already known and formulation of a purpose for reading.

◆ **Introduce Key Vocabulary**

Module 4 in this book addresses the principles and strategies important for the introduction of key vocabulary necessary for understanding the text. Use of the key words in several sentences spoken by the teacher and in the previewing discussion is highly recommended.

◆ **K-W-L**

The What I Know (K), What I Want to Know (W), What I Have Learned (L) framework (Ogle, 1986) is especially helpful for expository text reading. The strategy directs the teacher to elicit and formulate with the children their existing knowledge of the topic, and then to generate questions with the children before they begin to read. After reading, the children return to their initial set of questions to see if those have been answered. The class may also revisit what they thought they knew as listed in the (K) column to see if any ideas need to be modified. The chart is constructed, posted, referred to, and revisited as children read and reread the text.

One way to fill the "want to know" (W) column is to have students ask a good question by writing it on a post-it note and posting it on the chart for later reference.

What I Know (K)	What I Want to Know (W)	What I Have Learned (L)

◆ Provide Background Filler

If the text selection at hand is a story about bull-fighting in Spain, and the children say that they think French is the language spoken in that country and a bull fight is between two bulls, then the teacher needs to supply a substantial amount of background information before reading. She could use a map of Europe, pictures of Spain, examples of Spanish words, books about Spanish customs including bull-fighting, or information about this very old tradition and why it continues to be popular, to stimulate discussion about the topic. Many children with experiential or language limitations will have very little to add to a previewing exercise; time is better spent providing the background they need.

◆ Instruct Children to Browse the Text with a Purpose

Children will focus their attention on the text more readily if they can mark the text as they preview. If the text is consumable, children can make a limited number of question marks by words, pictures, subtitles, or other material they find puzzling at first glance. They can use small post-it notes to mark unknown words or concepts. Or, they can place post-it notes by the sections of text that they think will be most informative for them. These activities should be brief and should lead directly into a first reading.

◆ Introduce a Theme with Reference to Personal Experience

Young children often understand abstract ideas by experience and example until they grow mature enough to think globally and with perspective. Thus, narrative texts with powerful and engaging themes can be introduced by bringing up personal experiences that fore-shadow the reading. A good story is usually organized around a theme pertaining to common human conflicts—those that occur between individuals, between people and society, between people and natural events, or between people and their consciences or inner selves. The teacher can introduce a theme, such as the nature and importance of friendship, by talking about a special memory of childhood or adult experience, and then asking the children to share thoughts about similar experiences.

◆ Anticipating the Structure of Text with a Graphic Organizer

A main idea map or a story structure map can be introduced before a reading to remind students of the manner in which the expository text or narrative text is likely to unfold. Some of the information called for by the map can be supplied before reading, such as the main idea that the reading is about, or the names of the main characters and the central problem that they will encounter.

◆ Teacher Read Aloud, First Reading

Most texts in anthologies accompanying comprehensive reading instructional materials deserve several readings. The first one can be a sustained read through by the teacher as the students follow along, sliding their finger under the text. It is important for students to hear the entire text read fluently as a whole.

During Guided Oral Reading

The strategies that help children engage the meanings of a text deeply include asking questions at critical junctures; modeling the thought processes that you use as you make inferences or ask questions; helping children ask the questions in the group discussion; and constructing mental images as they read.

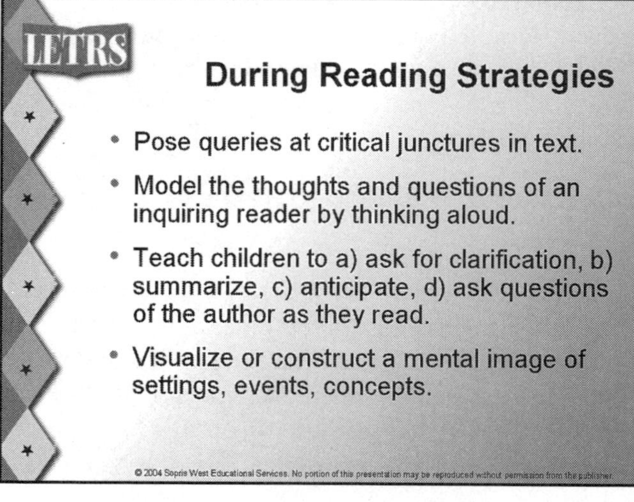

Slide 32

In guided oral reading, students read aloud designated sections of the text, pausing to clarify what is unclear, to ask questions, to summarize what has been read, or to anticipate what is ahead.

Oral reading can be done chorally with a group, alternately with well-matched peer partners, or simultaneously with everyone reading aloud quietly at the same time through the designated section of the text.

After students read key sections that the teacher has already identified in preparing to read the story aloud, the teacher asks queries or questions of the group that are designed to elicit deeper understanding. Well-designed queries will require longer, more elaborate, more thoughtful answers than the "closed," factual questions teachers often tend to ask.[11]

Examples of queries:

What was the reason for that?

Why do you think the character said that?

What does that have to do with what the character just said or did?

What does the author want us to think here?

Why did the author choose this word?

What's this all about?

Were you surprised here? Why?

What might happen now?

What do you wish would happen here?

Is that part clear to you?

So, what's happened so far?

What problem is this person trying to solve?

Queries should drive after *who* is doing *what*, and *why* they are doing it. *Why* questions are needed to identify what problem the story or selection is about, inferences about cause and effect relationships, the existence of actual or implied evidence, and the motives and goals of story characters. Guided oral reading is proceeding well if the students are doing more of the talking than the teacher during the teacher-student interchanges, and if they are making inferences about the text that go beyond the words themselves. If students are struggling with an insight, the teacher can also model her own thought process by saying aloud how she is making connections between ideas, how she is asking and answering her own questions as she reads on, and how she is reacting to specific passages.

---

[11] See *Questioning the Author* (Beck, McKeown, Hamilton, & Kucan) and *Bringing Words to Life* (Beck, McKeown, & Kucan) for full explanation of these strategies.

Students can be taught to ask their own questions. Rehearsal of question types is necessary to broaden the range of questions student ask. For example, the group can use cue cards with various questions designed to elicit paraphrasing, clarifying, predicting, summarizing, and elaborating the information given in the text, taking turns asking various questions drawn on the cue cards. These activities can become formulaic and rigidly implemented, however, unless the emphasis is maintained on a more free-flowing exploration of a text.

The construction of mental imagery during reading helps many students remember what they read. The teacher's questions and prompts focus on sensory images, such as how the scene might have looked in the mind's eye, where objects were located and what texture they were, what smells were present and how the characters moved through the episode. The goal is active transformation of verbal information into sensory images.

After Reading

Rereading a text is done for a specific purpose, such as finding evidence to support an inference, plot analysis, character description, or evaluation of the author's style. Summarizing and retelling are straightforward but powerful vehicles for promoting understanding.

Extensions to other projects are most productive when they lead to reading about the same topic from a different source.

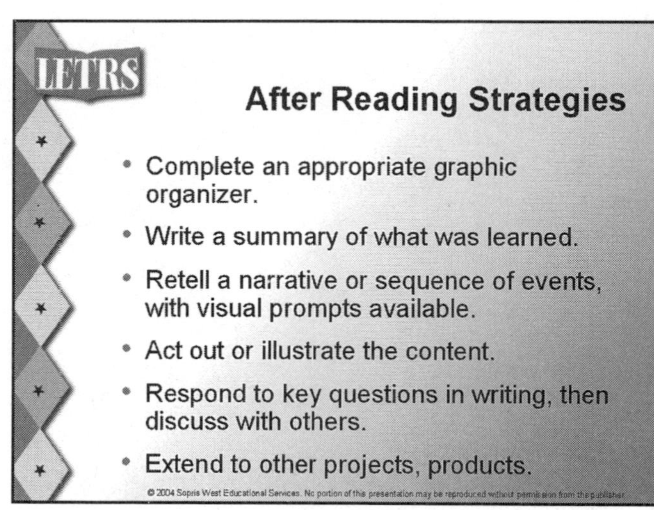

Slide 33

Students often need to revisit a text several times to process most of the ideas and information, literal and inferential. Activities are most powerful if they require active transformation of the key information in the text into a new representation of the ideas, such as an outline, summary, retelling, illustration or construction, dramatic rendering, or graphic depiction of ideas.[12] The after-reading activities should be designed in accordance with the original purpose of the reading.

◆ **Complete the Text Map**

Return to the K-W-L and complete the "What I Have Learned" section of the chart through dialogue with the class. Reconsider all the questions that were raised initially. Then talk the children through the

[12] Three-dimensional depictions of text structure.

"And what's the story behind the story?"

completion of an appropriate conceptual map or diagram, directing them to search the text again if necessary to find examples or supporting evidence for their assertions.

♦ **Retell the Narrative**

Reconstruct the setting, characters, problem, problem-solving attempts (episodes), climax, and resolution of the story, using a story map or storyboard. Then, ask students to retell as much of the story as they can remember while they look at the graphic organizer to jog their memory.

Some students will remember story sequence and details more readily if they actually walk through the progression of events as they are doing a retelling.

♦ **Dictate or Write a Summary**

Begin by paraphrasing topic sentences and listing those paraphrased ideas. Students need to practice putting ideas into their own words without losing the key concepts of the original.

Model many times over how to make a summary of a short passage or a paragraph; progress gradually to longer segments of text. Summarizing is difficult and in the beginning should be taught through extensive modeling and supported practice.

To summarize, children must be able to distinguish main ideas from supporting details. Details are generally omitted from a summary, so identification of the main idea of a key paragraph is a related skill that must be modeled and practiced often.

Use a chart, outline, or graphic organizer to support the translation of the summary into words. Select the main ideas of the passage through oral discussion and questioning, and note them on the graphic organizer. Paraphrase the main ideas in the text and show students where those ideas are located.

Summaries can be practiced with read-alouds, with videos or photographs, and with text the students read themselves.

◆ **Extend Beyond the Text: Write, Apply, Integrate**

Students will grasp deeper meanings more readily if the insights and information from their reading are applied in an endeavor that requires thorough understanding. Written responses to reading can differ in formality. Idea journals can contain personal responses and thoughts about reading intended as personal musings. Critiques and reports are offerings to a larger audience.

Having to write about what is read is similar to teaching about a topic; one must have a solid understanding in order to explain the concepts to someone else, whether the explanation is spoken or written down.

Research on Strategy Instruction

The National Reading Panel (2000) found solid evidence to support the value of the following comprehension strategies:

♦ Monitoring one's own comprehension

♦ Using graphic and semantic organizers

♦ Answering questions aimed at finding text-explicit, text-implicit, and outside-the-text information

♦ Generating questions

♦ Summarizing

♦ Using story structure as a guide

Overt, explicit instruction in the strategies good readers use enhances comprehension of children who are passive, inattentive, or superficial readers. Strategy instruction, however, cannot serve its real purpose if it is formulaic or if it becomes an end in and of itself. One important goal of strategy instruction is to help a child be meta-cognitively aware—that is, to monitor his or her own grasp of the content and then to do something active if comprehension is not occurring. A good reader uses "fix-up" strategies to repair a miscomprehension. Strategies should always be selected and taught in the service of reading and comprehending a specific text that has some value to the reader.

Text comprehension occurs most readily if the reader is engaged in an active dialogue with the text or the author of the text. Therefore, the text should be read for an established purpose. The teacher must help students anticipate the positive consequences of the reading: How will the information be used? Is the goal of the reading to appreciate language, to be moved, to understand something about human nature, to be entertained, or to be informed about a topic of discussion? Is it to produce a report, performance, or theme-related project?

The proven steps in any kind of strategy instruction are:

♦ Directly explain the strategy and why it is helpful.

♦ Model how to apply the strategy while thinking aloud.

♦ Practice application of the strategy with guidance and teacher feedback and assistance.

♦ Apply the strategy many times until it is used independently.

Finally, strategy instruction, according to Pressley and his colleagues, is most effective when it is flexible, dynamic, and involves the repeated and long-term practice of several powerful strategies used for the purpose of comprehending worthwhile text.

Exercise #9: Plan and Role-Play Text Comprehension Instruction

Select a text from those included with this book or from a reading selection that you will be teaching. Work with a small group. Prepare to teach the text by following these steps:

1. Read the story as if you were the reader.

2. Summarize the meanings that you want the students to take away from the reading.

3. Segment the text into chunks in which key ideas should be understood as the children read the story aloud.

4. Formulate key questions or queries that you would ask during those chunks or segments as the guided oral reading takes place.

5. Plan how you will introduce children to the text and motivate them to read attentively.

6. Plan how you are likely to revisit the text after it has been read through once or twice.

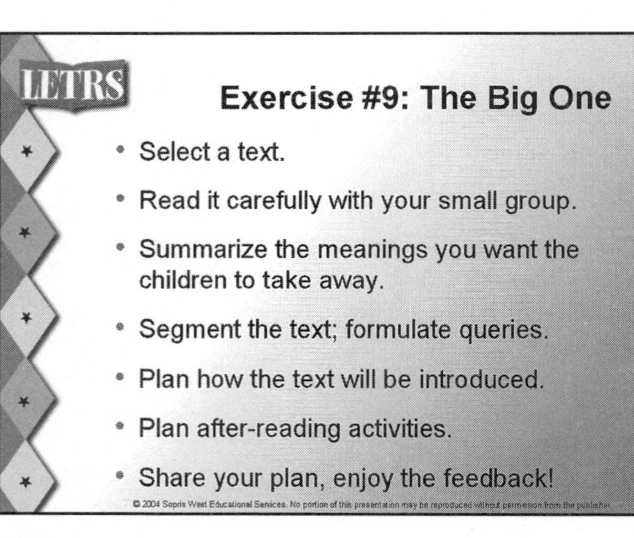

Slide 34

Leave about 1.5 hours for participants to complete this exercise. Model the activity with the class before putting participants into small groups.

First, select a text from the back of Book 2 that the group is familiar with from the vocabulary (Module 4) exercises. Then, ask the group to summarize the most important meanings that they would want the children in their class to take away from that text. Next, ask the group to identify critical junctures in the text at which questions should be asked during reading.

Next, Formulate questions that encourage the children to say more than a few words. Good queries probe the reasons why events are occurring and foster an understanding of how events are linked together.

Finally, plan the introduction to the text and after-reading activities that are going to help children deepen their understanding.

Participants should work in small groups. They should select a text (either narrative or expository). One person will take notes on the overhead transparency so that the group's insights and plans can be shared. Several groups should work with the same text so that groups can learn from each other. Encourage groups to follow the steps above. Circulate around the groups, asking "What are the most important meanings you want the students to get? At what junctures are you going to ask questions? What questions will you ask?" and so forth.

Debrief the whole group or ask representatives from small groups to report out. Each group is likely to devise unique strategies for teaching the text.

Exercise #10: Evaluate the Text Comprehension Instruction in Your Adopted Reading Program

Examine a typical text in your own adopted comprehensive reading program. What strategies are emphasized? How do the "before reading" routines differ from "during reading" and "after reading" routines? How much continuity is there from lesson to lesson? Are the language structures that are likely to challenge children's understanding taught explicitly? Would you add, delete, or change any of the suggested approaches to instruction of that text?

This exercise is advised only if participants are using the same core, comprehensive reading program. Identify the comprehension skills and strategies recommended for a unit you select. Encourage teachers to evaluate which ones they are most likely to teach and why. Are the comprehension instruction methods identified in this module compatible with the ones in the program?

Slide 35

Summary

Comprehension instruction involves much more than turning children loose with a roomful of good books or testing them on their silent or oral reading. Comprehension does not occur automatically if decoding instruction is effective and fluency is achieved.

Comprehension problems originate from multiple sources. Many children who do poorly on reading comprehension tests have fundamental weaknesses in phonologically based word reading skills and reading fluency, but those children often struggle with aspects of comprehension as well. Others are too inattentive, passive, or unmotivated to do the mental work of reading. Children who have limitations in verbal reasoning or language mastery will have difficulty with reading comprehension because they have broad weaknesses in language comprehension and use. Learners of English by definition will benefit from explicit, systematic instruction and feedback.

Some aspects of "book language" deserve special focus in instruction. Beyond vocabulary, these include idiomatic and figurative language, complex syntax, unusual sentence structures, and cohesive ties that bind the text together. Direct teaching of narrative and expository text structures, as well as other genres, is desirable.

Good instruction encourages more student talk than teacher talk. That talk, however, is aimed at specific goals: finding the main idea, clarifying ambiguities, interpreting difficult words or complex syntax, looking for the structure of the discourse, summarizing and retelling, or connecting meanings to information previously discussed or read about. Teachers overtly model mental processes during reading, such as asking questions and predicting where the passage is going, and explain why those mental activities are useful. They use specific comprehension strategies before, during, and after reading, and provide reinforcement to students who successfully practice those strategies. Effective teachers help students read varied texts and check their comprehension through follow-up tasks such as writing responses, completing graphic organizers and outlines, and applying what has been learned to a new reading.

A wide variety of interesting texts must be available to children inside and outside of school. Texts must include decodable stories, controlled vocabulary books, patterned books, and trade books of all kinds. Reading growth is impossible unless students read—early and often.

© The New Yorker Collection 2001 Gahan Wilson. Reprinted with permission.

"By God, for a minute there it suddenly all made sense!"

Reference List

Anderson, R.C., Spiro, R.J., and Anderson, M.C. (1978). Schemata as scaffolding for the representation of information in connected discourse. *American Education Research Journal, 15*, 433-440.

Beck, I.L., McKeown, M.G., Hamilton, R.L., and Kucan, L. (Eds.) (1997). *Questioning the author: An approach for enhancing student engagement with text*. Newark, DE: International Reading Association.

Beck, I.L. & McKeown, M.G. (2002) *Bringing words to life*. NY: Guilford.

Cain, K., & Oakhill, J.V. (1999). Inference making ability and its relation to comprehension failure in young children. *Reading and Writing: An Interdisciplinary Journal, 11*, 489-503.

Carlisle, J.F. & Rice, M.S. (2002). *Improving reading comprehension: Research-based principles and practices*. Baltimore: York Press.

Catts, H.W., Fey, M.E., Zhang, X., & Tomblin, J.B. (1999). Language basis of reading and reading disabilities: Evidence from a longitudinal investigation. *Scientific Studies of Reading, 3*, 331-361.

Dickson, S.V., Collins, V.L., Simmons, D.C., & Kame'enui, E.J. (1998). Metacognitive strategies: Research bases. In D.C. Simmons & E.J. Kame'enui (eds.), *What reading research tells us about children with diverse learning needs* (pp. 295-360). Mahwah, NJ: Erlbaum.

Dole, J.A., Brown, K.J., & Trathen, W. (1996). Effects of strategy instruction on the comprehension performance of at-risk students. *Reading Research Quarterly, 31*, 62-84.

Duffy, G.G., Roehler, L.R., Meloth, M.S., Vavrus, I.G., Book, C., Putnam, J., and Wesselman, R.(1986). The relationship between explicit verbal explanations during reading skill instruction and student awareness and achievement: A study of reading teacher effects. *Reading Research Quarterly, 21*, 327-352.

Fuchs, D., Fuchs, L.S., Mathes, P.G., & Simmons, D.C. (1997). Peer-assisted learning strategies: Making classrooms more responsive to diversity. *American Educational Research Journal, 34*, 174-206.

Gambrell, L.B., & Jawitz, P.B. (1993). Mental imagery, text illustrations, and children's story comprehension and recall. *Reading Research Quarterly, 28*, 265-273.

Gattardo, A., Stanovich, K., & Siegel, L. (1996). The relationships between phonological sensitivity, syntactic processing, and verbal working memory in the reading performance of third-grade children. *Journal of Experimental Child Psychology, 63*, 563-582.

Gersten, R., Fuchs, L.S., Williams, J.P., & Baker, S. (2001). Teaching reading comprehension strategies to students with learning disabilities: A review of research. *Review of Educational Research, 71*, 279-320.

Gillon, G. & Dodd, B. (1995). The effects of training phonological, semantic, and syntactic processing skills in spoken language on reading ability. *Language, Speech, and Hearing Services in Schools, 26*, 58-68.

Gough, P. B., & Tunmer, W.E. (1986). Decoding, reading, and reading disability. *Remedial and Special Education, 7*, 6-10.

Kame'enui, E.J., Simmons, D.C., & Coyne, M.D. (2000). Schools as host environments: Toward a school-wide reading improvement model. *Annals of Dyslexia, 50*, 33-51.

Lenz, B.K., Ellis, E.S., & Scanlon, D. (1996). *Teaching learning strategies to adolescents and adults with learning disabilities*. Austin, TX: Pro-Ed.

Mathes, P. G., Howard, J.K., Allen, S.H., & Fuchs, D. (1998). Peer-assisted learning strategies for first-grade readers: Responding to the needs of diverse learners. *Reading Research Quarterly, 33*, 62-94.

Maria, K. (1990). *Reading comprehension instruction: Issues and strategies*. Baltimore: York Press.

Oakhill, J. and Yuill, N. (1996). Higher order factors in comprehension disability: Processes and remediation. In C. Cornoldi and J. Oakhill (eds.), *Reading comprehension difficulties: Processes and intervention* (pp. 69-92). Mahwah, NJ: Lawrence Erlbaum.

Ogle, D. (1986). K-W-L: A teaching model that develops active reading of expository text. *The Reading Teacher, 39*, 564-570.

Palinscar, A.S. & Brown, A. L. (1986). Interactive teaching to promote independent learning from text. *The Reading Teacher, 39*, 771-777

Perfetti, C.A., Marron, M.A., & Foltz, P.W. (1996). Sources of comprehension failure: Theoretical perspectives and case studies. In C. Cornoldi and J. Oakhill (eds.), *Reading comprehension difficulties: Processes and intervention* (pp. 137-165). Mahwah, NJ: Erlbaum.

Pressley, M. (2000). What should comprehension instruction be the instruction of? In M. Kamil, P.B. Mosenthal, P.D. Pearson, and R. Barr (eds.), *Handbook of Reading Research, Vol.3*. Mahwah, NJ: Erlbaum.

Pressley, M. & Wharton-McDonald, R. (1997). Skilled comprehension and its development through instruction. *School Psychology Review, 26*, 448-466.

RAND Reading Study Group (2002). *Reading for understanding: Toward a research and development program in reading comprehension*. http://www.rand.org/multi/achievementforall/reading/readreport.html.

Scarborough, H. (2001). Connecting early language and literacy to later reading (dis)abilities: Evidence, theory, and practice. In S. B. Neuman and D.K. Dickinson (eds.), *Handbook of early literacy research* (pp. 97-110). NY: Guilford.

Shankweiler, D., Lundquist, E., Katz, L., Stuebing, K.K., Fletcher, J.M., Brady, S., Fowler, A., Dreyer, L.G., Marchione, K.E., Shaywitz, S.E., & Shaywitz, B.A. (1999). Comprehension and decoding: Patterns of association in children with reading difficulties. *Scientific Studies of Reading, 31*, 24-53, 69-94.

Stanovich, K.E., West, R.R., Cunningham, A.E., Cipuelewski, J., and Siddiqui, S. (1996). The role of inadequate print exposure as a determinant of reading comprehension problems. In C. Cornoldi and J. Oakhill (eds.), *Reading comprehension difficulties: Processes and intervention* (pp. 15-32). Mahwah, NJ: Erlbaum.

Vaughn, S. & Klingner, J.K. (1999). Teaching reading comprehension through collaborative strategic reading. *Intervention in School and Clinic, 34*, 284-292.

Williams, J. (1987) Educational treatments for dyslexia at the elementary and secondary levels. In R. Bowler (Ed.), *Intimacy with language: A forgotten basic in teacher education* (pp. 24-32). Baltimore: International Dyslexia Association.

Instructional Resources

Carlisle, J. (1991). *Reasoning and reading, Levels I, II, and III*. Cambridge, MA: Educators Publishing Service.

Carreker, S. (1993). *Multisensory grammar and written composition*. Houston, TX: Neuhaus Center.

Greene, J. (2000). *LANGUAGE !* Longmont, CO: Sopris West.

Greene, T. & Enfield, M. (1993). *Project read written expression: Framing your thoughts*. Bloomington, MN: Language Circle Enterprises.

Greene, V.E. & Enfield, M. (1994). *Report form comprehension guide*. Bloomington, MN: Language Circle Enterprises.

Klinger, J.K., Vaughn, S., Dimino, J., Schuman, J.S., and Bryant, D. (2001). *From clunk to click: Collaborative strategic reading*. Longmont, CO: Sopris West.

Appendix for Module 6: Comprehension Instruction Plan

A Home for Lizzie

Summary of Meanings for Students to Extract and Construct: The narrator (little girl in the picture) notices and then captures a back-yard creature, a lizard, whom she would like to be her friend and companion. At first the girl imagines that Lizzie the lizard's needs are a lot like hers. She makes a home for Lizzie as well as she can, hoping Lizzie will be happy in it. Quickly, however, the girl realizes that Lizzie is not happy and not doing well in the "home" she created. Realizing that the lizard's needs are different from her own, the girl takes Lizzie back to where she was found and lets her go, knowing that she has done the right thing for Lizzie.

Queries to pose at specific junctures in the text:

Par. #1, after "hello"	Who is telling the story? What could "Lizzie" be? What words give you a clue? How do you know Lizzie is alive?
Par. #3, after "bug"	What is this creature doing? Why does the girl think she is not moving? Why else might she not move? Is the girl thinking of Lizzie's feelings?
Par. #4, after "language"	Is the girl thinking about what Lizzie likes? Is the girl treating Lizzie like a person? How do you know? Why does the author wait to tell us what Lizzie is?
Page 2, bottom after "no"	In what way is the girl treating Lizzie like a friend, or even like herself? What does the girl want to happen?
Page 3, 1st par., "do"	How will Lizzie like this new home? Why?
Par. #2, "home"	Is Lizzie happy? Why not? If you were Lizzie, what would you need?
Par. #3, "backyard"	What new thoughts is the girl having here? In what way is she showing that she cares for Lizzie now? What is she going to do?

Ending

Why did the girl put Lizzie back on the rock? How did the girl change by the end of the story? Would you do the same thing as she did?

Preparation for Reading

Do you have a back yard to play in or a park near your house? Have you ever explored there or pretended that you were hunting for treasure? Have you ever found any interesting creatures in your back yard when you were exploring? This is a story told by a girl who finds something in her back yard that is very interesting to her. During the story, the girl has an important decision to make about her discovery . . .

After Reading

a. Compare these two types of homes. What do they have?

	A Home for the Girl	**A Home for Lizzie**
For sleeping		
For comfort		
For eating		
For shelter		

b. Have you ever captured a wild creature? What did you decide to do with it? [Make a class composite of back yard discoveries.]

c. Write a personal narrative about a discovery you have made while exploring your back yard or an area near your home.

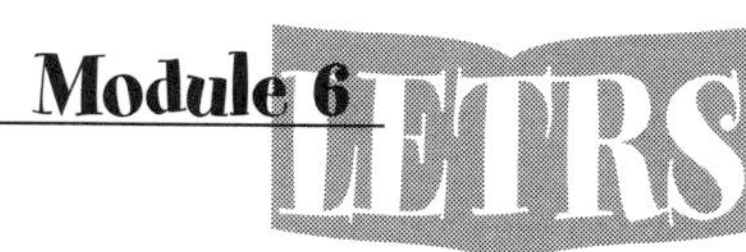

Animals Sharing Homes

Before Reading

Present the concept: Many people share homes with animals. For example, many people share homes with cats and dogs. The cats and dogs get shelter and food from the people, and the people get protection, companionship, and even jobs done by their pets. Both benefit from the arrangement.

Some animals share homes with each other. They share because both animals benefit from the living arrangement. The sharing is *mutually beneficial*—it is good for everybody. This story gives some examples of animals sharing homes. It also helps us understand the different ways that animals can help each other out when they live together (*cohabit*).

After Reading

Construct a "main idea" map or example chart of animals sharing homes:

Examples	Who Benefits and Why
Rhinos and oxpeckers	
Hermit crabs and anemones	
Gopher tortoises and mice, frogs, insects, possums, armadillos	

Vocabulary to discuss and elaborate: predator; reciprocity

LETRS
Language Essentials
for Teachers of
Reading and
Spelling

Glossary

affix: a morpheme or meaningful part of a word attached before or after a root to modify its meaning; a category that subsumes prefixes, suffixes, and infixes

Anglo-Saxon: Old English, a Germanic language spoken in Britain before the invasion of the Norman French in 1066

automaticity: performance without conscious effort or attention; a characteristic of skill mastery

base word: a free morpheme to which affixes can be added, usually of Anglo-Saxon origin

cognitive desktop: a figurative expression referring to the working memory capacity of the mind and the available attentional resources in consciousness

colloquialism: an expression used in informal speech

complementary antonyms: words that are categorical and dichotomous (either/or) opposites, such as *dead* or *alive*

concept: an idea that links other facts, words, and ideas together into a coherent whole

connotation: what is suggested by the word, in addition to the denotative or explicitly defined meaning

context processor: the neural networks that bring background knowledge and discourse to bear as word meanings are processed

cumulative instruction: teaching that proceeds in additive steps, building on what was previously taught

***derivational suffix**: a type of bound morpheme; a suffix that can change the part of speech of a root or base word to which it is added, such as *–ity, -ive, -ly*

direct instruction: the teacher defines and teaches a concept, guides children through its application, and arranges for extended guided practice until mastery is achieved

dyslexia: an impairment of reading accuracy and fluency attributable to an underlying phonological deficit

ELL: English Language Learner

explicit instruction: the teacher defines the concept or association the student is to learn, provides guided practice with feedback, provides additional independent practice, and checks to see if the concept was learned, retained and applied

expository text: factual text written to "put out" information

gradable antonyms: words that are on opposite ends of a continuum; their meaning is relative and depends on the perspective of the user

hierarchical networks: organizational systems in which items exist in categories ordered from high (superordinate) to low (subordinate)

idiom: a phrase or expression different from the literal meaning of the words; a regional or individual expression with a unique meaning

indirect vocabulary learning: the process of learning words through incidental and contextual exposures, rather than through direct and deliberate teaching

* Advanced concepts are indicated with an asterisk.

inflection: a type of bound morpheme; a grammatical ending that does not change the part of speech of a word but that marks its tense, number, or degree in English (such as *-ed*, *-s*, *-ing*)

integrated: when lesson components are interwoven and flow smoothly together

***lexicon**: name for the mental dictionary in every person's linguistic processing system

long term memory: the memory system that stores information beyond 24 hours

Matthew Effect: coined by Keith Stanovich; a reference to the Biblical passage that the "rich get richer and the poor get poorer," insofar as the pattern of language and reading skills development in individuals over time

meaning processor: the neural networks that attach meanings to words that have been heard or decoded

metacognition: the ability to reflect on and understand our own thought processes

***metalinguistic awareness**: an acquired level of awareness of language structure and function that allows us to reflect on and consciously manipulate the language we use

metaphor: words with nonliteral meaning, often expressed by an implied comparison of one thing to another or an unusual assignment of attributes ("the walls have ears")

morpheme: the smallest meaningful unit of the language

morphology: the study of the meaningful units in the language and how they are combined in word formation

multisyllabic: having more than one syllable

narrative: text that tells about sequences of events, usually with the structure of a story, fiction or nonfiction; often contrasted with expository text that reports factual information and the relationships among ideas

orthographic processor: the neural networks responsible for perceiving, storing, and retrieving the letter sequences in words

orthography: a writing system for representing language

paraphrase: express the thoughts in a sentence with different words

phoneme: a speech sound that combines with others in a language system to make words

phoneme awareness (also, phonemic awareness): the conscious awareness that words are made up of segments of our own speech that are represented with letters in an alphabetic orthography

phonics: the study of the relationships between letters and the sounds they represent; also used as a descriptor for code-based instruction in reading, e.g., "the phonics approach" or "phonic reading"

phonological awareness: meta-linguistic awareness of all levels of the speech sound system, including word boundaries, stress patterns, syllables, onset-rime units, and phonemes; a more encompassing term than phoneme awareness

phonological processor: a neural network in the frontal and temporal areas of the brain, usually the left cerebral hemisphere, that is specialized for speech sound perception and memory

phonological working memory: the "on-line" memory system that holds speech in mind long enough to extract meaning from it, or that holds onto words during reading and writing; a function of the phonological processor

phonology: the rule system within a language by which phonemes can be sequenced and uttered to make words

phrase-cued reading: the act of reading phrases that have already been marked or designated by underlining, spacing, or arrangement on the page

***pragmatics**: the system of rules and conventions for using language and related gestures in a social context

prefix: a morpheme that precedes a root and that contributes to or modifies the meaning of a word; a common linguistic unit in Latin-based words

reading fluency: the ability to read text with sufficient speed and accuracy to support deep comprehension

referent: a word that another word or words refers to, e.g., the referent for a pronoun is a noun

root: a bound morpheme, usually of Latin origin, that cannot stand alone but that is used to form a family of words with related meanings

scaffolding: providing extra structure or support that enables the learner to perform successfully

schwa: the "empty" vowel in an unaccented syllable, such as the last syllables of *circus* and *bagel*

semantics: the study of word and phrase meanings

semantic features: the specific aspects of meaning associated with a word and that distinguish that word

shallow word learning: partial or limited knowledge of word that may be constricted to one context or one meaning instead of several

sound-symbol correspondence: same as phoneme-grapheme correspondence; the rules and patterns by which letters and letter combinations represent speech sounds

structural analysis: the study of affixes, base words, and roots

suffix: a derivational morpheme added to a root or base that often changes the word's part of speech and that modifies its meaning

syllable: the unit of pronunciation that is organized around a vowel; it may or may not have consonants before or after the vowel

syntax: the rule system by which words can be ordered in sentences

vocabulary: the body of words known by the speaker of a language; receptive or listening vocabulary is the body of word meanings recognized in context, whereas expressive vocabulary is the body of word meanings known well enough that they can be used appropriately by the speaker of a language

vowel: one of a set of 15 vowel phonemes in English, not including vowel-r combinations; an open phoneme that is the nucleus of every syllable; classified by tongue position and height (high-low, front-back)

word recognition: the instant recognition of a whole word in print

Appendix A

Text Resources for Teacher Exercises

Contents for Text Resources for Teacher Exercises

A Home for Lizzie

by Beth Thompson • Art by Noela Young

I was in the backyard pretending I was a goldminer and searching for treasure when I saw Lizzie. She was sitting on a rock, not moving at all. She could have been a leaf or a twig, because her nubbly skin blended in with the dark gray stone. But she was watching me. Then she slowly blinked her shiny, black eyes. It was like saying hello.

I named her Lizzie. When I said her name out loud, she lifted herself up on her tiny toes as if she were going to tiptoe away. But she didn't go. I guess she liked her name.

I think Lizzie knew I didn't want to hurt her. When I touched her back, she twitched her long, skinny tail. Maybe she thought my finger was a strange, new bug!

The sun had warmed Lizzie's rock. Now the rock felt like the back steps under bare toes. "Does that feel good to your toes, too?" I asked her. But Lizzie only blinked a blink that could mean "yes" . . . or could mean "no." And I don't know lizard language.

I found an empty butter tub under the kitchen sink. It was smooth and white and just the right size for a lizard home. It had a plastic almost-see-through lid. Mom helped me punch holes in the lid. I made six holes, so Lizzie would get lots of air.

I picked a handful of grass and sprinkled it inside the tub. Then I showed it to Lizzie.

"Look, your very own room," I told her. "You don't have to share." She blinked. "It has air conditioning. And a nice green rug you can nibble on. Do you like it?" Lizzie blinked "yes" . . . but it might have been "no."

I set her carefully on the grass in the tub. Then I put on the lid. I peeked through the holes to see what she would do.

Lizzie didn't move at first. Then she tried to climb up the side of the butter tub, but it was too smooth. She slid back to the grass and sat very still. She couldn't hide against the white plastic or the green grass. She couldn't warm herself against the cold, smooth tub. She couldn't feel the sun through the plastic ceiling of her new home.

I took off the lid and held it over my head, pretending I was Lizzie. Six tiny bits of sun shone through a cloudy window that needed washing. The wilted grass felt limp and coarse. Then I sniffed the tub. It smelled like butter and plastic and soap-under-the-sink, not at all like the backyard.

So I took Lizzie out of the butter tub and put her back on the rock. She didn't make a sound or run away. She just sat there, blinking. But I knew this time she meant "yes," because now Lizzie was home.

LITTLE BEAR LOST

BY MARY KAY MOREL

BEFORE HER BROTHER was born, Blue Cloud had only a doll to play with. The doll, plump with buffalo-hair stuffing, wore a finely beaded dress stitched by Blue Cloud's grandmother.

But the first time Blue Cloud laid eyes on her new baby brother, she forgot all about the doll. The baby looked as warm and brown as the leaves that fell when frost lay on the grass.

When Little Bear started to cry, his mother gently pinched his nose as all good Lakota mothers did. "A new one's first lesson must be silence," she explained.

Grandmother nodded. "The cry of a Lakota baby can warn an enemy who might be looking for our camp."

Blue Cloud shivered at the thought of any Crow or Pawnee warrior who might be hiding in the willow brush near her people's village. Then she looked at her baby brother again and forgot her fears.

"May I hold him?" Blue Cloud asked.

Her mother nodded. Blue Cloud carefully lifted the baby. He was heavier than her doll, and soon her arms began to ache.

As Little Bear grew, he spent most of his time in a cradleboard. Riding on his mother's back, he was safe from harm's way. But Blue Cloud longed to carry him. She pestered her poor mother to let her hold the baby almost every day.

One afternoon Blue Cloud's mother looked especially tired. The air was as hot as the lodge fire in winter. The

Art by Bradley Clark
© 2002 by Mary Kay Morel

sun beat hard on the buffalo grass as the Lakota people traveled the prairie in search of a new campsite.

"Please, Mother," Blue Cloud pleaded, "let Little Bear's cradleboard ride with me on my pony."

Her mother sighed wearily. "Perhaps this would be a good time for you to learn to care for your brother. But look after him well."

Blue Cloud felt very proud and grown-up carrying the cradleboard slung on the side of her slow-moving pony. She secretly smiled when other girls gathered around her on their horses, admiring Little Bear. Soon Blue Cloud was receiving so much attention that she and her friends lagged behind the moving village.

"Look!" Blue Cloud suddenly said in surprise. "Our people are a long way from us."

Why don't we race to them and see who has the fastest pony?" Little Hawk suggested.

All the girls were excited at the idea of a horse race. They were ready to start when Blue Cloud suddenly remembered Little Bear. "I can't race with my brother on my horse!" she cried.

Lay him in the grass," Little Hawk suggested. "We'll only race a short distance."

Blue Cloud looked down at her sleeping brother. A large rock stood nearby. Would it really hurt to leave him resting there for a short time? Climbing down from her pony, she gently laid his cradleboard against the stone.

"Come on!" Little Hawk shouted.

Blue Cloud leaped back onto her pony. In a flash, they were off, girls in doeskin racing across the prairie, their horses kicking a cloud of dust into the air.

The race was short. When it was over, two girls squabbled over who had won.

"Let's run another," one suggested.

Again and again they raced. Blue Cloud felt proud when she won the third race. But suddenly she remembered

Little Bear. "My brother!" Blue Cloud cried, whipping her horse around. "I must find him."

Looking back on the sea of buffalo grass, Blue Cloud felt her heart sink. Where was Little Bear? Where was the rock she had rested the cradleboard against?

Quickly, she began the search. When Blue Cloud saw the dusty tracks of a coyote, her heart jumped. What if her brother was in danger?

Kicking the pony's ribs, she hurried faster. Soon Blue Cloud spotted the dusty trail of a rattlesnake. What if Little Bear had been bitten? Blue Cloud felt tears sting her eyes at the thought of something so terrible happening to her brother.

If only Little Bear would make a sound! But Blue Cloud knew that Lakota babies were taught never to cry.

Then she saw something that made her heart freeze in fear. A thin brown line far away on the horizon was moving toward her

Buffalo! A whole herd!

Blue Cloud's hands shook as she held her pony's rope. She slowed her horse to a walk and leaned forward, watching in terror. What if the buffalo reached Little Bear before she did? What if her sleeping brother woke from his nap to find a whole sea of huge, hairy beasts running straight toward him? Beasts strong enough to shake the earth like thunder and with hoofs as wide as a cradleboard?

A sob rose in Blue Cloud's throat. Suddenly she could not stop crying. For several moments she sat sobbing, not aware that the pony had stopped moving. Then she heard the thumping sound.

Blue Cloud looked down. Her pony's hoof was pawing against the side of a rock. Next to the rock lay Blue Cloud's brother, sleeping soundly in the shade where she had left him.

Blue Cloud's mother was terrified when she heard how Little Bear had nearly been lost. Her anger lasted for many moons. "It is not easy being a mother," she reminded her daughter time and time again. "A child is a great responsibility."

Blue Cloud could only nod and hang her head down in shame.

As time passed, Little Bear grew into a sturdy young boy. He loved chasing rabbits and listening to stories told before the lodge fire.

His favorite tale was the one his sister told of how he had been lost on the prairie. As lodge smoke rolled upward to meet the stars, Blue Cloud would shyly begin the tale. And in the years to come, even their mother could listen and laugh (a little, at least) with the rest of Little Bear's family.

How the Whale Got His Throat

by
Rudyard
Kipling

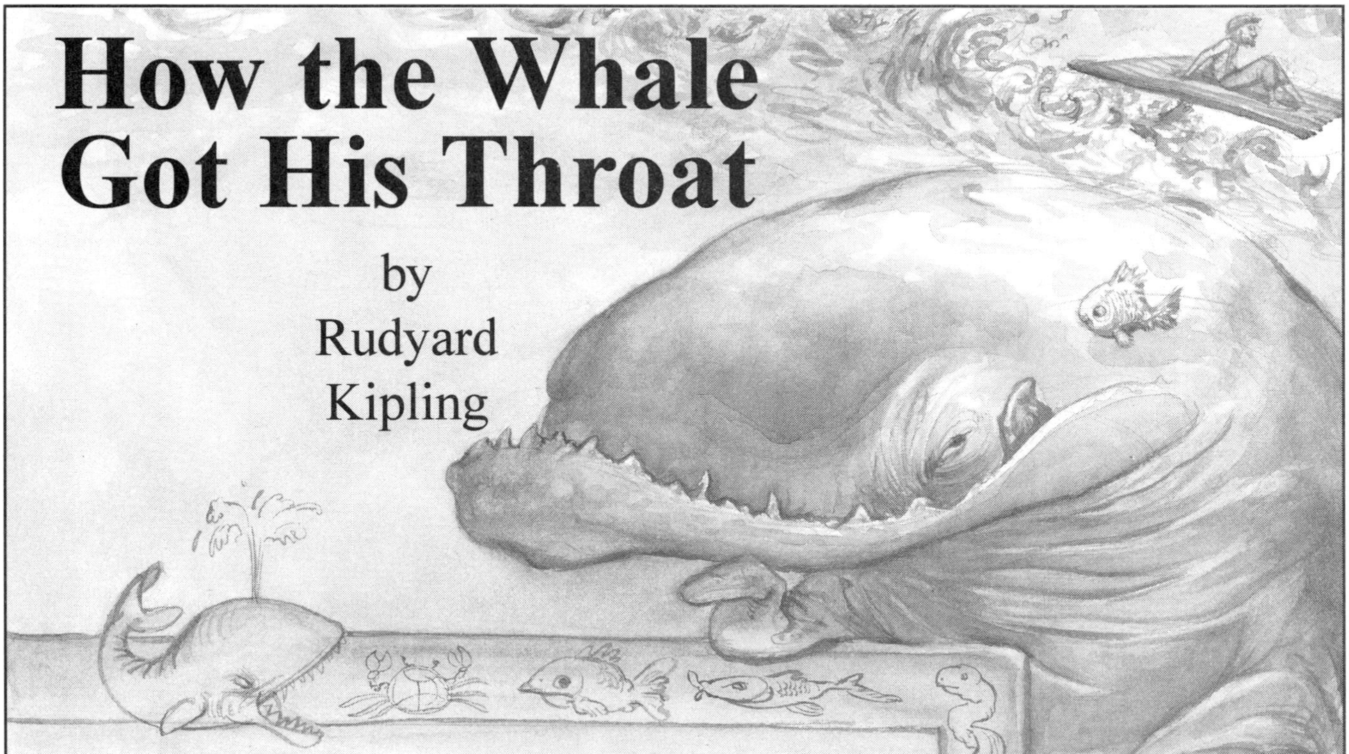

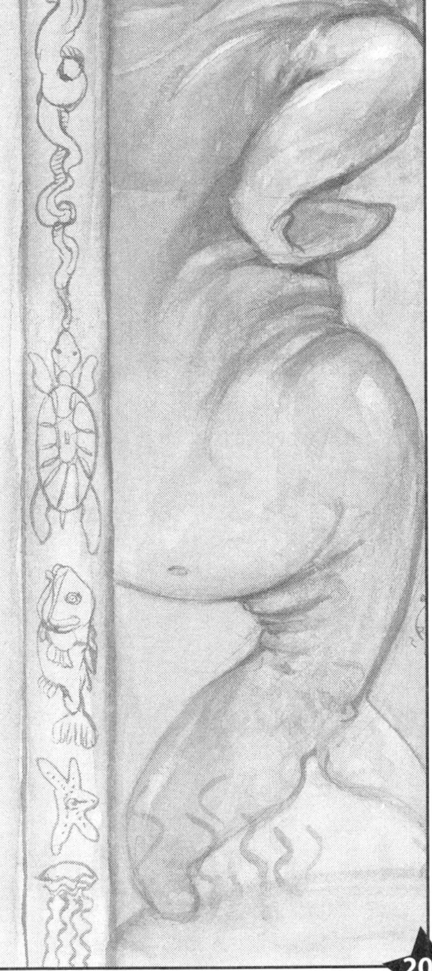

IN THE SEA, once upon a time, O my best Beloved, there was a Whale, and he ate fishes. He ate the starfish and the garfish, and the crab and the dab, and the plaice and the dace, and the skate and his mate, and the mackereel and the pickereel, and the really truly twirly-whirly eel. All the fishes he could find in all the sea, he ate with his mouth—so! Till at last there was only one small fish left in all the sea, and he was a small 'Stute Fish, and he swam a little behind the Whale's right ear, so as to be out of harm's way.

Then the Whale stood up on his tail and said, "I'm hungry."

And the small 'Stute Fish said in a small 'stute voice, "Noble and generous Cetacean, have you ever tasted Man?"

"No," said the Whale. "What is it like?"

"Nice," said the small 'Stute Fish. "Nice but nubbly."

"Then fetch me some," said the Whale, and he made the sea froth up with his tail.

"One at a time is enough," said the 'Stute Fish. "If you swim to latitutde Fifty North, longitude Forty West (that is Magic), you will find, sitting *on* a raft, *in* the middle of the sea, with nothing on but a pair of blue canvas breeches, a pair of suspenders (you must *not* forget the suspenders, Best Beloved), and a jackknife, one shipwrecked Mariner, who, it is only fair to tell you, is a man of infinite resource and sagacity."

So the Whale swam and swam to latitude Fifty North, longitude Forty West, as fast as he could swim, and *on* a raft, *in* the middle of the sea, *with* nothing to wear except a pair of blue canvas breeches, a pair of suspenders (you must particularly remember the suspenders, Best Beloved), *and* a jackknife, he found one single, solitary shipwrecked Mariner, trailing his toes in the water. (He had his mummy's leave to paddle, or else he would never have done it, because he was a man of infinite resource and sagacity.)

Then the Whale opened his mouth back and back and back till it nearly touched his tail, and he swallowed the shipwrecked Mariner, and the raft he was sitting on, and his blue canvas breeches, and the suspenders (which you *must* not forget), *and* the jackknife—he swallowed them all down into his warm, dark, inside cupboards, and then he smacked his lips—so— and turned round three times on his tail.

But as soon as the Mariner, who was a man of infinite resource and sagacity, found himself truly inside the Whale's warm, dark, inside cupboards, he stumped and he jumped and he thumped and he bumped, and he pranced and he danced, and he banged, and he clanged, and he hit and he bit, and he leaped and he creeped, and he prowled and he howled, and he hopped and he dropped, and he cried and he sighed, and he crawled and he bawled, and he stepped and he lepped, and he danced hornpipes where he shouldn't, and the Whale felt most unhappy indeed. (*Have* you forgotten the suspenders?)

So he said to the 'Stute Fish, "This man is very nubbly, and besides he is making me hiccup. What shall I do?"

"Tell him to come out," said the 'Stute Fish.

So the Whale called down his own throat to the shipwrecked Mariner, "Come out and behave yourself. I've got the hiccups."

"Nay, nay!" said the Mariner. "Not so, but far otherwise. Take me to my natal shore and the white cliffs of Albion, and I'll think about it." And he began to dance more than ever.

"You had better take him home," said the 'Stute Fish to the Whale. "I ought to have warned you that he is a man of infinite resource and sagacity."

So the Whale swam and swam and swam, with both flippers and his tail, as hard as he could for the hiccups; and at last he saw the Mariner's natal shore and the white cliffs of Albion, and he rushed halfway up the beach, and opened his mouth wide and wide and wide, and said, "Change here for Winchester, Ashuelot, Nashua, Keene, and stations on the *Fitch*burg Road"; and just as he said "Fitch" the Mariner walked out of his mouth. But while the Whale had been swimming, the Mariner, who was indeed a person of infinite resource and sagacity, had taken his jackknife and cut up the raft into a little square grating all running crisscross, and he had tied it firm with his suspenders (*now* you know why you were not to forget the suspenders!), and he dragged that grating good and tight into the Whale's throat, and there it stuck! Then he recited

the following *sloka*, which, as you have not heard it, I will now proceed to relate:

> *By means of a grating*
> *I have stopped your ating.*

For the Mariner he was also a Hibernian. And he stepped out on the shingle and went home to his mother, who had given him leave to trail his toes in the water; and he married and lived happily ever afterward.

So did the Whale. But from that day on, the grating in his throat, which he could neither cough up nor swallow down, prevented him eating anything except very, very small fish; and that is the reason why whales nowadays never eat men or boys or little girls.

The small 'Stute Fish went and hid himself in the mud under the Doorsills of the Equator. He was afraid that the Whale might be angry with him.

The Sailor took the jackknife home. He was wearing the blue canvas breeches when he walked out on the shingle. The suspenders were left behind, you see, to tie the grating with; and that is the end of *that* tale.

Mansion for a Mollusk

by Catherine Ripley

Here's the challenge—you're an animal called a mollusk with a soft, squishy body. But, uh-oh, you don't have a ribcage to protect your heart the way a human does. And, uh-oh, you can't flash away from danger the way a fish does—unless you happen to be a special type of mollusk called a squid or an octopus. And, uh-oh, you don't have a lodge to shelter you the way a beaver does. So just how do you protect yourself? You grow yourself a house! And that's just what most mollusks do.

The Florida horse conch has a two-foot-long shell for protection. It is big and strong enough to eat other large sea snails in their shells.

Picture of Florida horse conch

Picture of blue mussels

Blue mussels can't move—so they snap shut when trouble comes!

A Shell Is Like a House

The main job for the mollusk's hard, sturdy home is to protect the soft body inside. This is especially true for pearl oysters and mussels, which fasten themselves down and can't move. If danger comes knocking, they clam up tight as tight. Other mollusks, such as conchs, abalones, or whelks, carry their houses with them as they slide around the ocean bottom searching for food.

Like a house, a shell is also good protection against the weather. This is especially important for land mollusks. The shells of garden snails

This whelk travels on one big foot, which it also uses to pry open the shells of other mollusks, which it eats.

Picture of whelk

Right-Handed or Left?

Picture of snail

A snail shell is like a spiral staircase. The spirals go downward around a center pole to the opening at the bottom. For snails, the spirals get bigger and wider with each coil.

Snail shells can be right-handed or left-handed. Starting from the point, follow the coils downward. If they turn to the right, the shell is right-handed.

X-ray of a right-handed snail shell

---

prevent them from drying out. Land slugs, however, which are also mollusks, don't have shells. During hot or dry weather, many die because they can't keep their bodies moist.

Picture of spotted slug

Without a shell, this spotted slug needs wet, dark places to stay all slimy—and alive!

Growing a Home from the Inside Out

All mollusks start out tiny—smaller than your baby fingernail—and all mollusks have a mantle, which is a layer of flesh surrounding the body. This mantle produces a shell partly by secreting a material called calcium carbonate, which the mollusk gets from its blood, the water around it, and even the food it eats. (Calcium carbonate also makes up eggshells.) Mollusks keep building their shells their whole lives. Once a mollusk reaches full size, the shell just gets thicker and thicker. Knock, knock! Anybody home?

Picture of blue mantle

The blue mantle of a giant clam. Say ahh!

Animals Sharing Homes

Most wild animals live alone or with other animals like themselves. Some live out in the open. Others build nests or dig burrows. But not all animals build their own nests or dig their own burrows. And sometimes, two entirely different species of animals share a home!

Picture of rhinos

Red-billed oxpeckers eat, sleep, sunbathe, court, and mate on the backs of giant rhinos. Oxpeckers keep rhinos clean by eating ticks and flies found in their hides. In exchange for room and board, the birds warn the nearsighted rhinos of danger, by hopping and screeching and flapping their wings— even pecking the rhinos' heads if necessary!

When the European hermit crab grows, it moves into a new shell. It also looks for a sea anemone to attach to the shell. The anemone protects the crab by scaring away predators. And the crab gives the anemone a free ride to places where food is available.

Picture of crab

In hot, dry sandhills in Florida, the gopher tortoise digs a nice, cool burrow. But it doesn't live there alone! Snakes, gopher frogs, mice, and insects share the tortoise's home year-round. Armadillos, raccoons, foxes, and opossums drop in to find food, raise their young, or escape the grass fires that frequently rage across the sandhills.

Picture of tortoise

Appendix B

Answers to Applicable Exercises

Contents for Module Answers

Module 4 Answers

Module 6 Answers

Module 4 Answers

Exercise #1: How We Learn Words

Think of a word you have learned recently. What was the context for that learning?
What motivated you to learn and remember that word?

In the discussion, these points should arise: word learning occurs for a variety of reasons, including curiosity alone, the need to comprehend a passage, or the need to communicate with someone around a shared experience. Most people have to hear or read a word several times before they try to incorporate it into their own speaking vocabulary.

Exercise #2: Exploring the Use of Words in Context

Work with a partner. Choose an important word that is specific to a hobby or area of special knowledge that you have—a "jargon" word that a layperson would not know. Make up several sentences that use the word. Can your partner figure out what the word means? Could he or she define the word on the basis of the contextual uses you gave? How close was the meaning your partner came up with? What are the advantages and limitations of context use in word definition?

Context can help to a greater or lesser extent depending on the amount of redundant information that the surrounding text gives about the word. Context can be misleading. Exposure to a single contextual use of a word may not be enough to get the meaning; several exposures are often more helpful for narrowing down the word's meanings.

Exercise #3: Multiple Meanings

How many meanings and uses can you think of for the following common words: frame, check, pitch. Take one word and list all the meanings you know without using a dictionary. Then, check the dictionary for others you may have missed.

Frame: frame a picture; build the skeleton of a house; frame an innocent person accused of a crime; a sheltered box for growing plants from seeds

Check: bill at a restaurant; winning move in chess; body blow in ice hockey; check mark on paper; explore or look into (check up on...)

Pitch: throw a baseball to the batter; the angle of incline; black tar; try to sell an object or idea

Exercise #4: Categories

Put the following words on cards and then sort them into categories and subcategories. What do you need to know to accomplish this task?

mushing	Bruno	bones	fur/hair
jobs	Lassie	sniffing	retriever
kibbles	greyhound	famous dogs	legs
dogs	Rin-Tin-Tin	leading	spaniel
milkbone	tail	food	Fido
searching	terrier	breeds	body parts

DOGS

jobs	body parts	breeds	famous dogs	food
mushing	tail	terrier	Bruno	kibbles
searching	bones	greyhound	Lassie	milkbone
sniffing	fur/hair	spaniel	RinTinTin	(bones)
leading	legs	retriever	Fido	

Which graphic organizer in Appendix B would be most suitable for showing these word relationships?

Exercise #5: Structure of Definitions

Use the following format to make a definition for each word below.

A _______________ is (a) _______________ that (is, does) _______________.
(critical features)

Words to define:

River: _A river is a long, flowing body of water that goes downhill and that gets its water from many tributaries in a watershed._

Phoneme: _A phoneme is a single speech sound that combines with others to make words. Every language has its own inventory of phonemes. Phonemes may be consonants or vowels._

Bison: _A bison is a buffalo, a large brown animal with woolly fur that lives on the grassy plains of the Western United States and that once ran wild in very large herds before the west was settled._

Exercise #6: Semantic Feature Analysis

If the object at the top of a column has the feature designated on the left, mark a (+).
If the object does not have the feature, mark a (–). How extensively do these meanings overlap?
Are the words synonyms or not?

	OBJECTS		
FEATURES	cup	glass	mug
Have a handle	+/–	–	+
Made from clay			+
Made from glass		+/–	
Round shape	+	+	+
Taller than round		+	
For hot liquid	+/–	+	
For cold liquid	+/–	+	
Made from paper	+/–	–	–
Used for wine	+/–	+	–

Module 4 Answers (continued)

Exercise #7: How Groups of Words Are Alike

In what way are the following groups of nouns the same and different? In what ways do their semantic features overlap?

1. daughter, sister, niece   vs.   nun, waitress, actress

   Both groups are female; the first group are relatives.

2. rooster, bull, ram   vs.   hen, ewe, cow

   Both groups are farm animals; the first are male.

3. table, chair, pencil   vs.   water, cream, sand

   Both groups of objects are inanimate; the first group are solid and can be counted; the second are fluid and cannot be counted.

4. table, chair, pencil   vs.   faith, hope, charity

   Both groups are nouns: the first are concrete, the second abstract.

5. husband, brother, son   vs.   clerk, preacher, judge

   Both groups are people; the first are relatives, the second are professionals.

6. grandfather, mother, nephew   vs   brother, sister, cousin

   Both groups are relatives; the first are multiple generations, the second are the same generation.

Exercise #8: Antonym Pairs and Scaling

Check the antonym pairs as complementary (either/or) or gradable (opposite ends of a continuous scale).

	Complementary	Gradable
dead – alive	✓	
hot – cold		✓
above – below	✓	
fat – skinny		✓
married – single	✓	
fragrant – putrid		✓
angry – delighted		✓
hideous – gorgeous		✓
straight – bent	✓	
honest – devious		✓
winner – loser	✓	

Now take one of the *continuous* antonym pairs and fill out the scale from one extreme to the other with words that show degrees of meaning.

honest   straight   fair   dishonest   devious

←—————————————————→

Exercise #9: Apply Strategies to Teaching Text

Focusing on one or more texts at the end of this module, work with a small group to a) select the words that you would teach directly and b) devise strategies for teaching those words. Indicate whether you are likely to use the strategies before reading, during reading, or after reading.

This exercise can take an hour or more. Select a text that is appropriate for the group. The text on Animal Homes or the narrative, Little Bear Lost are excellent selections for this exercise. Give the groups 20 to 30 minutes to sketch out their instructional strategies for just the vocabulary part of the lesson. Use groups of 4 to 6 people. Give each group an overhead transparency or chart paper to support a brief presentation by the group. There are no "right" answers. Each group's approach will vary and the sharing will enrich everyone's knowledge of potentially productive approaches.

Module 6 Answers

Exercise #2: Summarize

Now refer back to your graphic organizer notes from the previous discussion. Verbally summarize the main points about the causes and influences on students' reading comprehension.

Comprehension is determined by a number of factors. It is influenced by the text itself, the verbal ability and background knowledge of the reader, the circumstances under which reading is done, and the purpose and nature of the reading assignment. To be understood, the text must be within the range of difficulty that the reader can handle, typically with 90% or more of the words recognized. Word meanings must be familiar and the text must be organized so that inferences are facilitated. The reader must have sufficient decoding ability and reading fluency to attend to the meanings in the text. The reader must be able to follow a logical structure and make inferences of many kinds. The reader must bring background knowledge to the task and connect to experiences beyond the text in order to fully comprehend. Finally, the environment in which reading takes place and the purpose of the reading task will influence how deeply and intentionally the reader reads.

Exercise #3: Locating Figurative and Idiomatic Language

Locate the metaphorical and idiomatic expressions any one of the accompanying texts. Pick one figurative or idiomatic expression. How would you explain the meaning of the expression to young students?

Mansion for a Mollusk

"if danger comes knocking"

Little Bear Lost

Blue Cloud felt her heart sink.
Something that made her heart freeze in fear...
Her [mother's] anger lasted for many moons.

How the Whale Got His Throat

He was a man of infinite resource and sagacity...
The 'stute fish [astute fish] ...
Once upon a time, O my best beloved

His mother had "given him leave to trail his toes in the water"

Exercise #4: Anticipating Comprehension Problems at the Sentence Level

Locate three complex or compound sentences in the accompanying texts. Can you describe what may be difficult for a student to comprehend? Could the sentences be simplified, rearranged, or broken down in some way to facilitate comprehension? What strategies do you already use to build children's sense of the sentence?

[KIPLING] – But while the whale had been swimming, the Mariner, who was indeed a person of infinite resource and sagacity, had taken his jackknife and cut up the raft into a little square grating all running crisscross, and he had tied it firm with his suspenders (now you know why you were not to forget the suspenders!), and he dragged that grating good and tight into the whale's throat, and there it stuck!

But from that day on, the grating in his throat, which he could neither cough up nor swallow down, prevented him from eating anything except very, very small fish; and that is the reason why whales nowadays never eat men or boys or little girls.